The Book of Syn

Dr Syn (Day of Syn 2012; photograph David Penfold)

The Book of Syn

Russell Thorndike, Dr Syn and the Romney Marsh

Keith Swallow

Edgerton Publishing Services

Pett, East Sussex

First published in Great Britain in 2013 by
Edgerton Publishing Services
Jasmine Cottage, Elm Lane, Pett, Hastings, East Sussex TN35 4JD
Tel. +44 (0) 1424 813003
Email enquiries@eps-edge.demon.co.uk

ISBN: 978-0-9548390-9-3

A CIP catalogue record for this book is available from the British Library.

Typeset in Garamond by Edgerton Publishing Services.

Printed and bound in Great Britain by Ashford Colour Press Ltd, Fareham, Hampshire

Every effort has been made to trace and acknowledge ownership of copyright of the illustrations used in this book. The publisher will be pleased to make suitable arrangements to clear permission with any copyright holders whom it has not been possible to contact.

Contents

Foreword

I first visited Romney Marsh in the mid 1960s. Being only four years old at the time, I cannot claim that it was love at first sight, but the Marsh was a place that quickly grew in my affections. At a time when other families were jetting off to Spain in the vanguard of cheap overseas package holidays, my lot was to join my grandparents in their modest bungalow at Greatstone-on-sea each summer. These were idyllic times, although I never let on to my parents; the guilt card was too easy to play.

Residing in the outskirts of London but yearning to be by the sea, as I grew older I read everything I could find about the Marsh. Inevitably, I soon stumbled upon one of Russell Thorndike's books. This was *Doctor Syn Returns*. The romantic mix of adventure and smuggling was captivating to a teenager, with the setting being an added bonus. I was hooked and next summer when visiting Hythe bought the remaining six volumes in the saga. I finished them within a week.

As the years have passed, my appetite for anything related to Romney Marsh has remained undimmed. I have re-read the Doctor Syn novels countless times and frequently find links to Thorndike's events, plots or characters in historical accounts. For some time I had considered bringing these together in a book, but was unsure that there would be sufficient interest. The advent of the internet caused me to reconsider; there are numerous sites and message boards that suggest a very keen interest, both in the Romney Marsh and in the Syn legend itself. Such interest is by no means confirmed to south-east England; many entries originate from America, where the children's TV series *Doctor Syn alias the Scarecrow* was one of the most popular that the Walt Disney Corporation has ever run.

More significantly (and as is common with the internet), I found that much of the information, whilst well-intentioned, is incorrect. There are some alarming inaccuracies, particularly where authors have clearly not read the books on which they are commenting. Having the advantage of owning copies of each of the books and (as I thought) *both* films, I started to research the subject in more detail. Having again wrongly assumed that I had access to all the source material, I was surprised to find – amongst other things – that there was a further related novel by Thorndike; that there was an elongated version of one of the 'canonical' novels published in America; that other authors had produced Doctor Syn novels; and that – however unlikely it seemed – there was a Hammer Horror Syn film starring Peter Cushing and Oliver Reed. There have further been plays (in which Thorndike himself took the lead role), a musical for schools and numerous comics produced by the Disney Corporation.

What I have tried to achieve in this book is to set the events of the novels in context and explore Thorndike's influences. I have included biographical detail of Thorndike and Syn, compiled a cast list of all characters featured and provided both a synopsis of each novel and a commentary on each of the related books and films. I have also tried to shed some light on the realities of smuggling at the time the novels were set and to highlight the places on Romney Marsh that meant most to Thorndike (and which feature in his stories). In summary, I hope that this book may be used as a reference point for those captivated by Thorndike's work, but who have yet to visit Romney Marsh, and also provide a greater level of insight into the phenomenon of Doctor Syn for those already acquainted with the area. In so doing, I have highlighted a number of errors that have been perpetuated in various sources. I am painfully aware that there will be other errors that I have overlooked and still more for which I am personally responsible. All I will say in my defence is that these are honest mistakes; I apologise for any such errors or omissions and will endeavour to correct these within future editions.

Keith Swallow
January 2013

Nina Thorndike and the author at the 2012 Day of Syn (photograph David Penfold)

Acknowledgements

I should like to take this opportunity to acknowledge those who have provided material and photographs. The Thorndike family have been most supportive and helpful and, in particular, I am indebted to Russell's son Dan and granddaughter Nina for their assistance. Special thanks are due to Sheila Jones of the Day of Syn Society and to David Penfold, who has guided me through the pitfalls of producing a first book.

Thanks are also due to the Random House Group Ltd, ITV, NBC Universal, Getty Images, David Ramzan, Joe Barnes, the Francis Frith Collection, Kentish Express; and the Ship Inn for permission to use images; to Philips and the Ordnance Survey for permission to reproduce the maps in Chapter 6; and to Nina Thorndike, Bruce Thorndike, David Penfold, Peter Mould, Mark Swallow, Judith Blincow (the Mermaid Inn) and the Day of Syn Society for provision of additional photographs. Photographs with no acknowledgement have been taken by the author.

Author's royalties will be distributed to local charities via the Day of Syn Society.

Dan and Nina Thorndike in a production of *As You Like It* at the Barn Theatre, Smallhythe Place (photograph: Peter Mould)

1

The Origins of Syn: Russell Thorndike – the Man and his Creation

Russell Thorndike 1885–1972

Russell Thorndike, creator of *Doctor Syn*, was the second child and elder son of Arthur and Agnes Thorndike, the product of two prominent but highly different families. His ancestry is well worth exploring, as it gives great insight into his career and interests.

In his biography of his sister, theatre legend Sybil,[1] Russell describes both his grand-fathers as 'sturdy and eccentric'. The paternal grandfather (Daniel) was a general who never saw action and never retired, whilst his maternal counterpart (John Bowers) was an authority on shipping who had only one significant voyage to his name! Despite these influences, it was religion that dominated both families. Herbert Thorndike – way back in the seventeenth century – had been a respected Church scholar who had written tomes on ecclesiastical law, before falling victim to Cromwell; John Bowers, who had run away from his Scottish home as a small boy and fended for himself south of the border, put all his sons into the Church. The story is told in the family that one of Bowers's daughters, the headstrong Agnes Mac-donald,[2] travelled to Bristol to listen to her brother preach his first sermon but was there captivated by the good looks of another young curate. This was Arthur Thorndike. Donnie, a very determined and ambitious young woman, determined there and then to marry him; and the story goes that barely a week had passed before she achieved her goal. Although this is partly true, it seems that the pair had previously met when involved in musical recit-als at Cambridge, where Donnie thought Arthur conceited and pompous. When she next saw him at Bristol, she did not recognise him from their earlier encounter. The pair were engaged within a fortnight but did not marry until September 1881, some four months after the events in Bristol.

After a honeymoon at Folkestone, Arthur and Donnie began their married life at Gains-borough, Lincolnshire, where their first daughter, Sybil, was born a year later. 18 months

---

1. *Sybil Thorndike*, Thornton Butterworth 1929.
2. She was rarely referred to as Agnes, but widely known as 'Donnie', a contraction of Macdonald – a maternal family name.

Minor Canon Row, Rochester, birthplace and early home of Russell Thorndike

further down the line, Arthur was offered and accepted a post as Minor Canon at Rochester Cathedral. It was in Rochester on 6 February 1885 that Arthur junior (the subject of this narrative) was born, although he was rarely known as such and his middle name – Russell – was used from an early age. Russell was not a name in particularly common usage in the nineteenth century, and its origin was in the maiden name of Daniel (the General)'s second wife.[3] Russell was to spend much of his childhood in Rochester, at first in the house in Minor Canon Row – just behind the Cathedral. The house is now in private ownership but for a long time bore a blue plaque denoting Sybil's residency; this has now been replaced by a tablet that additionally records Russell's occupancy. Subsequently, the family moved to a nearby vicarage after his father had been given the living of St Margaret's,[4] the largest parish in the area.

Russell's childhood was unconventional, but rich in variety. An early memory of his was of racing up and down the nave of Rochester cathedral, and playing hide-and-seek with Sybil in the crypt. The timing of his father's initial appointment to Rochester is interesting in terms of young Russell's development. Only 14 years had passed since the death of Charles Dickens, and many in the Precincts of Rochester Cathedral had known and still talked fondly of him. The Precincts still contained residents whom Dickens had used as the basis of some of his literary characters, and Dean Hole (who was a favourite of both Sybil and Russell) had been a close friend of the great man. Dickens was held in high esteem by many of Rochester's inhabitants, and Arthur Thorndike had a bust of him that took pride of place on his mantelpiece.

---

3. Their own second child had been christened Russell but sadly died in infancy.
4. This would have been either late 1891 or early 1892.

Rochester Cathedral: an
unusual playground

Ironically, his two elder children contrived to destroy this bust, having convinced themselves that it was a symbol of the devil.[5]

Russell was to have another sister (Eileen – born 1891) and a brother (Frank – 1895), but the proximity in ages dictated that he would be closest to his elder sister. Whilst Sybil also had a keen interest in music, both were passionate about acting and from an early age took to putting on plays on a homemade stage. In this they were to an extent following in family footsteps (their grandfather – the General – had been a keen amateur performer). Neighbours and friends would be roped in to assist, and family servants provided a (not always willing) audience. These early plays were almost always based upon the works of Dickens and the Bible but, as they grew older, the siblings would start writing their own.

From an early age, shock and horror intrigued and influenced the pair. Church grounds can be unnerving and, for kids with imagination, doubly so. Sybil recalled an incident where ghoul-

---

5. This seems to have arisen from the confusion over the phrase 'what the Dickens?' having been banned from the Thorndike household on the basis that it equated to 'what the devil?'.

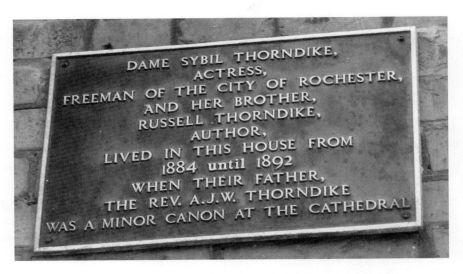

Plaque commemorating the residency of Russell and Sybil Thorndike

ishly-dressed mummers appeared unexpectedly over a wall when they were preparing for bed and Russell another where – following a November 5th bonfire party – they spotted four Guys swinging from a makeshift scaffold in the choir school playground. There were a fair few 'characters' who frequented the Precincts, and Russell identified a number of these as being 'scary'. These included a man with a long overcoat covered in 'pearlies' and brandishing scissors. He spent his time cutting paper silhouettes for anyone who crossed his path (whether or not they were willing participants) and subsequently formed the basis of a character in one of Russell's books.[6] Whilst many children display a fascination for morbid themes, the two took this to extremes: another early recollection of Sybil's was tying up her brother with a skipping rope to make a sacrificial offering to the Lord. On a later occasion – having found an entrance to a private vault in the graveyard – they spent hours lying on the damp grass watching the brass handles of a recently interred coffin growing dimmer. A significant event in their lives was being taken by Dean Hole to see Poole's *Myriorama*.[7] 'What a show that was . . . we nearly died that night. And yet we liked it'.[8] Inspired by this, they returned to their home-made apron stage and put on their own play *The Dentist's Cure* (sub-titled: *Saw their Silly Heads off*). Mother Donnie was incredibly ambitious for all her offspring and encouraged their acting and

---

6. The Wizard within *The Slype* (see also Chapter 3). Hard cover editions carry a picture of this character on the dust jacket.

7. Panoramas (moving pictures), which were accompanied by running commentaries, were the forerunner of the motion picture industry and very popular in their day. The Poole brothers developed this concept, and their *Myriorama* (which included themes of horror) was generally considered to be the finest of the genre.

8. *Sybil Thorndike*.

writing, but was less than enthusiastic about the content of some of their more gory productions and would shout out: 'mind the furniture!' when fake blood was being thrown around. Another great influence on the nature of the plays that they performed was the annual Mayday Jack-in-the-Green celebrations, which were then much more sinister than the watered-down affairs still staged today in a number of south-east towns.

After a number of kindergartens and smaller schools, Russell entered the Preparatory of the famous Kings School, Rochester before passing a voice trial for St George's Chapel, Windsor Castle and becoming a 'Child of the Chapel Royal' (a chorister). Here, one of a number of unforgettable incidents in the young Russell's life was being charged with guiding the legendary actor Sir Henry Irving[9] around the castle. On holidays from Windsor, he would lead expeditions with his elder sister and various friends to the Medway, where they would act out piratical fantasies on a number of wrecked barges and indulge sporting interests in tennis and cricket. Arthur took the family on hugely enjoyed holidays, at first (when the rest of the family was very young) to Broadstairs, but then further afield to Devon, Cornwall and Shropshire. Dalwood, near Axminster in Devon was a particular favourite. On these family holidays, Arthur would take the children on long bike rides and encourage them to take risks – an outlook that Russell would later say helped his development and confidence enormously. Later, holidays were taken in Ilfracombe with one of the Thorndike aunts, but without either parent. Arthur Thorndike's next appointment was to Aylesford,[10] described as *the plum of the diocese* on account of its great natural beauty. Aylesford was to become very dear to the hearts of all the Thorndike children[11] and further cemented their connections with Kent. Being born in Rochester, Russell was genuinely a Man of Kent, and his love of the county is very much from that standpoint, rather than that of a Kentish Man.[12] Within his writing, his characters speak for him: 'Kent's a great county, especially south and east of the Medway',[13] although that does not seem to extend to his birthplace – which he was to rename Dullchester in one of his novels. In *Sybil Thorndike*, Russell confirms that he loved the Kent coast even more than Devon and Cornwall and says: 'we saw our own Medway barges ploughing along, and knew that we belonged to that land'.

Deep in the south of the county, it was a rather nondescript village that was to play a key

---

9. Broadcaster and theatre critic Sheridan (son of actor Robert) Morley in his biography *Sybil Thorndike: a Life in the Theatre* recounts that both Arthur and Donnie were great fans of Irving, which may have been influential in them later allowing their children to pursue acting careers.

10. Strangely, there is also a Dickens connection with Aylesford church. Part of a family plot in the graveyard had been reserved for him, but not used (he was instead buried at Westminster Abbey).

11. At Aylesford, the vicarage tithe barn next to the kitchen garden became the siblings' new – and much more spacious – 'theatre'.

12. Kentish Men are those born to the west and/or north of the Medway. This is a very important distinction if you hail from the county – there is great rivalry between the two factions.

13. From the novel *Doctor Syn*.

part in the young Thorndike's development. Throughout her life, Donnie Thorndike displayed a habit of acquiring properties and, in the early 1890s, her attention was caught by Dymchurch. Although at this time Dymchurch could not be considered anything like a resort, it was an incredibly popular location with the acting and literary set and the weekends in the bar of The Ship Inn would read like a veritable *Who's Who* – a state of affairs chiefly attributable to one Hubert Bland. In addition to pursuing a very active philandering career, Bland was a leading light of the Fabian Society[14] and his holiday bungalow was open house at weekends with HG Wells, the Chesterton Brothers, E M Forster, Rudyard Kipling, George Bernard Shaw and (later) Athene Seyler and Noel Coward amongst the regular visitors.[15] Bland's partner in a very unconventional marriage was Edith Nesbit, known world-wide for her novel *The Railway Children*. Donnie's ambition for both herself and her children had seen her drawn into this literary circle (she was later thrilled to hear Oscar Wilde describe her as a 'witty young woman') and it was through this medium that she and her children were introduced to Dymchurch.

Back home, Russell was now the soloist in the Chapel Royal Choir at Windsor. He was disappointed to have to leave Windsor at the end of 1900 because his voice was breaking, but was briefly recalled when asked to sing at the funeral of Queen Victoria the following year. Whilst Russell clearly enjoyed performing and younger siblings Frank and Eileen[16] had both inevitably become drawn into the cast of Russell and Sybil's plays by this time, there was still no indication that the stage would provide a career for any of the family. Sybil – a very driven individual in the mould of her mother – had a career as a classical pianist mapped out, whilst Arthur desperately wanted his elder son to follow in his footsteps and become a parson: indeed, Arthur assumed that Russell would become his curate. Despite the family influence, a career in the Church was not for Russell, who yearned for greater adventure. As a young boy he had spent hours in a chicken shed at the vicarage (his 'study') writing the dramas that he would perform with his sister, and he saw his future very much as a writer and dramatist. A turning point for both was, strangely, a wrist injury sustained by Sybil in 1902. Her relentless ambition and drive had led to her practising the piano incessantly, resulting in her incurring what would now be termed a repetitive strain injury to her wrist. Having been advised to stop playing, Sybil turned to singing but was discouraged by the criticism of professionals, who felt that her voice lacked power. Russell then suggested, as an alternative, that they could both

---

14. Founded in 1884, the Fabian Society was (and still is) a socialist society committed to gradual rather than revolutionary social reform.

15. Coward relates that there would be an unholy scrum leaving London on a Friday night, everyone determined to get to Dymchurch early to secure a bed for the weekend. Seyler was later to buy a house in the village herself .

16. Eileen is the least known of the Thorndikes and relatively little has been recorded of her life. In 1919 she married Maurice Ewbank, a naval officer and had two children by him. Early in WWII she opened a drama school in Devon, but her business partner ran off with all the funds. After some other unsuccessful ventures, she had a nervous breakdown and regularly suffered from depression before dying of a brain haemorrhage at the age of 63.

take to the stage; in fact – whilst genuinely sympathetic to Sybil – he was delighted at the opportunity that this turn of events presented.

The Ben Greet Academy was advertising in the press, and they had both previously seen Greet and felt him to be a decent individual. Astutely surmising that of their parents their mother would be more amenable to the concept, they approached her to ask for funding. Donnie had had qualms about Sybil giving up the piano but – desperately wanting fame for her children – warmly embraced the idea of their acting. She wrote to Greet and the seed was sown, with the two being invited to enrol at the acting school in September of the same year. Russell later told his disappointed father that he hated the idea of being a parson and pointed out that it would have cost a lot to send him to Oxford to undertake the necessary study. Although in childhood surrounded by religion (and Sybil was later to marry into another highly religious family), both Sybil and Russell had spoken of a dislike of 'holy-bobs',[17] and Russell was to later say that he had 'never had much time for that sort of thing'.[18] He softened the blow to his father a little, however, by pointing out that, if he did take up acting, he would be able to protect his sister.

At this stage Russell, having left Windsor, was attending King's School, whose headmaster expressed the view that his father must be mad to let his son end his education and take up such an insecure career at just seventeen. Whilst others may have been sceptical, however, Russell and Sybil were highly excited at the prospect of a career on stage. Russell was later to confirm that the two and a half terms spent learning their craft at the Academy were amongst the happiest times of their lives. At the outset, Greet was away on tour and the Thorndikes' development was entrusted to his deputy, Frederick Topham. Topham's half-term assessment of Sybil was glowing, but he was less enthusiastic about Russell's prospects: 'the boy's harder to judge. He's odd and unexpected.' However, when Greet reurned, both siblings performed well in their formal audition and there is some evidence that, of the two, Greet was more impressed with Russell. Nevertheless, whilst Sybil was offered the opportunity to accompany Greet when the company went back to the USA, Russell was told that he was not old enough to tour. Instead, after making his first stage appearance as John Rugby in the *Merry Wives of Windsor* at the Theatre Royal, Cambridge, he was offered a part in a domestic tour of *The Eternal City* under J. Bannister Howard – with the promise of rejoining his sister the following year.

Russell clearly made a good impression in *The Eternal City*, and Greet kept his word by securing his release in 1905 (when the play was being staged in the Rhondda Valley), so that he could accompany Sybil – in England on her first leave – back to New York. It is quite apparent to any students of the Thorndikes that things always happened (or were made to

---

17. Their own term for overly reverential and solemn religious types.

18. Notwithstanding, he had some grudging admiration of the faith displayed by the likes of Sybil, Lilian Baylis and Athene Seyler. 'There is something splendidly primitive about both their religions' he wrote (of Baylis and Sybil).

happen) in their company and this voyage was to be no exception: the pair struck up an acquaintance with a young man who would remain a close friend for the rest of the time that they spent touring in the Americas. He was an older man, a professor from Princeton, and spoke of his passion for politics. There is more than a suggestion that Russell and Sybil convinced him that he should follow their example and give up his secure daytime job to pursue his first love. Whether this conversation was instrumental to what was to happen is, of course, open to conjecture; but the reality is that Woodrow Wilson went on to become the twenty-eighth President of the United States, holding this position for the duration of the First World War.

Thrilled though he was at the prospect of the opportunity to improve his acting ability, Russell confided in his sister that he was more excited at how seeing the world would aid him in his writing. In this he could not have been disappointed: there were experiences galore for a young man accustomed to comfortable living with servants on hand. These included a bear breaking into their bungalow in a remote mountain village in a quest for food; snakes invading a stage; and improvisation by the use of an execution shed scaffold when hosting Shakespeare in a court house. This latter event was at a small town called Cordele, in Georgia, where the company's train had been delayed by a derailment. Later in the day, Sybil and Russell went for a walk in the woods where they spotted an 'alarming red-haired gentleman' who kept dodging behind trees and boulders and who appeared to be stalking them. It transpired that this was an escaped murderer who had been sentenced to hang, and who was an expert marksman! This was another character that Russell subsequently weaved into his writing.[19]

During this tour, Russell's acting flourished and his reputation grew. He was prepared to take risks and to innovate in the pursuit of his art, and – amongst other memorable episodes – gave an acclaimed performance of Caliban in the *Tempest*. This involved one of a number of the outdoor sets for which Greet was well known and necessitated Russell swimming underwater in full costume to effect a dramatic entrance. In his three and a half years with the Greet Academy he played a host of roles, and it is reported that he became the first actor to give performances of Hamlet in three different versions of the text on the same day. Another distinction that has been recorded is his becoming the first professional actor to play the roles of King Lear, Richard II and King John.[20]

As the tour progressed, Sybil began to experience trouble with her vocal chords, and her condition grew steadily worse. She struggled on for a number of weeks, but was eventually granted permission by Greet to return to England accompanied, of course, by Russell. Whilst this condition was career threatening for Sybil, it had been exacerbated by her refusing to rest and their parents blamed Russell for the problem! This was something that Russell clearly resented, although there was a happy outcome: after observing a strict regime of silence pre-

---

19. McCullum, the red-bearded planter in both *Doctor Syn on the High Seas* and *Doctor Syn Returns*.
20. Whilst these are both impressive claims, it is difficult to see how they can be verified.

Westminster Dragoons: Russell (left) with brother Frank and father (Thorndike family collection)

scribed by a specialist, his sister made a full recovery. Russell later returned to America alone, to become Greet's leading man. Later still (in 1909), he joined Alexander Matheson Lang's World Tour, most notably performing in South Africa, India and China over a two-year period. These trips inevitably fuelled, and were reflected in, his subsequent writing; nephew John Casson, in his biography of parents Lewis and Sybil,[21] describes how Russell would come home with 'thrilling stories of diabolical torture.' On return from touring with Matheson, Russell joined the formidable Miss Annie Horniman's famed repertory company at the Gaiety Theatre, Manchester, where, for a brief time, he again teamed up with his older sister.

It was during one of the extended Thorndike family sojourns at Dymchurch that the spectre of war grew ever nearer. By now Sybil was married and her husband, Lewis Casson, saw the writing on the wall. Following news of the assassination of Archduke Franz Ferdinand, he insisted that they should all pack and return to London. He was not wrong: war was declared within the week. Typically, Russell saw this as a great adventure and immediately signed up with the Westminster Dragoons. 'I was the first to be involved' he was to proudly declare. The reason he was to give, however, was somewhat bizarre: '[I was] very keen to become a trooper because I had never been cast for one on the stage'. Brother Frank had also become caught up in the enthusiasm and, unbeknown to the rest of the family at the time, joined the same regiment.

---

21. *Lewis and Sybil: a Memoir* by John Casson, Harper Collins 1972.

Given the horrors that lay in wait, it is now difficult to understand the mood of the time and the way in which war was embraced in many quarters. But young men such as the Thorndikes couldn't wait to do their duty for King and Country. And at the beginning, there was much excitement for Russell, with the Westminster Dragoons being home to a number of close personal friends, including childhood pal Lawrence Anderson and the son of theatrical scene painter Joseph Harker. There was wider theatrical representation, which numbered (amongst others) baritone Charles Knowles and Lord Howard de Walden (whose family were great sponsors of the arts). There was also a splendid mounted band, which included a number of musicians very well known in London's theatreland. The Dragoons' London base was Vincent Square (next door to Arthur Thorndike's latest parish), which meant that the family maintained daily contact. Altogether, it was an auspicious start.

Having initially sailed to Egypt, by 1915 the Dragoons were in Gallipolli, where a colleague assisting Russell to carry a gun carriage slipped and fell. The carriage collapsed, with Russell trapped underneath. He suffered a dislocated spine and, whilst the injury would continue to trouble him on and off over the years, it led to his discharge and was arguably a lucky break: the platoon did not fare at all well and most of its members would be killed in the course of the war. Lewis Casson was also injured, albeit not seriously, but a real tragedy befell the family with the death of Frank. In many ways, Russell and his younger brother were very much alike, particularly in their *joie de vivre* and enthusiasm to throw themselves into any challenge. Frank was extremely good looking, articulate, popular and – according to many – had more natural acting ability than either Sybil or Russell. He seemed to have a glittering future ahead of him, but whilst on home leave had joked that he appeared on every church roll of honour except the Parish War Memorial; and that 'it would be a pity to miss that'. He also entered into a pact with his brother that, should either of them be killed, they would appear to the other immediately in a disguised form. His words were prophetic. A year after the Gallipolli landings (and following a return home to convalesce from a bout of fever and jaundice), Frank had applied to join the Royal Flying Corps and subsequently qualified as a pilot. After just four hours solo flying experience,[22] he was posted to France. He embraced flying with a passion and declared that this was now his reason for living. In August 1917, however, whilst on patrol, his plane stalled and crashed. Taken to hospital, his family were informed that he had received only minor injuries; but two days later came a telegram advising that he had died – at the tender age of 23. Russell swore that, on the evening that Frank must have died, a mouse had laid beside him on his pillow and refused to leave. Arthur broke down on hearing of his son's death and was unable to deliver that evening's sermon; Donnie also collapsed and Sybil had to take her place on the organ for the service. Whilst Arthur tried to hide his sorrow by

---

22. This was the norm, at a time when the average life expectancy for pilots was less than a fortnight.

publicly pretending how noble and glorious it was to lay down your life for your country, he never recovered. Two weeks before Christmas, he dropped dead at Sunday Evensong.[23] The official diagnosis was a heart attack, but most recognised that his death was from a broken heart.

Prior to being formally invalided out of the army, Russell had been temporarily transferred to desk duties in Cairo. But he was never one for the mundanity of an administrative job, and it bored him immeasurably. Still in great pain and with restricted movement, he did not make a success of it. However, he took great pleasure in subsequently recounting how he was frequently taken to task by none other than T E Lawrence (Lawrence of Arabia)! On eventually returning home, his appearance was a shock to his family. Sybil was to later recount: 'we'd seen Russell and Frank ride away with the regiment looking so jolly and fit . . . and now Russell looked an old man – bent nearly double – high spirits nearly gone – and just crawling along'. But, typically, Russell determined to make the most of his convalescence. Initially this involved hearing Sybil rehearse her parts but, while he was still incapacitated, Ben Greet took him back on and by 1916 was casting him in a few minor Shakespeare roles. Soon after, he joined one of the first Old Vic companies as leading man and – on occasion – producer-director, under Lilian Baylis. Although he was still far from full health, he played King Lear[24] at the Old Vic Theatre. One evening, the production carried on through an air raid. This was the night that Waterloo Station was bombed. The Old Vic Theatre is barely a stone's throw from Waterloo, and one explosion made the whole building shake violently. This was as Thorndike was due to deliver the line: 'Crack Nature's moulds all germens spill at once.' He immediately substituted 'Germans' for 'germens' and shook his fist to the sky – a gesture that was greatly appreciated and cheered by the audience.

While still in the army, Russell had continued to work on his great project. His writing style (influenced in part by Edith Nesbit) had matured and he had been greatly encouraged by the publication of his first dramatic work *Saul: a Historical Tragedy in 5 Acts* in 1906, in which Sybil had also supported him. But the natural storyteller within him demanded a wider canvas, and he yearned to develop his writing away from the religious genre. An incident that occurred while he and Sybil were first on tour in America[25] had sown the seed for his smuggler–vicar character Doctor Syn, and he worked for many months on a script. However, having realised that the cost of putting this on stage was then prohibitive, he turned it into a novel and this was published in 1915. It met with great success.

---

23. At this time Arthur had become vicar at St John the Less, in Westminster Road, London. As a mark of respect to the family, the street name was later changed to Thorndike Road.
24. To whom Sybil played the Fool.
25. See the second part of this chapter.

1918 marked not only the end of the war, but also the marriage of Russell. Family life was always important to the Thorndikes, and Russell's choice of bride was well received. Both Sybil and Russell were admirers of the actress Rosina Filippi[26] and Sybil not only considered her to be one of the greatest artists of her day but beseeched Russell not to marry until he had met Filippi's identical twin daughters. It was one of the twins – Rosemary Benvenuta Dowson – that Russell chose for his bride. Some sources have suggested that Russell had meant to propose to her sister Fanny instead, although this is most unlikely and probably due to a throwaway comment that he later made when the marriage was going through a difficult patch.[27] The ceremony took place on 17 August, at Kensington Parish Church.[28] Rosemary was herself an actress (as well as a talented musician) and kept her hand in with cameo roles in occasional plays.[29] For the most part, however, she was content to settle into domesticity and in due course raise their five children, the first of whom Daniel (Dan) was born in 1920.

Russell continued to take part alongside his sister in numerous productions and (amongst others) played Iachimo to her Imogen in *Cymbeline*, Leontes to her Hermione in *The Winter's Tale*, and Lysander to her Helena in *A Midsummer Night's Dream*. Most remarkably, Sybil played Gertrude (his mother) to Russell's Hamlet. In 1920, a significant event was to occur in the acting careers of both Russell and Sybil. Jose Levy had come up with the idea of opening a Grand Guignol at the Little Theatre[30] in London's John Adam Street. Grand Guignol (named after the main character in a French puppet show) was an interesting concept: a series of one-act horror plays designed to shock. This had proved to be a very successful medium across the channel, with Paris theatres selling out, but there were doubts that it could satisfactorily transfer to London. Strangely, Russell was amongst the doubters. Lewis Casson was chosen to produce and Sybil was also asked to take part. It is not surprising that Sybil thought this to be right up her and her sibling's street. She is quoted as saying to Levy: 'It's just what Russell and I have always wanted and if you don't have him you won't get me, because if you want horror, he's got a mind like a ghost story in a morgue'. Typically, Sybil got her way and Grand Guignol became established in England. At first, the Thorndikes and Casson cleverly concentrated on imagery to create fear rather than the more obvious props and copious amounts of fake blood that had provided the staple in France. Russell acted in six consecutive programmes, collaborating with Reginald Arkell in the writing of a number. Critical acting success came in Arkell's *Eight o'clock*, in which Russell played the part of a condemned prisoner during his last half hour.

---

26. Filippi was rumoured to be the half-sister of Eleanor Duse, who had found fame directing Shakespeare at the Old Vic. She had married brewer Henry Martin Dowson.
27. It is, however, well reported within the family that Sybil often confused the two.
28. The marriage certificate shows Russell's address at this time as 5 Great Peter Street, London.
29. And in *Scandal* (1932) Rosemary was to play the organ, whilst her mother took the part of Sybil's mother-in-law and Lewis Casson directed.
30. Later to become the Adelphi.

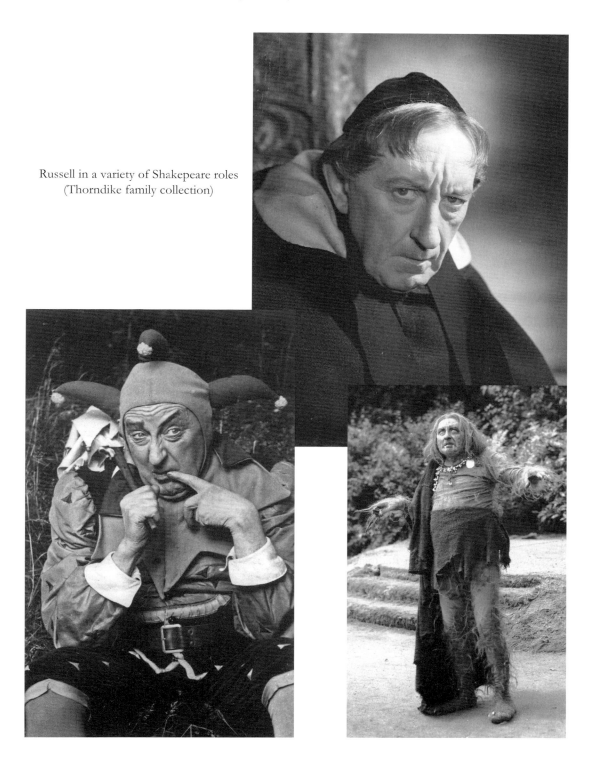

Russell in a variety of Shakepeare roles
(Thorndike family collection)

Russell was nothing if not resourceful. By this time he was living part-time in the rather grandly named Old Palace at Wrotham, and looking to put on a particularly gruesome Grand Guignol one-act play, *The Old Women*. Given past experience and the morals of the day, he and Casson (rightly) anticipated that they would struggle to get this past the censor and applied to put it on at Wrotham Parish Hall. Even such low-key productions had to be approved, but the Lord Chamberlain's Office presumably regarded this as an insignificant affair and passed the script. However, Russell was subsequently able to successfully argue that the licence duly granted applied to any venue in the country and after just one local performance transferred the play to London.

Russell himself took the part of one of the title characters,[31] who, to the strains of a requiem mass, gouges out the eyes of Sybil's character with knitting needles. The audience reaction must have delighted him: on the opening night a man stood up and shouted 'this is monstrous' before rushing out to be sick in the foyer. It was reported that the theatre was forced to employ nurses to deal with the casualties, although this smacks more of an early awareness of the power of publicity. Sybil added fuel to the fire by countering: 'it is a beautiful play, perfectly worked out. The only thing to which it can be adequately compared is the music of Mozart'. Russell was to say that it would be easy to write a 'lengthy book on the Grand Guignol days', although this was not to happen until 2002.[32] At the time, however, Russell himself produced a revuette with Reginald Arkell entitled *Oh Hell* lampooning the genre, whilst the *Daily Telegraph* was to write a leading article about the success of the venture.

In 1922, Russell was involved in what was claimed to be the first professional production of *Peer Gynt* at the Old Vic, and his performance in the title role attracted considerable critical acclaim. This was a role which Sybil – amongst many – felt could have been written for Russell. Peer Gynt was a dreamer, and Sybil was to say: 'Russell *is* . . . Peer Gynt . . ..a born romancer'. Russell would embroider tales, particularly when he had an audience, and, the more he told them, the more he convinced himself that they were all true. John Casson in describing Russell as a 'great favourite' also says: 'he had such wonderful stories to tell us of his own Munchausian adventures . . . to Russell happenings were never enough on their own. Being a writer he turned every event in his and other people's lives into a romantic adventure'. Jonathon Croall[33] asserts that 'his love of fantasy was greater than his ability to cope with reality', whilst his son Dan tells of some tall tales that Russell would recount in various public houses: 'everyone believed him because he was such a good actor'. Lewis Casson was to say: 'He lives and breathes in a world not of make-believe but of a reality wildly and often madly intensified by his own bounding imagination'. In the same vein, historian Tom Pocock (himself later to marry into the Casson family) described Russell as 'the best raconteur I've ever heard'.

---

31. La Bornesse.
32. *Grand Guignol: Freak Theatre of Horrors*, by Michael Wilson and Richard Hand.
33. *Sybil Thorndike: A Star of Life*, Haus Publishing 2008.

Russell's dream of recreating *Doctor Syn* on the stage had never faded, and by the mid-1920s he was in a position to do just that. The play was staged in the West End and taken on tour to a number of provincial theatres.[34] Inevitably, he took the lead role, and he could not have been disappointed with the reviews. *The Observer* wrote: 'Mr Thorndike plays the character with urbanity and charm'. The young Robert Morley, who became part of the touring cast, was to say: 'Russell was an immensely attractive and clever actor' and Morley was in awe of his ability to throw his voice. This production also offered Russell the opportunity to try his hand at stage management. Needless to say, he took to this like the proverbial duck to water, adding yet another string to his bow.

In 1927, Russell's second novel was published. This was *The Slype* – in many ways a typical Thorndike work, drawing on his upbringing in Rochester, his love of Dickens and referencing some characters who had earlier appeared in *Doctor Syn*. The *Manchester Guardian* review lauded it for its Dickensian quality 'and a whimsicality of manner and sincere love of humanity which by no means distantly recall the great Victorian'. To provoke comparison with Dickens must have been sweet music to his ears. Two years later, his biography of Sybil was published and, at the same time he was chosen to lead the Ben Greet Company on another Shakespeare tour of America. By now, Russell was the 'go to' actor for Shakespearian roles, his knowledge of the subject being extensive. Indeed, it was his proud boast that, should the bard's works be destroyed by fire, he would be able to reproduce all his plays virtually word for word![35] By the 1930s, however, the acting profession was undergoing great change, with the popularity of the theatre becoming increasingly threatened by the emerging medium of cinema. For some this was their making, but many established stage actors briefly flirted with the cinema without great success. It is not too harsh to say that Thorndike belonged in the latter camp, but both he and his sister (as well as Casson) strongly felt that cinema was an inferior medium. Nevertheless, he was not new to the silver screen and had made more than a dozen silent films in the 1920s, playing the title role in a number. Inevitably, many of his roles were Shakespearian and he worked alongside some of the major stars of the day, such as John Gielgud and Laurence Olivier. For the most part, Thorndike's later (talking) cinematic roles were minor and he often played figures of authority (doctors, priests and judges). His two most significant film credits were in 1933 and 1934 and both were typical of the time: quickly produced, low-budget British numbers trying unsuccessfully to compete with the big American films which were swamping the market. The first of these was *A Shot in the Dark*, described by studio Star as a 'whimsical yarn about two war weary sailors whose shore leave is interrupted by a trip to ancient Rome'. The cast included James Robertson Justice and Tommy Trinder. The second – *Fiddlers Three* – was also a product of Star and came a year later. George Pearson and

---

34. See Chapter 4 for more detail.
35. Asked (in 1920) how many Shakespeare characters he had played, he came up with a figure of 180 in 25 plays. This included no less than 16 parts in *Macbeth* alone.

Jack Hawkins co-starred in a British thriller 'in which a clergyman investigates the suspicious suicide of the town tightwad'.

By now, Russell's writing career was really starting to take off. The success of *Dr Syn* had resulted in his publishers pressing him to pen further *Syn* books and, between 1935 and 1940, he produced five of these as well as four other novels. His flair for storytelling translated easily into the written word, particularly where elements of horror or gore were involved. Indeed, on a number of book covers and dust jackets, Thorndike was awarded the sobriquet: *Master of the Macabre*.[36] But Thorndike's books covered not just fiction and included: an account of his life and times as a choirboy at Windsor Castle;[37] biographies (not only of sister Sybil but also a collaborative work with her of the great actress and family friend, Lilian Baylis); and Shakespeare commentaries. The love that he shared with his sister of Dickens's works was manifested in his retelling for children of both *Oliver Twist* and *Little Dorrit*. The *Doctor Syn* novels were certainly not his only foray into historical fiction, and the much acclaimed novel *The First Englishman* was set in the time of William the Conqueror and featured Hereward the Wake.

Russell always took an interest in his surroundings and in local history, and he would seek out sources of local knowledge; information so gleaned would often inform his own writing. This is no better illustrated than within the Dr Syn novels. Russell preferred to do most of his writing in his beloved Dymchurch, where he became fully integrated into the community. Here, in addition to patronising The Ship and other village pubs, he would write and perform sketches every Easter and Christmas in aid of the British Legion. These were exceedingly well received. He was unhappy, however, that Sybil and Casson would sometimes take it upon themselves to interfere, and complained that the pair would summon him from his lifeboat house to their nearby cottage to hear what he had written during the day. On occasion, Casson would refuse to serve him beer if he felt that insufficient progress had been made. For his part, Russell was becoming less reliable, spending more time holding court in the pub and often missing meals as a result.

In 1937, Russell's old friend Claude Soloman (a prolific writer with whom he had worked in his silent film days) bought the bombed London Playhouse and restored it to its former glory. This was a project dear to the heart of Russell and, five years later, he wrote a play for Soloman to put on there, entitled *The House of Jeffreys*. This was also adapted to become a detective novel.[38] It was typically part fact and part fiction and Russell wrote it whilst staying with Sybil and Casson in the latter's family home in north Wales. The leading role – Georgina Jeffreys – was written for his sister and was a classic Thorndike creation: a descendant of the notorious hanging judge who was a devout missionary perverted to cannibalism! Also true to

---

36. A title also used for one his books, a collection of short stories.
37. *Children of the Garter.*
38. The novel drew the following praise from no less than *The Times* critic: 'anything may happen; anything does happen. Mr Thorndike's masterly plot is indescribable'.

form, Russell was to play opposite his sister. Not for the first time, the two of them fought like cat and dog during the writing, as they re-entered their own world of *Grand Guignol*.

There is little doubt that, by this time, whilst Sybil's acting career was still forging ahead, Russell's had already peaked. His portrayals of Peer Gynt and Death in *Everyman*[39] (where he is widely reported as bringing a frightening authenticity to the role by making his eyeballs bulge and stand out like organ stops),[40] and his performances in *Doctor Syn* were the highlights of his stage career. Looking back on his life from a distance, it is clear that Russell's was a mercurial talent that didn't receive the recognition that it deserved, and, despite being an immensely popular actor of his generation, he was eclipsed by Sybil. Whilst this partly reflects the outstanding success of his sister, a number of commentators have made the claim that Russell was a more natural and gifted actor. Indeed, his brother-in-law Lewis Casson – never one given to hyperbole – is recorded as saying: 'Russell is the real actor of this family.' The reasons that Russell did not become a bigger 'name' are complex and probably reflect his make up. Ever one who lived for the moment, he would not always commit himself to the task in hand and, with so many different abilities and passions, he could not concentrate on just the one. He was bored by the mundane and the minutiae of life, such as the important tasks of budgeting and domestic management. As a result, his personal affairs were haphazard and he lacked the self-discipline to look after his finances. This is no better illustrated than by his selling of the film rights of *Doctor Syn* to London films for just £20, which was to disappear in the course of an evening at Chelsea's Pier Hotel.[41] For, although earning what must have been a considerable amount over his lifetime, he was never particularly 'comfortable' and was, at times, penniless. Dan recalls that: 'my mother was always short of money'. And, whereas Russell's own mother had accumulated and traded properties, Russell never owned a house but instead rented (or was a guest in) a series of homes. This lack of a permanent base also put pressure on a marriage that – despite a deep mutual affection – periodically showed signs of strain. Because of their financial situation, Russell and Rosemary frequently had little choice but to move. His financial failings – specifically his failure to submit income tax returns – resulted in bankruptcy for the first (but not last) time in 1952, and it was to be only very shortly before his death that full discharge was finally achieved.

Marriage had not altered Russell's feelings for his native county of Kent, and the locations of his rented properties included Wrotham as well as Dymchurch. However, as his family grew and his work required him to spend more time in London, it was not easy to find a suit-

---

39. *Everyman*, by Flemish monk Peter Dorland, was a constant in the lives of both Russell and Sybil. Sybil played in it at the Old Vic in 1915, whilst Russell's first appearance was at the Rudolf Steiner Hall in NW1 in 1923 – with Greet, Sybil and Eileen also in the cast .

40. An ability he was to use widely – see Sybil's comments re: the birth of *Doctor Syn* (second part of this chapter).

41. Thorndike's son, Dan, says that this transaction was his father's biggest mistake. The consequences were certainly far reaching, even precluding the screening of video recordings of plays performed on Romney Marsh in the twentyfirst century.

Rosemary and Russell pictured in the mid 1960s (photograph Bruce Thorndike)

able base. Donnie's large leased house in Oakley Street, Chelsea (which she had secured for a peppercorn rent) had increasingly become the hub for both the Thorndikes and the Cassons. Donnie had become depressed following the death of her husband and took to the bottle – sometimes keeping the neighbours awake with her raucous singing of hymns through the night. Sybil and Casson had moved in full-time to keep an eye on her, but moved out in 1937 to allow Russell and Rosemary the luxury of sufficient space for themselves and their children. But Russell's drinking was also increasing and his behaviour grew more eccentric over time. He would regularly go missing during performances, and even celebrated producer Robert Atkins had to send 'runners' to bring him back from various public houses in time for his scenes during open-air performances in Regents Park. During one production in the north of England, the usual search of local pubs proved fruitless and Russell's understudy was prepared. Minutes before curtain up, however, he was found queuing for admission to his own play. He explained that he had heard so many rave reviews that he wanted to see this Russell Thorndike for himself, to ascertain just how good he was!

The darker side of Russell's behaviour was marked by sporadic bouts of violence: at home, objects would fly and, on one occasion, he attacked his wife with the handle of a bayonet. Rosemary, for her part, had been a devoted wife, who had sacrificed her career for her marriage. She had been a wonderful mother to her children, but, with all of them having flown the nest and her husband frequently absent (touring or at the pub), she became increasingly lonely. As a consequence, she also took to alcohol and the domestic situation became quite strained.

There were some growing tensions within the wider family, too. Arguments had always been a part of the family fabric: John Casson wrote that 'when a Thorndike is on the rampage, no one dares to laugh'. Notwithstanding, Sybil and Russell remained close, although Sybil expressed increased anxiety as to his behaviour. Jonathon Croall relates that she was also concerned on behalf of one of Russell's daughters, who was witnessing much of her parents' drunken quarrelling (Sybil even talked about arranging therapy, although the sub-text was that she felt that it was Russell who should go down this route). Sybil for her part thought that Russell had a downer on her ('Russell has always taken me as a joke, and always will'), whilst Russell was convinced that Lewis saw him as a 'lowbrow' and less intellectually gifted. He had a little 'dig' at Casson in his biography of his sister, saying (with Casson clearly in mind): 'I don't like disciplinarians, especially when they don't discipline themselves'. Such family squabbles often ignore the bigger picture, though, and Russell came to rely more and more on Casson to help him with his financial and domestic affairs.[42] Russell also freely admitted to a lack of practical skills, particularly where that great invention of his age – the motor car – was concerned. Indeed, whilst Casson was fascinated by cars, Russell never learned to drive[43] and so became increasingly reliant upon him for transport – particularly for visiting his beloved Dymchurch.

Many of his fellow actors attest that, despite his drinking, Russell was always the complete professional and was never drunk on stage. Playwright Ronald Harwood concurs with this but also recalls that, in the early 1950s, Russell's props included make-up bottles filled with gin. It is perhaps due to the tales of his drinking that the parts he was to be offered decreased in both number and significance as he grew older – in contrast to the career of his sister. In later life Russell took to drinking pints of bitter rather than shorts, although this was as much due to his straitened circumstances as to any change in taste. Having grown up in the company of drinkers, he could be suspicious of teetotallers and, in his biography of Sybil, referred to his sister (albeit in an affectionate way) as a 'tea-fiend'. This was not strictly the case as – particularly in later life – Sybil was also known to imbibe quite regularly. Nevertheless, Russell's acting days were by no means over and, throughout the 1950s, he played Smee to considerable acclaim in J M Barrie's classic *Peter Pan*. The *Manchester Guardian* (which appears to have been a staunch follower of his career) said of his Smee: '[it is] a bewildering mixture of the genial and the sinister, the whimsical and the unkind'. Television appearances were fleeting, but included involvement in the BBC *This is Your Life* tribute to his sister in 1960. Russell was to continue

---

42. This was also clearly demonstrated when Russell's home was bombed in 1940. Lewis generously accommodated both Russell and sister Eileen (herself a victim of the bombing campaign) at his ancestral home in north Wales.
43. Russell was required to drive a short distance in one of his films and ironically managed to crash the vehicle.

Russell pictured at home in
Foulsham, c. 1970
(photograph Bruce
Thorndike)

acting right up until 1969, by which time he was well into his eighties and too weak to work on the stage, although this did not preclude him giving lectures on his long and distinguished stage career.

In their later years, Russell and Rosemary put any earlier differences behind them and lived happily together. But, after the death of Rosemary in 1970, Russell's health, not helped by his war injury, deteriorated further. His youngest daughter, Rhona, was at the time living in Mileham in Norfolk and, so that she could keep a closer eye on him, found him a home in nearby Foulsham. The property in question must have been very appealing: it was King's Head House – a former pub. Here, for a time, Russell attained a new lease of life, holding court to numerous neighbours who had once been regulars in the same establishment.

Despite his prolific output of books and plays, Russell had never been a great letter writer but, when his son Dan had made a 300-mile round trip dash to see him between his own

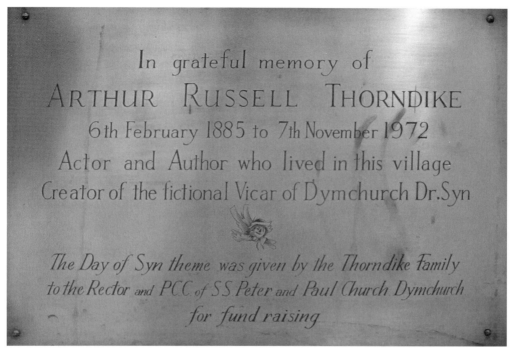

In grateful memory of
ARTHUR RUSSELL THORNDIKE
6th February 1885 to 7th November 1972
Actor and Author who lived in this village
Creator of the fictional Vicar of Dymchurch Dr. Syn

The Day of Syn theme was given by the Thorndike Family
to the Rector and PCC of SS Peter and Paul Church Dymchurch
for fund raising

Memorial plaque within St Peter and St Paul, Dymchurch (photograph David Penfold)

performances in a West End musical, he promised that he would 'write more often'. Three days after this conversation – on 7 November 1972 – he died peacefully at his home.[44] Sybil wrote to her actress friend Gwen Ffrangcon-Davies: 'my darling old Russell was so full of fun, though feeble – well God rest him'.[45] The oldest of four children, she had seen all her siblings die before her. Sybil helped to organise Russell's service of thanksgiving, which was held some three months later at St Paul's, Covent Garden. The service included a reading by Dan and – most movingly – a rendition of *O for the Wings of a Dove*, which Russell had himself sung at the funeral of Queen Victoria some 71 years before.

In a moving obituary, Sheridan Morley said: 'a proud and long-standing member of a theatrical clan, Russell Thorndike remained dedicated to his wife, sister and overacting in approximately that order'. I'm sure that Russell himself would have appreciated and been amused by that. A plaque within St Peter and St Paul church in the village of Dymchurch provides a per-

---

44. The death certificate records the cause of death as bronchopneumonia, oeripheral arterial disease and heart failure. It also shows his occupation as 'author', whereas his marriage certificate shows 'actor and author'.

45. Sybil had celebrated her own ninetieth birthday less than a month earlier but been upset that Russell was too ill to attend a tribute held at the Haymarket Theatre.

manent memorial to his life and times. He was survived by his five children – Dan, Dickon, Jill, Georgia and Rhona – all of whom have appeared on the stage. Dan[46] was with the National Theatre for 17 years and is credited with speaking the first line at the Olivier Theatre. He has actively promoted the Syn legend and has performed in revivals of plays based upon his father's creation. Russell's three daughters all subsequently moved to Canada and one of his grandchildren, Lucy Peacock, is a well established classical actress in that country.

A filmography and bibliography can be found in Appendices 1 and 2 respectively.

The Character *Christopher Syn*

It was whilst touring with Ben Greet in Spartanburg, South Carolina, that a pivotal event occurred, one which was to define Russell Thorndike's writing career and one with which many readers will be familiar – so often has it been told. Events are taken up by Sybil in a foreword she wrote for the first Arrow reprint of *Doctor Syn* (in the form of a 'Dear Russell' letter):

Do you remember a long journey to Spartanburg, South Carolina – I, rigid with fear and thrill, open-mouthed – you, unfolding horror upon horror – the day Dr Syn was born?

Do you remember how on arriving at the hotel, some kindly fate playing up to us so nobly, arranged for a perfectly good murder to take place on the front steps right under our windows – and how the corpse lay there all night, and we being too frightened to go to bed so sitting up most of the night, I making countless pots of tea, while you with bulging eyes gloated over the double-dyings and doings of that splendid criminal, Dr Syn?

It was a far cry from South Carolina to the Romney Marsh, but I think it was some longing for home and the Kent lands that made you develop his story with that background instead of the more obviously thrilling country in which we were travelling.

What a pal the old parson-smuggler became to us! I know for me he joined the merry band – the Men of Kent – the Dickens men of Kent who made the white roads famous.

I envy those who are to make his acquaintance for the first time. I remember with thrill the feeling I had when you first showed him to me. Here was another of those creatures of the family of Daniel Quilp[47] (Our first great love, wasn't he?). Creatures that are above the ordinary standard of right and wrong – tho, even if they murdered their favourite aunt would have been forgiven – they being so much larger and more loveable than aforesaid Aunt.

---

46. Although a serious actor, Dan is probably best known to television audiences through his portrayal of Lord Whiteadder in the sit-com *Blackadder* and for an appearance in *The Avengers*.

47. A character in Dickens's *Old Curiosity Shop*. Whilst in Dayton, Ohio, the siblings founded *the Quilp Club* – but refused to admit any other members!

Was Syn a play or a novel first? I forget – He walks in Romance and it matters not at all to me if I meet him again in prose or verse or in actuality – poking his head out of a dyke in our beloved Marsh. I shall say Good Luck to him in whatever form he may appear – the souls like us who love a thrill will be jollier for the meeting.[48]

A number of commentators have cast doubt on the strict authenticity of all this but, apart from the issue of whether all parties involved in this episode would have seen the fates as 'kindly', it all rings true. Russell himself was to tell a similar tale:

We arrived on the Sunday and had to rehearse *The Tempest* that evening in the hotel. During our rehearsal a revolver shot sounded outside the window. That shot turned out to be a momentous one in my life, as you shall hear. Following the shot came a great shouting and the noise of many feet. We heard the word 'Murder!' called by the gathering multitude on the side-walk. I dropped the prompt book and dashed to the window followed by Sybil and the Company . . . Well it was murder. A young man had shot his stepfather dead for being unkind to his mother . . . The murdered man was left lying on the side-walk and when we went to bed, the corpse, with a bullet hole in its hard-boiled shirt, was still gazing with glazed eyes up at Sybil's window. Sleep for Sybil was impossible. She asked me to go and sit with her. I kept having another look out of the window. Sybil kept making another pot of tea. And we talked, and that night the first idea of Dr Syn was born. That dreadful night we piled horror on horror's head, and after each new horror was invented, we took another squint at the corpse to encourage us.[49]

What intrigued Russell the most was how the crowd not only sympathised with the killer but hailed him as a hero, chairing him into the local bar. This planted the idea within him of a chief character removed from the traditional stereotype: an avenger who was prepared to defy the law to achieve natural justice. *Doctor Syn* was written not in South Carolina but – fittingly – in Dymchurch, although not published until 1915, when Thorndike was still serving in Gallipoli. It is not difficult to draw a parallel between Thorndike himself and his title character patrolling the Dymchurch sea wall, spyglass in hand. Just from where the name Doctor Syn derives, however, has been open to debate. There is of course the play on 'sin'. It has been suggested that the seminal Robert Louis Stevenson work *The Strange Case of Dr Jekyll and Mr Hyde* (published in 1886) was an influence on Thorndike and many other authors, and that use of old-English (in choosing the letter 'y' over 'i') partly reflects this.[50] However, there are other possibili-

---

48. From *Doctor Syn* by Russell Thorndike, published by Arrow Books. (Reprinted by permission of The Random House Group Limited).

49. *Sybil Thorndike.*

50. This is also the likely reason for Russell's surname being spelt 'Thorndyke' by a number of sources. Thorndike himself changes the name of Syn's chief protagonist *Collier* (a historical figure) to *Collyer.*

ties. As already identified, Thorndike was very close to his elder sister (widely known as Syb to friends and family) and it may be more than coincidence that the names are so similar. The first three letters of *synod* are also a possibility. Some members of the Thorndike family believe that the roots are in the Greek prefix 'syn' which translates as 'together', and which would fit with the character's all-for-one philosophy. More likely, however, is that it is a contraction of the word 'syntax'. James Finn refers in his Mersham[51] village journal to a parson (of the village) noted for his loquacity – 'he was a veritable Dr Syntax'. This is a name in turn 'lifted' from the writer William Coombe and caricaturist Thomas Rowlandson (based on Doctor William Gilpin, one-time headmaster of Cheam School). Finn was writing of the late 1800s, and it is very likely that Thorndike was aware of Finn's work (reasonably well-known in smuggling literature) – and/or that of Coombe and Rowlandson. Most significantly, Dan Thorndike recalls his father owning a china plate bearing a depiction of Doctor Syntax.[52] Whatever the truth, it is undeniable that both Syn and Thorndike displayed a veritable gift of the gab.

The settings for the Syn novels and Syn's daytime occupation clearly owe much to Thorndike's own family background. The qualification held by Syn – Doctor of Divinity – was one that was greatly respected by Russell. This partly reflects his admiration for Dean Hole (who was so qualified) but additionally his early aspirations: before he grew disillusioned with the church, he had envisaged earning the 'DD' adornment himself. Indeed, he taunted Sybil that he 'would be a Doctor' someday, a qualification to which Sybil – by dint of her gender – could not aspire.[53] Although there is no evidence of clergymen on Romney Marsh leading smuggling operations, such characters did exist in other parts of the country (most notably the Reverends Matthew Mundy and Ambrose Stapleton in Devon). If there were no smuggling parsons on the Marsh, however, there were those who turned a blind eye, condoned or benefited from the activity. One such was Richard Barham, author of *The Ingoldsby Legends* and vicar of Snargate Church from 1817. Whilst there is no suggestion that he was actively involved with the freetraders, he was certainly sympathetic towards them. Barham has been put forward as a possible influence on Thorndike, and it is worth recording that he was tutored at Brasenose College, Oxford, the same *alma mater* as Christopher Syn.

Even more relevant to this account is the tale of a piratical vicar in the village of Brede – a few miles outside Hastings and very close to the Romney Marsh. The story is of John Maher, parson of St George's Church in the early nineteenth century. Reverend Maher sported a hook in place of his left hand, a legacy – he informed anyone who enquired – of an accident involving the Oxford Mail Coach. The truth, however, was much darker, the loss result-

---

51. A village to the north of Romney Marsh.
52. Research shows that the firm Clews produced a limited *Doctor Syntax* series of plates at the turn of the twentieth century .
53. Many years later, Sybil was to become an honorary Doctor of Manchester University, and lost no opportunity to remind her brother of their childhood spat!

ing from his former life as a pirate on the Caribbean Seas. During this earlier phase of his life, Maher had had a bosun by the name of Smith, but the two had fallen out and Maher had given Smith the slip and travelled back to England alone. Smith vowed revenge and swore to travel the world until he tracked down and destroyed his former Captain. Before long he found himself in a Hastings tavern hearing tales of a parson in the neighbouring village who had a hook in place of a hand. Further investigation confirmed to Smith that this was indeed his man. The following day, Smith confronted Maher and promised to break him – which he did, by threats and blackmail that eventually drove the parson insane. If this story is familiar it is because this was author J M Barrie's inspiration for the character of Captain Hook in his classic *Peter Pan* (and Hook's sidekick Smee was certainly based upon Smith); but there is also a link to Doctor Syn. The concept of a seaman returning to English shores to seek out his one-time pirate captain who has adopted a new persona as rector of a village church very much reflects the circumstances in which Syn and Mipps were re-united. Further, although the initial partings are dissimilar, the Maher/Smith rift bears comparison with the plot of *Doctor Syn*: Syn maroons the mulatto who swears his revenge and eventually turns up in Dymchurch, sending the vicar to the point of madness. The above may sound like conjecture, but I would strongly argue the link. Whilst Barrie was not part of the 'Dymchurch set', he and Russell shared numerous literary friends, some of whom – including Wells and Kipling – were regular guests of Barrie's at nearby Brede Place. Thorndike first got to know Barrie through his sister's season with Charles Froham (the producer of Barrie's plays) and through Barrie's presidency of the Play Actor's Society. Both Russell and his sister regularly acted in Barrie's plays (Sybil playing Wendy to Russell's Smee in *Peter Pan*)[54] and, although much of this post-dates the development of Doctor Syn, the Thorndike family confirms that they were friends from early days. In short, there is a lot of circumstantial evidence to support the theory that Thorndike and Barrie were close enough to discuss and even share literary ideas. Thorndike is quoted as saying that he felt that there was a lot of himself within the character Smee, and it would seem that Mipps is very much modelled on the latter.

There has been another suggestion that part of the Syn persona may derive from the double life not of a vicar but another public figure, a former Bailiff (Mayor) of Hythe. This was a certain Roger Stares who once famously received information from four local men that another inhabitant (William Dranton) was engaged in the smuggling of horses from England to France. The response of Stares, actively involved in local smuggling himself, was to arrest and imprison the informants – and he has been subsequently described as 'Hythe's own Doctor Syn'. It would seem more likely, however, that this is an understandable attempt by the Hythe tourist authorities to cash in on the legend.

---

54. Russell first played this role in 1941 at the Adelphi, but also later in ten revivals of *Peter Pan* (right through the 1950s).

2

Books of Syn: The Canonical Novels

The 'canonical' Doctor Syn novels number seven,[1] as follows:

Vol 1 *Doctor Syn on the High Seas* (first published 1936)[2]
Vol 2 *Doctor Syn Returns* (1935)
Vol 3 *The Further Adventures of Doctor Syn* (1936)
Vol 4 *The Courageous Exploits of Doctor Syn* (1939)
Vol 5 *The Amazing Quest of Doctor Syn* (1938)
Vol 6 *The Shadow of Doctor Syn* (1944)
Vol 7 *Doctor Syn* (1915)

This list is not in chronological order of writing, but sequential in terms of settings and events. The main reason for this anomaly is that Thorndike wrote *Doctor Syn* in 1915 as a one-off, and so had no real problem in killing off his leading character at the end. When he next took up his pen to write of Doctor Syn some 20 years later, he thus had to write of previous events, with all the constraints which that imposed. In literary fiction, Thorndike is not unique in this: Conan Doyle, for example, had to address the same issues with Sherlock Holmes. Thorndike, however, was not one inclined to half measures, nor to make life easy for himself. The second related book that he wrote was not even part of the saga, but a sequel of sorts (*The Slype*) which centres on the discovery some 100 years later of Mipps' diary. The next that he wrote was *Doctor Syn Returns*, followed by the *Further Adventures of Doctor Syn*. Accordingly, the elusive first volume of *Syn's* adventures (dealing with his earlier life) became the fourth of the canonical novels to be penned!

   With the completion of *Doctor Syn on the High Seas* Thorndike clearly felt that the saga was indeed concluded, and its preface states: 'to the memory of John Buchan[3] under whose auspices Doctor Syn was first published, I respectfully dedicate this volume, which completes the Doctor's history'. It is no coincidence that he delayed writing the opening novel until then because, by definition, much of the action would have to be set away from Romney Marsh. Thorndike was never happier than when writing of his beloved Marsh and, accordingly, although *High Seas* is a well constructed story and a good read, it is surprisingly short. We get

---

1. Full publication and other details can be found in Appendix 3.
2. This was originally entitled *The Adventures of Captain Clegg*.
3. Best known as the author of the *Thirty-Nine Steps*.

very little detail about Syn's life as Clegg and, indeed, 12 years of his life is compressed into less than three per cent of the book. But, through this, Thorndike achieves what he set out to do by filling in many of the gaps and establishing the background necessary to support the novels set subsequently in time.

Thorndike, however, was pressured by his publisher for further instalments and another three novels were to follow. A stronger London connection begins to creep in now, and in *The Amazing Quest of Doctor Syn* Thorndike ventures further afield and features North Wales heavily within the plot. In *The Shadow of Doctor Syn* – the final novel to be written (and published some 29 years after Christopher Syn first saw the light of day) – Thorndike explores the French end of the smuggling business, against the background of the French Revolution. This volume was published in 1944, when events in France were once again very much to the fore. There are signs that he had consciously decided that this really would be the final volume, particularly as he arguably fills in the remaining gaps. Hence we learn for the first time in the saga that a Hedge Lane bookstore is used to pass messages to and from France; and that messages are passed between London and the coast by means of tunes played by the Dover Stagecoach[4] and by the positioning of cattle within fields.

Because of the time that elapsed between the writing of his first and subsequent novels, there are some understandable stylistic differences – particularly in terms of the length of chapters. Thorndike tended to include many chapters in his early books, but gave way to fewer – longer – chapters subsequently.[5] This arguably reflects the way that Thorndike matured as a writer. Nevertheless, the original *Doctor Syn* is perhaps the best 'yarn'. Yet in this, Syn is something of a different character, more ruthless (evidenced by his threatening to turn King's Evidence against his colleagues; and his preoccupation with rooting out the mulatto at the time that the Squire's son needs rescuing from the press gang). He is also less meticulous and takes greater risks. Some of the other cast members undergo change, too, as the saga progresses. Strangely, Mipps starts to speak in local dialect for the first time in *Shadow*. By the time that this volume had been completed, however, all local angles had been exhausted: the Marsh was overflowing with contraband and Syn had run out of Cobtree daughters to seduce. It was time for him to hang up his cassock.

---

4. The commonly-featured tune being *The British Grenadiers*. This is yet another 'nod' by Thorndike to his childhood. When growing up he frequently had to listen to Sybil practicing her piano pieces; this was one of her favourites.
5. *Doctor Syn* – his first novel – comprises 40 chapters. *Amazing Quest* – the fifth novel to be written – has only eight.

The front and back covers of the 1972 Arrow editions of *Dr Syn on the High Seas*, *Dr Syn Returns* and *The Further Adventures of Dr Syn* (Reproduced by permission of The Random House Group Limited)

The front and back covers of the 1972 Arrow editions of *The Courageous Exploits of Dr Syn, The Amazing Quest of Dr Syn* and *The Shadow of Dr Syn* (Reproduced by permission of The Random House Group Limited)

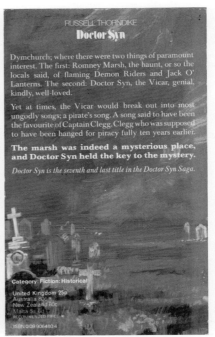

The front and back cover of the 1972 Arrow edition of *Dr Syn* (the first book to be published, but the last chronologically) (Reproduced by permission of The Random House Group Limited)

Plots

Although each book is complete and free-standing in its own right, when they are read sequentially, there is an added dimension. In terms of the whole saga, the apparent dichotomy of the parson/buccaneering smuggler roles is explained early on when Syn is cuckolded by Nicholas Tappitt. The parson turns to the heavens and cries: 'Cursed be the name of the Lord . . . I am a dead man with nothing to fear' (*High Seas*). There is a delicious irony in Syn's odyssey: on the one hand, the pursuit of Tappitt and, on the other, his own demise at the hands of the mulatto who has overcome great odds (including apparent death!) to wreak his own terrible vengeance.

The stories are essentially formulaic: smuggling exploits with a popular hero struggling against seemingly insurmountable odds, sometimes with a romantic sub-plot. There are a number of common themes: the locals claiming that smuggling does not exist (or if it does that it is organised by Sussex men); ever more senior Dragoons and Riding Officers being despatched to Dymchurch to wipe out smuggling for once and for all; young bucks setting out from London for adventure and the reward on offer for catching the Scarecrow; and Syn's great friend Tony Cobtree being oblivious to Syn's wooing of his daughters, which ultimately results in their deaths. Further, 'formulaic' is sometimes taken to extremes. In *Returns*, for example, the Squire's daughter Charlotte (Syn's lover) is shot whilst dressed as the Scarecrow as she lights the Aldington beacon; in *Shadow*, the Squire's daughter Cicely (Syn's lover) is shot whilst posing as the Scarecrow, but manages to light the beacon before dying in Syn's arms back at the Vicarage. And in the latter book, Cicely reveals her knowledge that Clegg, the Scarecrow and Syn are one in a passage that exactly mirrors the events of the chapter: *Charlotte names her Three Loves* within *Returns*.

The lines between good and evil are sometimes blurred, particularly the issue of trading with the sworn enemy, France. Thorndike, however, set out to write adventure yarns and these are good ones of the genre. Within this context it is legitimate for the author to offer mitigation for the actions of his heroes and to blacken his enemies at every opportunity. Thus, Mipps advises that Clegg 'has killed men by the hundreds but only men that were better off dead. And in all the ships he scuttled, he never left even an enemy to drown' (*Returns*). Two of the 'bad guys' (Tappitt, *High Seas*; and Foulkes, *Shadow*) are afforded the sobriquet *Bully*, and for the most part Syn adheres to a strict code. He insists, for example, that Brotherhood rules – that fights must be staged fairly and to the death – must be observed. In similar vein, weakness is despised, with the beadle being depicted as a coward and contempt shown for the Welshman Jones who – in justifiable fear for his life – is exhorted by Syn to seek 'courage to play the man' (*Amazing Quest*).

Allied to this is the strong group dynamic, with incredible loyalty shown by Syn to his men, be it through the Brotherhood when he is involved in piracy or to his smuggler followers in his capacity as the Scarecrow. Any dissension is mercilessly quelled, not least because of the danger of disillusioned colleagues turning King's Evidence – many smugglers did indeed live in fear of being betrayed in this way. When dark deeds have to be done, it is usually Mipps who has to act: it is he, for example, who scuppers their own ships *Pit of Sulphur* and *Imogene* with the attendant deaths of their former colleagues. Syn is oblivious to what his lieutenant has planned, although – typically – he benefits from the actions. There are very few incidents where Syn commits a violent act without justification – a notable exception being the murder of the Chinese cook (Yellow Pete) for having the temerity to protest at the mutilation and marooning of the mulatto (*High Seas*). Other killings are mostly in the course of fair struggle, as a penalty for extreme cowardice or dictated by the need to protect the collective group.

In this context even the highwayman Jimmie Bone is a man of high principle, who makes a point of never robbing a parson; who risks his liberty to alert the Squire when his daughter Charlotte lies dying (*Returns*); is outraged by 'traitors' trying to ship gold to France (*Returns*, again); and who always pays tithes on his ill-gotten gains. In contrast, Syn's enemies are usually men of low principle, whose faults include (in the case of Captain Blain in *Courageous Exploits*) being dishonest and hypocritical! In various duels to the death, Syn always has the upper hand, but the cowardly villain invariably commits a foul (in *Shadow*, for example,

Foulkes hurls a burning torch at him, which is the prelude to Syn mercilessly despatching his opponent with a thrust of his sword through the neck). Other villains struck down in similar style are Bully Tappitt (*Returns*), Raikes (*Further Adventures*) and Dolgenny (*Amazing Quest*).

There is also jingoism by the bucketload. The contention that Clegg would never attack English ships or sailors is again redolent of the patriotism of a bygone age that borders on racism. Mrs Waggetts holds 'anyone born beyond Hythe or the Kent ditch to be foreigners', so a Spaniard is deemed to be 'beyond the pale'! (*Amazing Quest*). Indeed, the Spanish come in for a lot of criticism, with the Governor of Santiago branded as lazy merely by dint of his nationality (*High Seas*). The French do not fare much better, with Robespierre (*Shadow*) described as 'politically courageous although physically an arrant coward'. More alarmingly, in *High Seas,* Syn shoots the captain of the *Intention* for wimpishness and 'demeaning himself in front of a nigger'; and in *Doctor Syn* announces that he is off to preach to the 'smelly blacks'. In defence, it must be said that Thorndike was perpetuating attitudes of the day.

Plot synopses for the novels can be found in Appendices 5 to 11.

Historical context and parallels

The novels are all set in the eighteenth century (although arguably the events of *Doctor Syn* could spill over into the early nineteenth). In most of the novels individual dates are quoted, although the last (the first to be written) is an exception. Many commentators state that *Doctor Syn* is set at the turn of the century, and some that it is definitely the early nineteenth. The narrative advises us that it is set in the times of George III, which only narrows things down to within 60 years. The events conclude one week before England declares war with France and, although this is useful, it is not as helpful in pinning down precise dates as it would have been in other centuries. There was hardly a significant time during this period that England was not at war with France, although the two most likely years are 1793[6] (the beginning of the French Revolutionary Wars) and 1803 (the start of the Napoleonic Wars). That it is more likely to be the former lies in the fact that the ages of some of the characters are divulged and can be cross referenced to books set earlier in the saga (but penned subsequently). At the start of the book we learn that Denis Cobtree, the Squire's son, is 18. If the latter date (1803) was applicable this would have made his father 57 at the time of his birth, which would appear improbable from other events. More significantly, Imogene is depicted as being 17 in *Dr Syn*, and a 1793 setting is fully consistent with her being a babe in arms in 1775 in the only other book in which she features (*Returns*).[7] The French Revolutionary Wars commenced in February 1793 whilst the events of the preceding volume (*Shadow*) extend to at least late 1793, so there would have to be some crossover in any event.

With only one other possible exception, the dates of the events spanned by each book are

6.   The film *Captain Clegg/Night Creatures* (see Chapter 4) sets the action in 1792.
7.   Against which, at least one version of the stage play sets the action in 1804.

mutually supportive. *Amazing Quest* identifies the date only once – as 1780. This novel is the first in which Jerk appears in the saga, and we learn that he is 12. This is very unsatisfactory – given that the character is still a schoolboy in *Doctor Syn* at least 13 years later. If set in 1780, the novel predates *Courageous Exploits* (but it is worth noting that Arrow have consistently identified *Courageous Exploits* – set in 1781 – as the fourth and not the fifth, sequentially). A likely explanation of this is that there is a misprint that has been perpetuated, and that the date of commencement of *Amazing Quest* should be 1790. Such an explanation would fit Jerk's character better and would also be supported by a reference early on to the Squire giving his 17-year-old son (Denis) shooting lessons – which would again be consistent with events and a 1793 setting of *Doctor Syn*. The picture is far from clear and such an explanation would suggest that volumes 4 to 6 were not written sequentially, as it would be natural to assume.

Where necessary, Thorndike sets the political context and there are some fairly acute observations in relation to the political backdrop. The unpopularity of the English in Spain during the eighteenth century – as related in *High Seas* – is a case in point, as is the smuggling of English aristocrats out of France during the Reign of Terror (*Shadow*). In a number of the novels, reference is made to the unease of many sailors who were itching to fight the French but who had been pressed instead into waging the war against smuggling. Not only were these men less than happy at spending their time crawling through ditches on unfamiliar ground, but there was understandable reluctance to fight their fellow countrymen. In reality, there was often sympathy for the smugglers – who had a lot in common with the sailors – and in other circumstances the adversaries would have been natural allies. Even if suitably motivated for their work, in the event of conflict sailors were ordered to 'fire low' whilst the smugglers were not so constrained – given the tariff that applied in the event of capture. These aspects are particularly well covered in *Doctor Syn*.

Issues of the day in relation to the Royal family are also well observed. There are a few mentions of the reigning monarch, George III – who is on occasion referred to by his popular nickname of the day, Farmer George. His eldest son, the Prince of Wales (the future King George IV) features more prominently, riding to hounds with the Scarecrow and forming a close friendship with Syn. Thorndike's portrayal of him as a hard-riding sportsman is much in keeping with the reality. The Prince of Wales was additionally a famed womaniser, and within *Shadow* there is reference to the socialite Maria Fitzherbert – who became the Prince of Wales' first mistress (the two were to marry in a ceremony that was later declared illegal under English civil law).

Thorndike additionally reveals a close interest in Jacobitism. This was the political movement dedicated to the restoration of the Stuart dynasty and – during George III's reign – both the King and the Whigs[8] were targets of the Jacobites. The reader learns from *High Seas* that

8. The Whig party developed from opposition to the religious policies of Charles II and was the forerunner of the Liberal party.

the decline of the Syn family was in part due to fighting for the Jacobite cause; and in *Doctor Syn,* Collyer suggests that profits from smuggling runs are in part being used to fund Jacobite activity. Denis Cobtree protests: 'my father is no Jacobite…a sound Whig'. In *Amazing Quest,* the plot centres on a tontine formed by ancestors of Syn and Jones 'fighting for what must now be considered the wrong side'; the two are conscious that this matter should not be discussed in front of a Justice of the Peace – because of its Jacobite origins. The number of references throughout the saga is somewhat incongruous as the south of England was not a hotbed of the Jacobite movement (notwithstanding that some agents based in France would land on this part of the coast when undertaking spying missions).

Mummers plays[9] are featured in both *Courageous Exploits* and *Further Adventures* (and within the latter are a crucial plot device). These were very much a part of Kentish life during the period concerned, and their inclusion owes much to Thorndike's roots as they were performed widely in north Kent (which includes his home town of Rochester) but very rarely in the south of the county. Passion plays[10] were, however, a regular feature of Marsh life and these would commonly be performed in the village church.

The preoccupation of Thorndike's characters with the Marsh ague is also authentic to the period. The ague was a form of malaria (spread by mosquitoes that thrived because of the way that the Marsh was cultivated and drained), and it caused high mortality rates until the 1730s. Even after this time, it remained a major problem until the completion of the Royal Military Canal in 1806, which greatly improved the drainage of the area. Rehabilitation was hindered by the prevalent damp conditions and, even today, sufferers from bronchial conditions complain that the low-lying land of the Marsh is not conducive to good health. One of Thorndike's influences – Reverend Richard Barham – was a sufferer and so preferred to live on the higher land at Warehorne rather than at Snargate, although he was rector of both parishes.

Finally, the Doctor of Divinity qualification would have entitled Syn to a Deanery, although Dean of the Peculiars – one of titles used by him – is not a *bona fide* one. This was another useful plot device developed by Thorndike to allow his character the option of moving outside the area at will, but – in order to allow him to preach from the pulpit at Rye – his flock would have had to extend from the Diocese of Maidstone to that of Chichester.

---

9. Mummers plays are folk plays which date – probably – from the fourteenth century. They are a form of early pantomime fare poking fun at the failings and failures of the year gone by. The name derives from the Greek word for 'mask' – a standard prop for actors even at that time.

10. Passion plays are related to mediaeval mysteries and highlight the events of Easter, from the Last Supper to the Resurrection. Although never retaining their fifteenth-century popularity they were to be re-enacted for many centuries and still survive in some areas to this day.

Influences and characters

In 1883, Robert Louis Stevenson's classic *Treasure Island* was published, a novel that was to influence and set the tone for most subsequent piracy tales. This was a favourite book of Thorndike's and undoubtedly some parallels can be found, not only within *High Seas*. The dual persona of Syn also resonates with the subject of Stevenson's *The Strange Case of Dr Jekyll and Mr Hyde*, as previously identified.

There is much to be found of Thorndike himself between the pages of his Doctor Syn novels. Early on in the saga, the duel in *High Seas* reflects his fascination with his paternal grandfather's duelling pistols. And the pirate adventures later in the same volume recall his childhood games played out on the rotting Medway barges. Although there are many parallels that may be drawn between the author and his leading character, there is even more of him to be found within Syn's henchman, Mipps. Mipps is a central character in all the books, and spends much of his time in Thorndike's favourite hostelry:

> Here (in the old Ship Inn) . . . [he] would recount many a tale of horror and adventure, thoroughly encouraged by Mrs Waggetts, the landlady, who had perceived the sexton's presence to be good for trade[11]

Despite his strange, unappealing appearance (frequently remarked upon within the novels) and a reluctance to wash, Mipps is not without female admirers – notably the widowed Mrs Waggetts. Mipps makes it clear that he is not interested – his main purpose in life is to serve Christopher Syn. To avoid any accusation of homosexuality (which would have been a significant issue at the time of publication), hints are dropped of Mipps's past. Hence in *Further Adventures*, Mipps recalls a young girl in Savannah; and in *Returns* he speaks of a girl 'I once knew at Saratoga'.

Throughout the novels, Thorndike weaves into his stories parts of his own life, passions and experiences. His love of the theatre is often given an outlet, and there are numerous thespian references within the Syn books, with Shakespeare plays, the Sheldonian Theatre and Drury Lane all featured. The best example of this can be found in *Shadow*, where a meeting between Syn, Sheridan and Kemble provides a most interesting cameo. Richard Brinsley Sheridan and Phillip Kemble were, of course, real-life giants of the theatre: Sheridan a playwright[12] and manager of the Drury Lane Theatre who subsequently became a Whig MP; and Kemble a Shakespearian actor. The two were well known to each other, but were to fall out badly when Sheridan became proprietor of the Drury Lane Theatre. The timing of Syn's fictional

---

11. From *The Return of Dr Syn* by Russell Thorndike, published by Arrow Books. Reprinted by permission of The Random House Group Limited.
12. Thorndike himself played a major role in the film adaptation of one of Sheridan's plays – *The School for Scandal* – in 1923.

meeting fits the facts almost perfectly, and Syn's questioning of Sheridan as to why he 'forsook Old Drury for Westminster' reflects a topical issue of the day. There are further – separate – references to Sheridan in other volumes. It is also of note that, in Crockfords, Sheridan opines that the Scarecrow would have made a good Hamlet – a role played more than once (and to critical acclaim) by Thorndike himself.

Similarly, references to a number of Thorndike's own literary influences can be found within the Syn novels. His and Sybil's shared love of Dickens has already been alluded to by Sybil (within her introduction to *Doctor Syn*). The revelation (within *Returns*) that the brig *City of London* was formerly the *Gog*, with a sister ship the *Magog*, also reflects Dickens: Gog and Magog are biblical characters represented as giant figures within the Guildhall, City of London (commemorating the only two survivors of a brood of giants) who come to life in *Master Humphrey's Clock*. The character Barsard (*Shadow*) would appear both in name and deed to derive from Solomon Pross (also known as John Basard, informer and spy) in *A Tale of Two Cities*. There are also 'nods' to Shakespeare: for example, the landlord of the Mitre Inn in the City of London – Bubukles (*Courageous Exploits*) – takes his name from the description of a character in Henry V; and in the same volume, the smuggler Old Katie is compared to the Fat Woman of Brentford (from *The Merry Wives of Windsor*).

Neither are the Classics ignored, with Syn frequently depicted with his head in a volume of Virgil or Homer (even when captaining the *Imogene*!). In *Shadow*, Aunt Agatha makes mention of Hannibal's ride across the Alps, whilst in *Doctor Syn*, Syn rhetorically asks whether it was Hannibal or Hamilcar who could not stand the sight of blood – a line later faithfully reproduced in the 1937 film version.[13] A chapter title within *Doctor Syn* – *Scylla or Charybdis* – references the two perils of Greek mythology described by Homer. Even at the time, not many readers would have been that familiar with the legend – and a less pretentious title would have been *Between a Rock and a Hard Place*.

In terms of locations, when plotlines dictate a departure from Romney Marsh, Thorndike weaves in other places from his own experience. Hence, when Syn begins his odyssey of revenge in *High Seas*, he calls in on the Carolinas (familiar from Thorndike's early touring days).[14] London and Oxford – theatrical haunts of Thorndike – appear quite regularly and, in *Amazing Quest*, Syn ventures to North Wales. In this novel, Porthmadog and its environs (particularly Bron-y-Garth) feature heavily. The significance here is that Thorndike's brother-in-law's ancestral house was known as Bron-y-Garth[15] – and Thorndike spent much time there as a guest of Lewis Casson and Sybil. In *Doctor Syn*, Mipps alludes to diabolical events that he

---

13. See Chapter 4.
14. This influence also extends to Thorndike's use of language. In *Doctor Syn*, for example, he uses the word 'trash' – this was not in common usage in the United Kingdom until long after the novel's 1915 publication date.
15. The literal translation of Bron-y-Garth is 'Breast of the Hill'. Casson and Sybil spent a part of their honeymoon there, and Casson later inherited the property.

has endured in China and, after Syn's dénouement, flees to a Penang monastery – with descriptions drawn from Thorndike's touring days with Matheson Lang.

It is often suggested that many of the character names within his novels are taken from people known to Thorndike, and from tombstones in the local churchyard. The former is abundantly true as, just like Dickens, he weaves acquaintances into his cast. Although names are sometimes changed, this is not always the case and there are frequent references, for example, to both the Wraight (boat building) and the Henley (fishing) families. These families were well established in Dymchurch during Thorndike's residency, in just these professions.[16] Even Thorndike's grandfather's first wife[17] is acknowledged in the name of a major character. Possibly the most glaring and interesting example, however, is a character who appears only once – and fleetingly – in the saga. This is Lord Noel of Aldington (*Amazing Quest*), and this can only be a jocular reference to his friend Noel Coward, who at the time this novel was written had just moved to a farmhouse (Goldenhurst) at Aldington. Where the graveyard source is concerned, there is less evidence. Clearly, the well quoted example of the physician Doctor Pepper fits the bill (although the tombstone – prominently sited close to the church door – bears the Christian name Solomon and not Sennacherib). Otherwise, neither the tombstones that remain today nor Parish records bear out this part of the theory. Some names, however, clearly reflect Thorndike's background. Examples include the Cobtree family name (Cobtree Manor Park is small country park at the foot of the North Downs in his father's parish of Aylesford) and Briston, a small Norfolk village with a connection to Rosemary's family.

Some characters are – to varying degrees – based upon historical figures. A 1791 Directory does not list any physician in Dymchurch but it is likely that the role of Sennacherib Pepper owes much to a Brookland surgeon, Doctor Hougham, who features in smuggling literature. Arguably the most interesting of the smuggling parallels comes from *Further Adventures*, specifically those passages that describe the Scarecrow's betrayal by Ransley. Chapter 5 of this book discusses the real-life activities of the Ransley clan, and there are some remarkably accurate historical details reflected by Thorndike. The grandmother, for example, advises Syn that her husband was sent to Van Diemen's land, and that she did not join him because he had promised to escape. Van Diemen's land is the former name of Tasmania, to which the real George Ransley was exiled. Although his family did join him, not all travelled with him at the time. The grandmother talks fearfully of Hawkhurst, and George Ransley was not only part of the Hawkhurst Gang, but its one-time leader. Although there is no record of a Shem Ransley (cast by Thorndike), certain details of his sons' fictional exploits would match with George's cousins James and William Ransley (born in 1774 and 1778 respectively).

---

16. In addition, the Wraight family ran the local garage. The Wraights feature in smuggling lore and are still well represented within the village today.

17. The General's first wife – Faunce – secured an annulment to her marriage, but was rarely referred to within the Thorndike family who (along with many of that generation) did not approve of divorce.

Solomon Pepper's gravestone.

Still within *Further Adventures* (and also in some other subsequent volumes) there are a number of references to the Bow Street Runners, including the visit to Dymchurch of 'the famous Jerry Hunt'. This would appear to be a fictional character, although the Bow Street Runners (formed in 1750) had a high profile at the time in which this novel was set (1776). Syn advises that Hunt's boss is Sir John Fielding; Fielding was again a real figure, instrumental – alongside his half-brother Henry[18] – in establishing the Runners, the forerunners of the modern police force. Thorndike's keen interest in naval and military history is also manifested in the names of some key figures. The characters Admiral and Colonel (later General) Troubridge, for example, are undoubtedly based upon the famous military family of that name. This included Thomas (one of Nelson's 'Band of Brothers', who distinguished himself in the Revolutionary and Napoleonic Wars – the timing of which is again fully consistent with the setting of the Syn novels), his son Edward and grandson Sir Thomas St Vincent Hope Cochrane. Sir Thomas was the father of Ernest Troubridge, who served with distinction in World War I. Thorndike took a very close interest in their exploits; so much so that 'T. St. V. Troubridge' was credited with the role of General Manager in the Dr Syn play staged at the Strand Theatre![19]

---

18. Author of *Tom Jones* and *Moll Flanders*.
19. See Chapter 4.

An interesting character who appears in both *Further Adventures* and *Shadow* is Slippery Sam. Sam, in his lonely farmhouse on Stone Street, is no figment of Thorndike's imagination. Sam Jackson was a real-life incorrigible smuggler, following a 'trade' that had been in the family for generations. He headed a widespread operation, which was centred on his home[20] on Stone Street (near the village of Petham, just north of Lympne). He masterminded the smuggling of goods from all over the county and also participated in runs. Arrested and imprisoned at Maidstone, he overpowered his guard, covered himself in axle grease and escaped through a small window, earning a nickname and degree of immortality.[21] Another historical name 'borrowed' by Thorndike is Quested (*Shadow*). Jonathan Quested is described as a Dymchurch smuggler and, whilst there is no authenticated record of a Jonathan, the Quested clan (notably Cephas but also James) is infamous in local smuggling lore. Appendix 12 – which includes a complete list of characters from the novels – indicates all such connections, where known.

Origin of the Clegg and Scarecrow names

A key development within the saga is Syn's adoption of the alias *Captain Clegg*. This derives from an incident (*High Seas*) in which a fly is seen to terrorise a herd of cattle. The *Clegg* (sometimes *Cleg*) is a bona fide name (in Scotland as well as other parts of the globe) for a species of horse fly. It has a particularly vicious bite which can cause extreme irritation (to humans as well as animals) and makes very little noise (in Ireland it is known as *the Silent Doctor* because it arrives quietly and administers a painful injection). The name is thus perfectly suited to the role that Syn has in mind, and seemingly well chosen by Thorndike. However, the likelihood is that the idea was 'borrowed'. At the time that Thorndike was penning his first novel, playwright St John Ervine was writing a play with Sybil very much in mind and consequently had much contact with the family. The play – which subsequently premiered in 1914 and did indeed star Sybil Thorndike – involved a woman who had to become a silent killer and murder her scientist brother in order to save the world from a deadly bomb. The play took the name of its title character: *Jane Clegg*.[22]

Whilst the third persona of Syn – the Scarecrow – might be assumed to be a novel plot device to initially save the villagers of Dymchurch from the hangman's noose and subsequently to lead the smugglers, even this would appear to be rooted in Thorndike's past. When he was 13, Russell had witnessed a performance by Sybil in a musical operetta entitled *Jebediah*

---

20. The fourteenth-century listed property now forms part of a holiday accommodation complex (*Slippery Sam's Holiday Cottages*).
21. Although this story is often told and glamourised, his demise is more often overlooked by those of a romantic disposition; the truth is that his luck eventually ran out and, in 1760, 'Slippery Sam' was hanged for the killing of an Excise Officer.
22. This was a role which Sybil would reprise many times in her career.

Slippery Sam's Farmhouse, Stone Street, Petham

the Scarecrow. At the time he commented how the producer had missed the chance to introduce blood and gore aplenty. The production made quite an impression on him and, not for the first time, he would store this away for future reference.

Incidents

A number of the stories within the books derive from bar room tales (including some that are based on fact), although most of Thorndike's time as character-in-residence at The Ship post-dates the writing of his earliest novels. More reflect Thorndike's keen interest in history. An important source of reference for Thorndike was the seminal 1923 two-volume publication by Lord Teignmouth and Charles Harper: *The Smugglers.*[23] The Romney Marsh features heavily in this account, and Russell was fascinated to find many families of his acquaintance featured.

Other links to local history include the terrible fate of Knarler (working for Farmer Finn), who attempts to level Aldington Knoll (*Courageous Exploits*), in defiance of an ancient curse

---

23. This prized possession is still in the hands of the Thorndike family today.

'that some say was laid upon the Knoll by the Holy Maid of Kent'. The Holy Maid of Kent was one Elizabeth Barton, a servant girl of the sixteenth century given to 'visions'. In reality these were probably epileptic fits but the girl was manipulated for political purposes before being branded a fraud and executed by Henry VIII. Whilst there is no suggestion that she laid a curse upon the Knoll, she lived at Aldington; and tradition has it that any interference with Aldington Knoll will result in bad luck – the barrow being guarded by ghouls. These ghouls are supposedly the spirits of local sailors who drowned nearby, but it is very likely that the story was instigated by the smuggling fraternity, to keep others away. It is tempting to draw the conclusion that the name of Farmer Finn derives from the family of the local Lydd brewery; this could be the case, although, if it is, the credit is not due to Thorndike. This becomes apparent when studying the poem *Aldington Knoll, the Old Smuggler speaks* by Ford Madox Ford.[24] In this, not only is the character (Finn) the same, but a labourer from outside the village undertaking the task of levelling the Knoll unearths a sword and skeleton before dying in identical circumstances to those that befall Knarler. Ford wrote this poem when he and his bride lived at Bonnington, before moving to Aldington, and it was included in a volume called *Poems for Pictures*, published by John MacQueen in 1900.[25] It thus predates the writing of all the Syn novels.

The incident that results in the renaming of the Sea Wall Tavern as the City of London at the start of *Returns* also illustrates how Thorndike the author – as in his own life – at times combined real incidents and fiction. The novel records the vessel *City of London* coming to grief off Dymchurch in November 1775. Whilst the winter of 1775/6 was a particularly cold one, there were no major storms leading to loss of shipping. The events, however, have much in common with those surrounding the wrecking of the *Vryheid*[26] in November 1802 and of the *Courrier de Dieppe* in 1867. The former was an East Indiaman sailing from Amsterdam and the victim of a violent storm. Although managing at one point to anchor off Hythe, she dragged her anchors and subsequently broke up on the large groynes and jetties of Dymchurch Wall, with the loss of 450 lives – a tragedy very similar to that described in *Returns*. The *Courrier de Dieppe* had only four crew on board, but Dymchurch rector Reverend Charles Cobb effected an heroic rescue of the one surviving member – and this would appear to be the inspiration behind the tale of the local vicar (Bolden) being killed whilst trying to rescue the survivors of the *City of London*.[27]

---

24. aka Ford Madox Hueffer (he changed his name just after WWII when such foreign names were deemed to be a great handicap).

25. See *The Last Pre-Raphaelite – The Life of Ford Madox Ford*, Douglas Goldring, Macdonald and Co 1948.

26. Referred to in some sources as the *Melville Castle*, the vessel's original name. The change to Vryheid followed its purchase by a Dutch consortium.

27. If you are looking for additional sources that Thorndike may have drawn on for this pivotal episode, the wreck of the *Northfleet* off Dungeness in 1873 may be one such. Over 300 perished in this disaster, and one of the rescue tugs sent to assist was named the *City of London*.

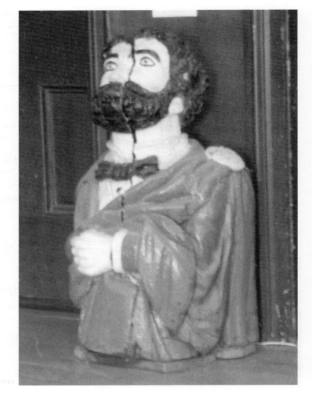

The figurehead from the *City of Delhi*
(Photograph Mark Swallow)

Within the novel, the same incident results in the stricken ship's figurehead being salvaged and displayed above Wraight's boatyard in the village. Wraight's Boatyard in Dymchurch did, for a time, sport such a figurehead – clearly the source of Thorndike's inspiration. Such was the popularity of his books that a number of travel guides have stated that the figurehead really did come from a ship by the name of the *City of London*. Furthermore, so believable was the tale that in the 1970s the figurehead was subjected to a rash piece of vandalism, with drunken teenagers smashing it open with an axe in a bid to find the string of pearls secreted there by Syn! Subsequently, the figurehead was presented to the New Hall Museum where staff effected repairs. It has recently been identified as originating from the *City of Delhi*, a vessel wrecked off Galloways (near Dungeness) in 1867. The rather garish colours with which it was painted led to a belief that the ship may have originated from the Mediterranean. One of the Wraight family has since confirmed, however, that it had been repainted in colours that corresponded to the only tins of paint that were available in the yard at the time! The figurehead can still be seen in the Dymchurch Museum, with the damage clearly visible.

Some other events recounted in the novels would appear to have strong parallels with Thorndike's own activities, both within and beyond Dymchurch. In *Returns*, the Squire gives Syn permission to erect a hut on the sea wall behind Grove House, a 'snug retreat' in which

Sycamore House is now a Bed and Breakfast establishment. A blue plaque records Edith Nesbit's residency

he was to write his sermons. It again does not require too fanciful an imagination to see a connection with Thorndike writing his early novels in an upturned boat under the sea wall. And in the same novel, bodies from the wreck of the *City of London* are initially laid out at Sycamore Farm, a farm of which there is no record but which would appear to draw its name from Edith Nesbit's home (Sycamore House).[28]

Dymchurch Village

Thorndike's descriptions of Dymchurch are also — as far as can be ascertained — authentic to the period of which he writes. A good example can be found within *Amazing Quest*, in which we learn that the front door of the Ship faces the sea wall. This would at first sight appear to be wrong, but the repositioning of the main road at the end of the nineteenth century resulted in the pub now appearing to be back-to-front.[29]

---

28. Later, Thorndike would himself rent a house in Sycamore Gardens.
29. See also Chapter 6.

The original front entrance of The Ship Inn prior to the road realignment

In this area, historian George Frampton has undertaken some interesting research.[30] He concludes that Thorndike's descriptions of the church are accurate in every detail but that church accounts show that a bassoon had been purchased and was in use in the late eighteenth century; accordingly, the schoolmaster (Rash) may have backed the singing with his violin, but would not have led it. In terms of Rash's occupation, although the Forster Elementary Education Act (which established compulsory schooling) did not come into being until 1870, vestry minutes of 1777 record the provision of 'money, clothing and faggots of food, children boarded out and school provided'[31] and the existence of a Sunday school is noted in 1798.

From the turn of the twentiethth century (and possibly earlier), there was a prominent gipsy encampment at the northern end of Dymchurch, close to where the firing ranges now start. Some residents (particularly children) reported the encampment as being quite intimidating and accordingly gave it a wide berth. Thorndike, however, greatly admired the gipsies' skills with – and knowledge of – horses and this was almost certainly the inspiration for scenes that involve Syn horse trading with the community.

---

30. Article in *Bygone Kent* vol 19; no 7.
31. In all likelihood, this was just for the needy of the village.

The current front entrance of The Ship Inn after the road realignment

Other local connections

Many other examples of Thorndike's familiarity with local custom can be found within the novels. In *Doctor Syn*, Jerry Jerk initially names his newly-acquired plot of land *Lookout Mountain*. Marshmen tend to refer ironically to any hillock above sea level as a mountain – indeed, one of the clubs that currently 'operates' in the area is the Romney Marsh Mountain Rescue Society(!). And in *Further Adventures*, the Scarecrow instructs his Night-riders to put on their backstays – these are adapted wooden shoes[32] to aid walking over shingle, familiar to residents of Romney Marsh (particularly those living close to Dungeness). The main legitimate activity on the Marsh at the time was sheep farming, and the local term for a shepherd was (and remains) *looker*; this is acknowledged in a scene within *Shadow*, where (near Lympne) Russell recounts that: '[a] watcher was lookering his sheep'.

In the early Syn novels, there is only sparing use of local dialect, although a very good example: 'the Scarecrow was his dog-fish in the kiddle-net' can be found in *Further Adventures*. Kettle (or keddle) net fishing was an activity almost exclusive to the Romney Marsh coastline,

---

32. Sometimes referred to as 'baxters'.

and to snare a dogfish in the net would spell disaster as much of the catch would be damaged or destroyed. Hence, this was very much a local term to describe somebody with a 'bee in their bonnet'. During the last Syn novel that Thorndike wrote (*Shadow*), his knowledge of local dialogue had grown to the extent that he uses it liberally – necessitating the use of numerous footnotes (only sparingly used within the other volumes).

Public Houses

There are a significant number of public houses featured within the Syn saga and, with one exception,[33] all are real. Most are traditional pubs with genuine connections to the smuggling trade and all were operating in Thorndike's lifetime.

There are three Dymchurch pubs referenced by Thorndike: the City of London, the Ocean Inn and The Ship. The former features heavily in *Returns*, where it initially appears as the Sea Wall Tavern (the name change occurring after the wrecking of the *City of London* as previously described). Although there was no Sea Wall Tavern in Dymchurch, there is evidence of the Ocean Inn having changed its name: at one point it became the Victoria Inn before reverting to its original name in 1958. Prior to this it may also have been the Good Intent (the census return for 1841 shows a pub of this name in the village although it is not clear if this was a separate entity). Certainly in 1910 it was known as the Victoria, so Thorndike's use of a change of name for one of the village pubs may again be partly based on his local knowledge.

Whilst it can be taken as read that Thorndike's accounts of the pubs on Romney Marsh were fully authentic (from personal experience!), this extends to other Kentish pubs such as the Chequers at Aylesford (in one of his father's parishes) and the Rising Sun at Canterbury. There also two London hostelries mentioned significantly in the novels – the Mitre Inn in Ely Place and the Ship Tavern in Whitehall – and both are of considerable interest to students of Thorndike. The Mitre claims to have links to both smuggling and Charles Dickens – and Mitre Square certainly features within Dickens's novels. The inclusion of the Ship Tavern further underlines Thorndike's acting and theatrical background: whilst the pub dates back to 1650, the Whitehall Theatre was built on the site in 1930. Thorndike and his fellow thespians would often decamp after appearances at the Whitehall Theatre to the 'new' Ship Tavern – which was rebuilt directly opposite.

Continuity

The order in which he wrote the books inevitably caused Thorndike a few headaches in terms of achieving consistency and he does occasionally get caught out where dates are concerned.

---

33. The Staunch Brotherhood, Santiago.

In addition to those anomalies already highlighted, within *Returns* Syn's return to Dymchurch is recorded as being in November 1775, at which point Charlotte Cobtree is said to be 19 years of age. In the same book, Syn presents a set of pearls to her on her 21st birthday. Given that there is every indication that this takes place in the summer, this would have to be 1777, yet *Further Adventures* – the next volume sequentially – commences in 1776.

As well as confusion over dates, the hanging of Tappitt (as Clegg) caused some further difficulty. In the penultimate scene in *Doctor Syn*, Syn tells his congregation from the pulpit that Tappitt was formerly one of his own (Clegg's) men, rather than his deadliest enemy; the subsequent changes were clearly needed to sustain the events in *High Seas*. Also within *Doctor Syn*, the Squire displays incredulity that Syn would ever wish to leave Dymchurch – notwithstanding that a similar scenario occurs/will occur(!) within *High Seas*. And in *High Seas*, Syn's first encounter with Mipps makes it plain that Tony Cobtree is fully aware that Mipps is involved with the 'free trade', a situation seemingly incompatible with Cobtree's later sincerely stated beliefs that there is no smuggling within his jurisdiction.

Where the plots are concerned, there are a few other minor inconsistencies. One of these relates to the circumstances surrounding Clegg's ambush in Havana, as recounted in *Returns*. Mipps recalls how Syn had sold a cargo of goods to the red-bearded planter (McCallum) but that, when he attempted to collect payment, McCallum had alerted the authorities and Syn was only saved by torching the venue. In *High Seas*, however, we are told that Syn (Clegg) had looted McCallum's cargo.[34] In *Courageous Exploits*, it is explained that, because Troubridge is not a Roman Catholic, he is unable to comprehend why Syn cannot betray a secret of the confessional. Syn is portrayed as a cleric of the Church of England, so the implication here that he may be Catholic is rather puzzling. However, this is not the only inconsistency to be found in this area. Given Thorndike's background, it cannot be considered that he was ignorant of the sensitivities of different denominations, so it may be that his writing reflects his increasing ambivalence toward religion.

Overall, however, it is a measure of Thorndike's skill as a storyteller that, despite the constraints that he placed upon himself, there is so little contradiction or inconsistency. Furthermore, there is much that is complementary. Of note here is Clegg's shanty. This appears in its entirety in *Doctor Syn,* and Thorndike cleverly manages to weave the derivation of individual lines into other novels. For example, in *High Seas* 'Here's to the feet wot have walked the plank' is attributed to an incident where Syn watches Mipps crossing a Marsh dyke.

Occasionally, the morality referred to earlier is compromised. Lapses include Syn reminding Mipps (*Courageous Exploits*) that grooms who have failed them in the past 'have disappeared into the mist'. This does not sit too comfortably with the portrayal of Syn as a great humanitarian, who entertains murder only for the most extreme transgressions and displays of treachery. We are reminded in the same volume that no one has been killed 'who didn't

---

34. One of MacCullum's trading ships – the *Santa Mariana* – is also wrongly referred to as *Santa Maria* in *Returns*, but this may be the result of a printer's error.

deserve it' and also told how well those exiled in France (as prisoners) and their women-folk are cared for.

If one ventures deeper into the realms of the pedantic, there are some historical continuity breaches. The issue of the mummers plays has already been raised. A similar point of interest concerns the pirate England, referred to by Syn and Mipps on a number of occasions. Syn, indeed, claims to have killed England and informs the Squire that he is leaving Dymchurch to retrieve England's treasure (*Doctor Syn*). Mipps often favourably compares Clegg to England, and avers that he served under the latter. Although not one of the best known of the day, Edward England was an English pirate who operated mostly off the coast of Africa and in the East Indies.[35] By common consent, he died in 1720 or 1721, which makes the claims of Mipps and Syn impossible. Mipps himself, although rarely referred to by Christian name, is Septimus early on, but in *Shadow* has become Didimus.

Publication issues

Early editions of the novels are now rare, though not impossible to track down. The first edition of *Doctor Syn* spells Thorndike's surname as *Thorndyke,* which makes it even more of a collectors' item.[36] More significantly, many reprints of *Doctor Syn* omit the chapter *The Tower of Silence*, in which Mipps recounts a further tale of his experiences in China. Adjoining chapters have had to be amended to achieve continuity, and it is unclear how or why this change came about. Further, the incident towards the end of the book where Mrs Waggetts is seized from the *Ship* and hanged from the inn sign has also been completely omitted from most reprints. One can only speculate as to whether this was deliberate (i.e. deemed to be too bloodthirsty and gratuitous for the target audience).

It is the Arrow editions with which readers will be most familiar. Whilst Arrow have done more than most to keep the legend of Doctor Syn alive, there are a number of errors contained within their publications. Many of these are minor: for example, on at least two occasions, *Amazing Quest* refers to the village of *Brookland* as *Brooklands*.[37] The Arrow back cover summary of *Doctor Syn* relates that 'Clegg was supposed to have been hanged for piracy fully ten years earlier'. If this was the case, then Thorndike had made a significant error when he wrote *Returns*, because the hanging took place in 1776 (i.e. at least 17 years previously). The

---

35. This is not the only time that historical fiction has been linked to Edward England; it is widely accepted that one of his colleagues, a Captain Johnson, was the role model for Robert Louis Stevenson's Long John Silver.

36. *The Scarecrow Rides* (see chapter 3) repeats this mistake as do some later re-prints. Some sources claim that the family name was changed, but this is not the case.

37. Brooklands was a motor racing circuit of high renown at this period, and lies some 90 miles from the Marsh. Other volumes refer to the village correctly.

1972 Arrow editions are worth a special mention for the quality of the artwork on the covers. These are mostly accurate depictions of scenes from the novels,[38] and some of the Romney Marsh settings are very recognisable. *Returns* depicts the Night-riders out at night with Fairfield Church instantly identifiable as a classic Marsh backdrop (although Fairfield Church is not specifically mentioned within any of the novels). On the cover of *Doctor Syn*, the illustration is of three men peering into a tomb in a graveyard. This is clearly St Peter and St Paul, Dymchurch, but the scene does not relate to any incident within the book. It is reminiscent, however, of scenes from both the London and Hammer films[39] where it is claimed that Syn *was* hanged as Clegg, but cut down and revived; his coffin (full of stones) was later opened for inspection to confirm the theory. The novels have it that Tappitt was hanged as Clegg, but was not even buried at Dymchurch. We learn instead (*Returns*) that he was hung in chains and buried on unconsecrated land at cross-roads by the Kent ditch. Other publications (notably those issued under the Hutchinson [Universal Book Club] banner) omit whole chapters from the novels.

In 1998, Liz Skilbeck of the Romney Bookshop re-published the original *Doctor Syn*, under licence from the Thorndike family. Between 2010 and 2012, the related Romney Publishing re-issued this, along with *High Seas*, *Returns* and *Further Adventures*, with cover illustrations by local artist Charles Newington.[40] Ms Skilbeck also intends to re-publish the other volumes in due course. Availability of all the novels has greatly increased with the advent of the internet, and advances in desk-top publishing have also resulted in more versions appearing on the market. In both cases examples can be found of typing errors and omissions resulting in some meaning being lost. Some copies of *Doctor Syn* are marketed under the title: *Doctor Syn – a Smuggler Tale of the Romney Marsh* (which incorporates Thorndike's original subtitle); and other volumes may contain similar subtitles.

---

38. See the pictures of the covers on pages 28–30.
39. See Chapter 4.
40. Creator of the Folkestone White Horse.

3

Alternative Syn: Related Novels and Books

In additional to the seven canonical novels, there are a number of further books that can be linked either directly or indirectly to the adventures of and characters within the Syn saga. Two were written by Thorndike himself.

The Scarecrow Rides – Russell Thorndike

This novel by Thorndike is an expanded re-telling of *Doctor Syn Returns*. It was published in 1935 (the same year as the original) in the United States, by Dial Press. It erroneously shows the author's name as Thorndyke[1] and it is not clear why two versions of the same novel should be produced. Some sources have opined that *Doctor Syn Returns* could not be published in original form in America for copyright reasons, but this is a far from satisfactory answer. This extended version runs to an astonishing 344 pages, featuring 40 chapters. The list of chapters makes interesting reading as it shows that most of the additional narrative comes at the start of the novel. A comparison of the chapter titles within the two novels can be found in Appendix 4.

A number of sources have claimed that *The Further Adventures of Doctor Syn* received similar treatment and was repackaged as *The Scarecrow Rides Again* by Dial Press in 1937. This may be the case, although this author has not managed to track down any definitive evidence of such a book.

The Slype – Russell Thorndike

This further book by Thorndike – a murder mystery – was set in Rochester (his birthplace), but uses the fictional name Dullchester.[2] Published in 1927, it was written after *Doctor Syn* but before any of the other Syn novels. It is set some hundred years later.

An extract from the introduction to the Cape edition sets the tone:

---

1. The only other twentieth-century example of this spelling in his published works is the first edition of *Doctor Syn*.
2. It is probably more than coincidence that Dickens had earlier ascribed an alternative name to Rochester (Cloisterham, in the unfinished *Mystery of Edwin Drood*).

To reveal that the Slype is a deep, dark and sinister alley with high and terrifying walls connecting the Deanery with the Cathedral in a sleepy old Kentish town, is no betrayal of the secret of this book. For that eerie and disquieting chasm played an intimate part in the disappearance of a Dean, the concealment of a Canon, and the strange conspiracy revolving about the cathedral plate.

The book is a pleasant enough read, but for those with an interest in Romney Marsh and more particularly the Doctor Syn saga, the significance lies within Chapter 43. This is entitled *Mipps: His Booke*. The storyline revolves around the chance discovery of a journal which Mipps had written with the intention of sending it anonymously to Captain Collyer. He had omitted to forward it, however, and it only surfaces much later in a Penang[3] market amongst a pile of junk. At the front of the journal is the message:

> If this book should fall into the hands of any good Christian what can speak the good King's English like as what I is now a-writing in, let him forward the same to one Admiral Collyer of the Royal Navy . . .

There follows a detailed account by Mipps of his smuggling exploits and his confession to being Clegg's carpenter. He makes out that he has great respect for Collyer ('a brave and worthy officer') and that the journal is a pre-deathbed confession. He tells of treasure which he and Syn had been unable to reclaim on account of Collyer routing them from the Marsh and gives details of its whereabouts in a house in Dullchester. In this account, Mipps also relates that he is pleasantly situated in a Chinese monastery overlooking the sea, having 'outwardly turned Buddhist for my immediate convenience' and the heavy presumption is that the specific location is Penang. All of this accords with the closing passage of *Doctor Syn*, but does not answer the question of whether this was merely a stopping-off point for Mipps or his final destination.

There are also other references within Mipps's journal to past smuggling activities. As it is being read to an assembled throng by the Dean, one of the audience – a fisherman by the name of Jubb – is overcome with mirth. He then produces a letter that Mipps had sent to his (Jubb's) grandfather, who was a contemporary of Mipps (and, moreover, a fellow-smuggler). This tells that the journal contents are a fabrication, a joke at the expense of Collyer, because jokes have been thin on the ground since Mipps departed Romney Marsh. However, the real joke is on Mipps for – by an incredible coincidence – there is in fact treasure secreted in the house he so identifies!

In addition to again basing a number of characters upon real-life acquaintances, the name of one of these – the central figure Dan Dyke – derives from Thorndike's eldest son, who was seven at the time this book was published.

---

3. Thorndike again drawing on his touring experience.

Christopher Syn – William Buchanan[4]

It has been widely reported that, in 1956, American author William Buchanan stumbled across *The Further Adventures of Doctor Syn*. Notwithstanding the existence of *The Scarecrow Rides*, it appears that he considered that there was no American copyright (on either the books or the name *Doctor Syn*) at the time and he determined to adapt this for the American market. It is this book that has probably given rise to most of the inaccuracies surrounding the Syn legend. *Christopher Syn* was published by Abelard-Schuman of New York in 1960 and the dustjacket and flyleaf credit Thorndike and Buchanan with joint authorship, although strangely the hard cover carries only Thorndike's name. There is an acknowledgement that the book is itself 'adapted in part' from *Further Adventures*, although some of the sub-plots are 'borrowed' from other Syn novels, confirming that Buchanan had read more than just the one. These include Syn impersonating the Head of the press gang (from *Courageous Exploits*).

The book formed the basis for the 1964 Walt Disney film, but copies are very hard to come by. Accordingly, some commentators have made assumptions (based upon either the contents of the Disney Film or *Further Adventures*) without having read the Buchanan version.

Some commentators have also claimed that the yarn is spoilt by the poor and inaccurate descriptions of Romney Marsh and that, when the author subsequently visited the area for the first time (to attend the Day of Syn),[5] he expressed his regret that his own account had been so wayward. This – if true – is a little surprising; there is not a great deal of descriptive text within the novel. There's some talk of swamps and an implication that Dymchurch had a cobbled high street, but the only major 'crime' seems to be to confuse Romney Marsh with Kent as a whole – i.e. that the area was renowned for producing hops, cherries and apples in addition to wool and mutton. It may be that reviewers have been misled by the title-page illustration by Harry Horner, which suggests that Dymchurch is more of a Wealden village, with a bizarre interpretation of an English country church. The line – '(General Pugh was determined to destroy) a marsh that was old when kings began' – is a direct 'lift' from Kipling's *Puck of Pook's Hill*, and its use suggests that Buchanan was well versed in the literature of the area and – accordingly – that he would have had a reasonable idea of its topography.

Throughout the book there is the regular use of Americanisms, which sit a little incongruously for the British reader, but this is not unexpected. More pertinently, Buchanan uses the setting of *Further Adventures* to weave in a link to the American War of Independence (*Further Adventures* begins in 1776, which coincides exactly with the American Declaration of Independence). Much of the book does indeed comprise huge chunks of Thorndike's novel reproduced word for word and, understandably, the changes that do occur are largely the result of alterations to the plot to better suit an American audience. Notwithstanding, it is puzzling why Buchanan should retain the names of most characters but change the names or roles of

---

4. Buchanan (1930–1995) also sometimes went by the names William Buck and Will Ray Buck.
5. See Chapter 7.

others. For example, whilst Sir Henry Pembury remains, the Squire of Dymchurch (Tony Cobtree) becomes Sir Thomas Banks. Schoolmaster Mr Rash also remains, although he is a much older man – he has spent 55 years in the choir – and inexplicably leads the church choir rather than playing the violin (which is now taken up by Mipps). He is further noted as being partially disabled and holding a torch for the Ship landlady, Mrs Waggetts – who is additionally credited with having brought up the orphaned Slippery Sam! Syn himself appears to have had ten years taken off his age and, whilst there is reference to his time at sea with Mipps, there is no suggestion that piracy was involved. The village of Dymchurch is portrayed as being riddled with underground passages.

In this novel, the forces of law and order are led not by Faunce or Troubridge, but by General Pugh. Whilst Cobtree is married with three daughters and a son, Squire Banks is widowed with one daughter, Jenny (his only son having died at the hands of the press gang). Jenny Banks is a masked Night-rider (going by the name of Curlew) who – like Charlotte and Cicely in other instalments of Thorndike's – loves both Syn and the Scarecrow. Buchanan maintains that she is unaware that they are the same, which is rather preposterous as, in the opening scenes, the two are seen entering Mother Handaway's stables in costume and then leaving together in their daytime personae! It is also rather unbelievable that Buchanan portrays Mother Handaway as being unaware of the identity of the Scarecrow.

In the opening scene, the occupants of the Dover stage are Pugh, Brackenbury, the Archbishop of Canterbury and a dishevelled wayfarer on whom the Archbishop has taken pity.[6] The coach is stopped not by highwayman Jimmie Bone (completely written out of this version) but by a party of Dragoons, searching for an American spy. The additional passenger is the spy in question, who leaps from the coach, taking Pugh's briefcase in the process. He flees but collapses (and dies) outside Mother Handaway's stables. The usually reclusive Mother Handaway – although illiterate – recognises the papers as something that may be of interest to Mipps and takes them to Dymchurch.

In a scene otherwise faithful to *Further Adventures*, Syn receives this new information whilst maintaining a journal within the covers of official Parish ledgers. However, instead of containing the names of his enemies and their misdemeanours, this is remarkably filled with quotations from the American revolutionary James Otis and philosophers such as Voltaire. In discussing these with Mipps, in addition to the rather predictable homilies relating to personal liberties and freedom, Syn pontificates on the dangers of high-speed travel that could result from the inventions of the industrial revolution!

In contrast to *Further Adventures*, where the customs officer Fragg and the traitor Brazlett are both murdered, in this version Fragg is allowed to escape. Buchanan has replaced Brazlett with Rash who – as a result of his 'acquired' disability – is bitter that he has not been able to join the Night-riders and seeks to sell out his fellow villagers so that he can start a new life in London. At the farewell party thrown in his honour he is not hanged in his chair by the

---

6.   In *Further Adventures*, the occupants are Faunce, Troubridge, Syn and the Archbishop.

Scarecrow; a dummy is used instead. Rash is repentant and even forgiven by those he has betrayed. Again, some critics have seized on this to suggest that Buchanan's book is not as dark as Thorndike's and that this is what appealed so much to Disney (with a family audience in mind). There is some truth in this, although it may be the murderous side of the title character that concerned Buchanan; against this, Pugh is a very dark character, and there is no lack of killing. The sequence of a number of key events is quite different and another two significant characters are also added to the mix. The first of these is an escapee from the press gang, Charley Cullen. He is a friend of the Squire's late son and the sympathetic Squire harbours him. Cullen has served in America, an experience that has helped him identify with the Revolutionaries' cause. The second is a seven-year old orphan (Robin), who has travelled from Steyning in search of his press-ganged brothers. He is cruelly lured to his death by Pugh, who by now has developed a deep hatred of Dymchurch and its inhabitants.

Two further plotlines are reminiscent of Thorndike's *Courageous Exploits*. First, in the manner of Captain Blain, Pugh starts to suspect that Syn is the Scarecow. And a much fiercer Mrs Waggetts – who carries knives, loaded pistols and a meat cleaver under her petticoats! – emulates Old Katie by claiming to be the Scarecrow. Syn, meanwhile, has by now overseen the marriage of Philip Brackenbury to the Squire of Lympne's daughter Kate. Pugh's feelings towards Dymchurch intensify when, with the aid of the Scarecrow, Cullen and the Brackenburys flee the village and set sail for America. He determines to teach the residents a lesson by demolishing the sea wall and by threatening to publicly torture the villagers until such time that the Scarecrow is identified. In the mayhem that follows, the Squire, Mother Handaway and many others are drowned. The Scarecrow is caught in the flood and his horse Gehenna subsequently found dead. Pugh's body is later found washed up on the French coast. All believe that the Scarecrow is amongst the victims, which leaves Syn to – presumably – live happily ever after with his beloved Jenny. To complete the happy ending, news is received that the Brackenburys have safely reached the New World.

The book includes an introduction by the English actor James Mason, who advises that he discovered Dr Syn in his teenage years and was captivated by Thorndike's original novel. Mason himself displays some ignorance about how this particular version came about and, in truth, his introduction adds little.

Dr Syn alias The Scarecrow – Vic Crume

This novel is nothing more or less than a film tie-in. Published by Pyramid Books under the Disney banner in November 1975, it coincided with a re-release of the film and is a retelling of the story aimed at a much younger (8–12-year-old) audience. Vic Crume was prolific in this role, penning numerous such works for Disney to accompany film releases. Thorndike and Buchanan are both credited and the novel is illustrated by Joseph Guarino. Following very good sales, it was reprinted in January 1976.

The plot is, as one would expect, very close to the film version and at times the narrative replicates dialogue from the film. There are some new characters introduced: smugglers by the names of Scannel and Ben Davis, as well as a friend of Mipps known only as Sam.[7] At one point, Mrs Waggett (*sic*) sends a message to Dover via the village cobbler, a profession that has not previously been identified in Dymchurch. But these are only minor characters. There is more detail as to why Bates is a wanted man – with Crume careful to point out that the American grievance was at the injustice of having to pay taxes without being granted representation. This is well handled for the target audience. Sir Thomas's groom is given the name Hobbs whilst Syn's pony (Buttercups in one of the Thorndike novels) goes by the less than flattering name of Fatty.

In keeping with the Disney rather than the Buchanan plot, it is the Squire's daughter (Kate) who is pursued by Brackenbury. Consent to Kate's marriage is given only after Syn points out to Sir Thomas that Brackenbury must have shielded young John Banks when the rescue of Harry was effected.

Son of Syn – Chris George

This book, by local author Chris George, is undoubtedly the least known of the Syn-related titles. As it has never been formally published, copies are very scarce. Thorndike only briefly mentions that Syn has a son and implies that Nicholas Tappitt murders the boy on learning that Syn (and not he) is the father. George bases his story on the premise that Tappitt's claim – that Syn junior was abducted by Red Indians – is truthful. The plot involves the boy Christopher Almago[8] Syn being adopted by a Mohican Indian tribe; marrying a beautiful squaw – Blue Moon Sky – and eventually ending up in Spain (his mother's native land). The couple have a daughter, Christina Sky, who marries a Spanish Count.

On the Trail of Doctor Syn – David Ramzan

Sub-titled *A journey through the adventurous life and times of Kent's most famous pirate, smuggler and parson*, this limited edition large-size 80-page glossy paperback was published in 2010. Purchasers prior to January 2011 were entitled to enter a competition to locate the source of Syn's treasure chest on Romney Marsh. This book provides a background to the novels and main characters and contains some good artwork and photographs. The author has worked in the media and attempted to sell a series that would have brought Dr Syn to a new television audience. He advises that there was firm interest from a film production company, and that a well-known actor[9] was lined up for the title part before the project became another victim of copyright restrictions. Many of the storyboard images are reproduced in Ramzan's book. The

---

7. This would not appear to be the same Sam who appears in *Further Adventures*.
8. The middle name – Imogene's maiden name – has been added by George.
9. This was Gareth Hunt, most famous for his role in the *New Avengers*.

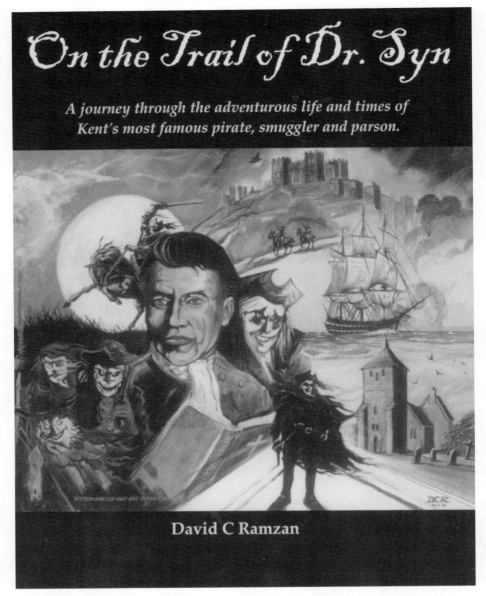

The cover of David Ramzan's book (image used with kind permission of the author)

only current known sources are internet auction sites.

.

4

Screen Syn: Film and Other Media

Films

To date there have been three film adaptations of the Syn saga. Full cast details of each can be found in Appendices 14–16. A fourth film has often been rumoured to be in the pipeline, but has yet to come to fruition.

Doctor Syn (1937) – 75 minutes

Following Thorndike's rather less than shrewd move in selling the film rights for a pittance,[1] it was London Films that produced the first of the Syn films in 1937.

Plot

This is generally faithful to the original *Doctor Syn* novel – with much verbatim dialogue – although there are some significant departures. But to condense any book to 75 minutes on the screen requires changes to be made and there can be no criticism by Thorndike, who wrote the screenplay! In this storyline, the man hanged as Clegg at Rye was in fact Syn rather than Tappitt. He was not hanged 'until he was dead', however, and the viewer is advised that the rope was soaked in acid by his friends, allowing him to survive. Accordingly, Clegg's grave is empty – a fact revealed by the mulatto when he opens it with Clegg's harpoon.

The ending also changes, with the escape rather than death of the title figure (in fairness, it would be difficult to envisage any other ending for a film of this type), and the denouement takes place in the Court House rather than the church. In this scene, Collyer asks what Syn was before spending nearly 20 years as Vicar of Dymchurch; Syn wittily replies: 'a comparatively young man!'. Stretching credibility, Syn interrupts his daring escape to undertake the marriage of Imogene (his own daughter in this version) to Denis Cobtree.[2] His final act before departure is to arrange the blowing up of the oasthouse by Doubledyke Farm, which

---

1. See Chapter 1.
2. In the book this marriage takes place after Syn's death.

Promotional poster for the 1937 London Films film (© itv)

conveniently contains all incriminating evidence of smuggling in the locality. Even more conveniently, the mulatto is in the oasthouse at the time!

When Collyer earlier sets his trap to confirm his suspicion that Syn and Clegg are one and the same, a stuffed dummy is used. This contrasts with the novel, in which Morgan Waters acts as decoy. Other departures include: the identity of Syn (as the Scarecrow) being known to his henchmen; the identity of her father (Clegg) only being broken to Imogene by Rash; the casting of Jerk as Waggetts's nephew, who lives in The Ship; the existence of a secret passage between the pub and Mipps's coffin shop; Clegg acquiring a forename (*Nathaniel* – depicted on his gravestone); and the revelation that Collyer pursued Clegg around the world for two years.

There is further a rather unbelievable plot device, which involves Collyer firing a shot at the scarecrow in a field and subsequently finding blood on it (the significance being that Syn, who subsequently sports a bandaged wrist, was hiding behind the scarecrow[3] at the time!). A major scene in which Collyer marches his men half way around the Marsh at night over rough and muddy terrain and through ditches, only to find themselves back where they started from, is more reminiscent of a tale from *Returns*, which had already been published by the time that

---

3.   The Scarecrow has a signalling function in this plot.

The mulatto contemplates an enforced stay at Camber Sands! (Meinhart Maur; © itv)

work started on this film. Similarly, the presentation by Rash to Imogene of a valuable cross (it was formerly her mother's and has been stolen by Rash from Syn's study) and the consumption of a glass of wine by Collyer that turns out to be nothing of the sort have overtones of other novels (*Returns* and *Further Adventures* respectively).

To strengthen boundaries between good and bad, the mulatto is demonised by having been made responsible for the death of Clegg's (Syn's) wife, thus justifying the awful punishment meted out to him. The role of the mulatto is an interesting one and it has been said – fairly – that such a character could not be portrayed on screen today in the same way. He is demonised and kept in chains, and is a long way removed from the constraints of political correctness. The portrayal is faithful to the book, however, and reflects attitudes prevalent at the time. It has also been pointed out that the book *Doctor Syn* was released a year after D W Griffith's *Birth of a Nation*, which too featured a ruthless mulatto with few redeeming features. Syn's smuggling exploits are justified in the film by the revelation that he has put the proceeds into poverty relief and a new school house for the village.

There is some good attention to detail within the film, which is independent of any narrative in the novel. One scene, for example, involves smugglers turning around a signpost to confuse their pursuers. The distances shown on the signpost are: 'Ashford 12 miles' and 'Ivy-

The mulatto, Collyer (Roy Emerton) and the Bosun (Wally Patch) searching the cellar of The Ship Inn
(© itv)

church 2 miles'; this places the spot close to St Mary's Bay – which is entirely consistent with Collyer having taken his charges on a short march from Dymchurch. The place that Pepper identifies as the apparent source of phantom activity is Doubledyke Farm. This is not mentioned within the novel, although it does feature in other volumes. There is no farm of that name on Romney Marsh, but Coldharbour Farm – to which the smugglers change its name within the film – can be found at Old Romney.

Location and cast

The film is certainly watchable and was shot partly on the Marsh (Rye featuring prominently, with the marooning scene taking place at Camber Sands). There is also some interesting casting, and the signing of George Arliss for the title role would have been considered something of a coup by the producers. Arliss was a major British (stage) star of the period, who had made a successful transition to the early 'talkies'. His was a strange career, however. For a time he could do no wrong and, after receiving an Oscar for his portrayal of Disraeli, was feted; but he was subsequently castigated by critics for wooden acting. Although undoubtedly a strong box-office draw when this film was made, it is questionable whether Arliss (whose last film this was to be) was an entirely appropriate choice for the pirate turned smuggler–parson. He was over 70 years of age at the time, although not

Syn (George Arliss) with Imogene (Margaret Lockwood) and Denis Cobtree (John Loder) (© itv)

greatly older than the character he portrayed (Syn would have been around 63 at the time of his death). But, whilst he well displays the humanitarian side of Syn's character, he hardly passes for the swashbuckling demon rider of Romney Marsh and there is no suggestion of the sailor's rolling gait in his deportment. Perhaps this is harsh; after all, it would be more meaningful to consider what the author thought of this portrayal – and the fact that Thorndike dedicated his next novel (*Amazing Quest*) to George Arliss 'who so brilliantly brought Doctor Syn to life on the screen' suggests that he was more than satisfied. A young and relatively unknown Margaret Lockwood was a success in the role of Syn's 'secret' daughter and it was this film that brought her to the attention of Gainsboro and ultimately stardom, although, as some critics noted, the most demanding aspect of her role was to look pretty. Particularly well cast as schoolboy Jerry Jerk is George Moffatt.[4] Although 18 at the time the film was made, Moffatt passes for younger (Jerry being portrayed as a 12–13 year old in the book). Roy Emerton is less well cast as Captain Collyer, giving a very unconvincing performance.

A point of interest for those with a fascination for the cinema is the technique of undercranking the camera for the fist fight between Syn and Rash. Although fairly common for the time to enliven the action, it does now appear very dated. The film was re-issued on video in

---

4. Older readers and film enthusiasts will recall him as one of the long-suffering sidekicks (alongside Moore Marriott) of William Hay in *Oh Mr Porter!* and a host of other Hay films of the day.

the UK by the Pickwick Group Ltd in 1995 as part of a series of Margaret Lockwood pictures, at a budget price. It is now also available on DVD (as a US import).

Captain Clegg/Night Creatures (1962), Universal/Hammer-Major – 82 mins

Origins

When film producer John Temple-Smith approached Hammer with the idea of a remake of the 1937 film, he had secured what he believed to be the complete rights for owners Rank. John Elder[5] was tasked with writing the screenplay, which, although based on the original film, introduced other elements from Thorndike's novels.

While all of this was taking place, Disney were working on their version of a Doctor Syn film. Stealing a march, Disney had acquired the book rights and copyrighted the Syn name; they then threatened to sue Rank for breach of copyright. Although Temple-Smith believed he had sorted out this angle, Disney claimed that the rights he had acquired only applied in the event of a straight remake of the London Films production based on the 1915 novel. Any deviation – including development of the Scarecrow character – would therefore constitute breach of copyright. Disney had a case, although had it gone to court the outcome would have been by no means certain. Rank, however, were not prepared to put this to the test, and filming had already started (but under the *Hammer Horror* banner). Elder had ascertained that Disney would not contest the use of the Scarecrow character if the Syn name was dropped, and in accepting this he decided to substitute the name *Dr Arne*. He was overruled, however, by Temple-Smith and by leading actor Peter Cushing; the name that they came up with was *Dr Blyss*. Many critics not in possession of the full facts have dismissed this (the continued use of a surname without a vowel) as a cheap gimmick. The reality is that, because filming had already started, a name was required that could be dubbed over some of the earlier takes and it was felt that the retention of a single-syllable name would preclude the change being obvious. That this was unsuccessful is borne out when one watches the film.

Location

Temple-Smith and director Graham Scott spent some two weeks searching for a suitable location for filming. Hammer claim that they looked at Romney Marsh but decided that it could not provide the backdrops required for an eighteenth century period film. This is a strange claim – Disney had no such problem – and the more likely reason is that the two locations on the final 'shortlist' – Denham and Waltham St Lawrence – were both close to the Rank Studio in Bray, Buckinghamshire. The Hammer publicity machine seemed to go into overdrive in relation to this film and made much play of the fact that Denham – the final choice – had 'retained its olde worlde charm'. In the end, little of the film was actually shot at Denham –

---

5.   aka Anthony Hinds.

the majority of scenes being shot at Bray Studios, and many of the properties (e.g. the pubs and village buildings) were just studio props that were used in numerous Hammer movies. Other locations were also used, including Fingest Mill[6] and Chobham. The film undoubtedly suffers from not being shot on the Marsh, particularly as in a key scene the iconic Kentish oasthouse has to make way for the rather more ubiquitous windmill.

Plot

The film is set in 1792 which is a reasonable start in terms of faithfulness to Thorndike's novel. The opening title, is also highly promising:

> . . . the Romney Marshes – flat and desolate – was (*sic*) the land of a proud and inde- pendent people. Their shores faced the shores of France – and many was the ship- load of wine and brandy smuggled across the sea in defiance of the King's revenue men. Many legends have come from this corner of England – but none so widely believed or widely feared as the legend of the Marsh Phantoms – who rode the land on dark misty nights – and struck fear into the hearts of all who crossed their paths..

Because of the restrictions imposed by Disney, there are many similarities with the 1937 ver- sion, particularly the premise that the churchyard contains the grave of Clegg. Earlier events are covered by the marooning of the mulatto,[7] tied to a tree on a coral reef to which is nailed the sign: 'Thus perish all who betray Captain Clegg'. Imogene is again Syn's (Blyss's) daughter and unaware of her parentage until advised by Rash; and the mulatto is also depicted digging up the grave of Clegg, who cheated the hangman by being cut down before he was dead. Some of the spoken lines are identical, including Collyer's assertion to Imogene that he chased a vessel bearing her name across the seas for two years. Syn/Blyss repeats the humorous ban- ter from the earlier film that before becoming Vicar of Dymchurch he was a comparatively young man, although also claiming that he has been in post only 10 years (the London Films interpretation of nearly 20 years is much nearer the mark). Although the Scarecrow is not inanimate, he is certainly not depicted as a horseman and there is a recognisable plot device involving the Scarecrow being grazed by a bullet. Being a Hammer film, however, there are inevitably some twists and there are a number of plotlines that are unfamiliar.

The arrival of Collyer in Dymchurch is heralded in typical Hammer style. His presence is the result of a tip-off by an informant, a villager by the name of Tom Ketch.[8] Ketch himself

---

6. Film aficionados may be interested to know that this windmill is the one more widely known from *Chitty Chitty Bang Bang!*
7. This is portrayed as taking place in 1776, although the incident was certainly earlier (probably 1775) – as depicted in both *High Seas* and *Returns*.
8. Note that the alias afforded Jerry Jerk by Mipps on his initiation into the Nightriders in the novel *Doctor Syn* is *Jack* Ketch – the traditional name for a hangman (after a particularly poor exponent of the art).

falls to his death in a ditch after being scared senseless by the Marsh Phantoms as Collyer makes his way to the Marsh. On arrival, Collyer demands to see Ketch and is taken to him – laid out in Mipps's coffin shop![9] Highly significant is that the Scarecrow is not Syn/Blyss, although the film leads you to believe this is the case until near the end. The Scarecrow is actually the likeably roguish Squire's son – Harry Cobtree in this version. The *modus operandi* of the smugglers is the use of Mipps's horse-drawn hearses to transport smuggled spirits (more faithful to the novel than the 1937 film in this respect).

It is also explained that the mulatto was rescued from the island on which he was marooned by the very sailors with whom he is now serving. For the supernatural element of the story to be removed in this way seems highly inappropriate for a Hammer film! The mulatto's escape from chains is facilitated by the murder of his 'minder' by Rash. With the coffin shop coming under increasing suspicion, a decoy is used to lead the King's Men out on the Marsh, while the contraband is secreted in a local mill. Less significantly, Doctor Pepper's frequent sorties onto the Marsh at night are to treat patients for the plague rather than marsh ague (presumably deemed too difficult to explain). Blyss is annoyed that the Squire offers Collyer the use of his barn as he wants the sailors as far away as possible, whereas in the novel Syn freely offers the vicarage barn as he wishes to keep an eye on them.

As in both the original novel and film, Rash[10] (innkeeper rather than schoolteacher) is prepared to turn traitor to his fellow smugglers and – as a result – Harry Cobtree is arrested, but then escapes. Blyss's denouement is familiar although taking place at the church (as per the novel) and not the Courthouse (London Films). In a highly dramatic confrontation, Collyer rips off Blyss's collar to reveal the hangman's scar and to denounce him as Clegg. Blyss appeals to the villagers – stressing the good he has done for them – and they respond appropriately, allowing Blyss and Mipps to escape via a secret tunnel to the coffin shop. In keeping with London Films' version, Blyss *en route* hurriedly marries Imogene and Harry (this time using a ring removed from a curtain rail!) before finding the dead body of Rash, harpooned by the mulatto. The mulatto also harpoons Blyss as he tries to protect Mipps and Blyss is then lowered into his own (Clegg's) grave – an unusual ending to a highly unusual film.

Although clearly not to the taste of all who take an interest in Thorndike's creation, it is a passable film. There is a dry underlying humour and the special effects are particularly notable for the time: the Marsh Phantoms are both scary and convincing.[11] The film has received some good reviews, and not just from those close to the Hammer organisation. One appar-

---

9. Not content with being afforded two different forenames by Thorndike, Mipps now acquires the name Jeremiah (!).
10. Rash is married in this version, but still pursues Imogene!
11. Les Bowie's achievements in relation to the marsh phantoms have been roundly praised. The effect was achieved by the use of black body suits for both horsemen and horses, with luminous paint used to depict skeletons. With spotlights placed either side of the camera, the result was an image similar to that produced by a car's headlights picking out road signs at night.

ently independent source has posted a review on the internet that describes it as: 'one of Hammer's finest films yet unseen for years . . . it's a wonderful little movie . . . a neglected gem from a more simplistic age'.

As with the 1937 version, the portrayal of the mulatto caused some problems. Although political correctness had still not entered the dictionary by this time, there were significant concerns about public perceptions of a coloured man being chained and used like a dog, and Hammer were certainly uneasy concerning the reaction of the censor when this character was scripted. In this version, the crime attributed to him was the rape of Clegg's wife (with the rather alarming implication that he *could* be Imogene's natural father). Although much play is made of the fact that the mulatto has had his ears removed, no effort has been made to portray this on screen (the make-up team on the London Films version addressed this much more satisfactorily).

Don Banks was commissioned to write the music, and songs from the film include *The Flowing Can* and *True Courage*. The traditional sea shanty is courtesy of fiddler Harold Gee, who reportedly took some exception to being asked – for reasons of authenticity (i.e. mimicking a drunken sailor) – to 'play badly'!

Cast

The casting of Peter Cushing in the title role illustrates that this was by no means a low-budget, production-line number. Elder wanted Christopher Lee to play opposite him as Collyer – which would have been a classic Hammer pairing – but, alas, it was not to be. Patrick Allen got the part of Collyer and, in the eyes of many critics, was not a success.

Cushing – a household name for his screen portrayal of vampire hunter van Helsing in the Dracula films – was an interesting but perhaps unsurprising choice for the title role. Like Thorndike, he was Kent-born and he lived at Deal, only a few miles up the coast from Dymchurch. Cushing was also interested in local history and seemingly loved the part. During filming he was quoted as saying: 'for years I've nurtured a secret ambition to play a pirate on screen . . . Captain Clegg? He's my kind of buccaneer.' This for once was not standard hype from Hammer: Cushing not only insisted on input to the script, but also made notes for his own adaptation of a Syn story. He subsequently completed the screenplay in 1972, which was given the working title *Awaiting Revenge*. Unfortunately nothing came of this, although his hand-written draft sold for a healthy sum at auction in the 1990s.

The role of Mipps is taken by Michael Ripper,[12] another screen stalwart of the time and a fine character actor. Ripper was not a large man and, when a distraught Mipps was required to carry Blyss/Syn's lifeless body, Ripper was unable to support the weight of the much larger Cushing in a slow walk to the grave. Accordingly, a lighter dummy had to be constructed for use in the longer shots. For the close-ups, Cushing had to be supported at the shoulders and knees by two members of the production team.

---

12. Ripper had once appeared in a film alongside Russell Thorndike (*Richard III*, 1955).

This promotional poster demonstrates that marketing was not limited to
a local audience (courtesy of Universal Studios Licensing LLC)

The rest of the cast list is also fairly impressive. Oliver Reed[13] performs well in the role of
Harry Cobtree and Yvonne Romain – who had a brief but successful screen career – emulates
the performance of Margaret Lockwood in looking pretty. The part of the mulatto was played

---

13. One of the more scurrilous rumours surrounding the choice of locations is that Reed – a renowned
drinker – was well acquainted with the pubs around Denham, and refused to be parted from them!

by Milton Reid, an ex-wrestler. It was claimed by Hammer that he got carried away during the fight scene with Cushing, who sustained some significant bruising.[14]

Release

Filming was completed in November 1961. Two weeks later, work began on *Phantom of the Opera*. The two films were to comprise a double bill, which premiered in June the following year and went on general release later the same month. Although reviews had been generally favourable, audiences at the time were less enthusiastic. This was despite – or maybe because of – some aggressive marketing and strange stunts by Rank. These included the use of an electronic clock in cinema foyers with a flashing red light and a series of publicity cards left in phone booths. One of these cards read: 'what could be better than a street promotion featuring a really trim girl in a provocative pirate rig?' A four-page newspaper – *Horror News* – was also printed to promote the double bill. Other spin-offs from the film – which still occasionally surface on internet auction sites – included a Scarecrow costume.

Captain Clegg was a working title and was only subsequently used in parts of Europe. In the United States the film was released as *Night Creatures*. A measure of its success – or Rank's perception of its appeal – is that it was additionally dubbed and released in France (*Le Fascinant Capitaine Clegg*); Germany (*Die Bande des Captain Clegg*); and released elsewhere in Europe and South America. At the time of writing it has not been shown on British television for well over 25 years. It also remains the only Cushing Hammer Film not released on video or DVD in this country. Distribution rights to *Night Creatures* are held by Universal International, and the movie gets occasional TV airings in North and South America. Rumours continue to surface of a UK DVD video release, but (appropriately enough!) 'pirate' copies (recordings from USA television airings) are widely available on internet auction sites and clips can be viewed on YouTube and Vimeo.

Dr Syn alias The Scarecrow (1963/4)

This is probably the best-known of the films and led to significantly greater awareness of the Syn legend in both the UK and USA. It was commissioned soon after Disney's successful *Zorro* serialisation, which also featured a popular masked figure. The Walt Disney Corporation had acquired the rights to the William Buchanan novel *Christopher Syn* and, importantly, also felt that they had acquired the right to exclusive film usage of the name Doctor Syn.

Plot (UK Film)

The screenplay is by Robert Westerby. Although based on the Buchanan book, there are some significant variations, including the conclusion. One of the main differences is the develop-

---

14. Such claims have to be treated with some scepticism, as Hammer had a history of seeking publicity angles.

ment of the character of the American spy. Buchanan does not afford him a name; but in this film he is Simon Bates who, having been sentenced to death for preaching sedition (for advocating independence for the American colonies), survives his ordeal when fleeing the stagecoach. He makes his way to Dymchurch, where he finds a natural ally in Christopher Syn. The scene is set by Syn justifying to Mipps their smuggling activities in terms of the harshness of the law, which restricts freedom and independence. As well as instantly aligning the Scarecrow and Bates as fellow outlaws, it also nicely addresses the moral issues for the benefit of the viewer. Bates seeks sanctuary, hands over the documents stolen from Pugh and is then secreted in Mother Hathaway's cottage.[15] Other departures from Buchanan's work include it being the squire's youngest son John Banks[16] who takes the role of Curlew, rather than his sister. Syn does not pursue a love interest and it is the Squire's daughter – Kate rather than Jenny – who is the object of Brackenbury's affections.

In pursuit of his mission to stamp out smuggling on the Marsh, Pugh orders the burning of houses and then pressurises the farmer Ransley[17] to turn King's Evidence. In a scene that combines two storylines, he is given 48 hours to come up with a list of names of fellow smugglers. Their conversation, however, is overheard by young John Banks, who in turn informs Syn. Ransley instead determines to make a new life for himself and his sons, financing this action by diverting some of the barrels of rum from the next night's run. The Scarecrow learns of the plan and, after Brackenbury is informed, the Ransleys are duly captured and brought to trial. The Prosecutor (Fragg) demands the death penalty, whereupon Syn enters the courtroom and outlines his theory that the kegs may not contain liquor. They are of course full of seawater, although in another scene otherwise faithful to *Further Adventures* it is Syn and not the Prosecutor who opines that a man cannot be hanged for carrying seawater. The Prosecutor is branded incompetent by Pugh and is stung into trying to prove him wrong.

Fragg pays Ransley a visit and strikes a deal. Ransley is thus persuaded to produce the list of names to qualify for his reward; the Scarecrow's spies have again been busy, however, and the pair are ambushed. A kangaroo court is staged for the benefit of Fragg, who is forced to watch as Ransley is tried, convicted and sentenced to be hanged (whilst tied to his chair). The lawyer, however, is allowed to flee in terror before the sentence is carried out. Ransley remains in the chair but is cut down before his life has expired. This is rather confusing as in the same scene in *Further Adventures*, it is Brazlett who is the victim and there is no such merciful ending, whilst in *Christopher Syn* the quarry – Rash (!) – is replaced with a dummy.

The escapee from the press gang is not Charley Cullen (the friend of the Squire's son), but the son himself – Harry Banks. Banks has spent some four years in service and the circum-

---

15. This is an interesting change of name – Buchanan sticks with the original Handaway. One can only assume that Disney was trying to trade on the popularity of Shakespeare in the United States (Anne Hathaway being the Bard's wife).

16. As in the Buchanan novel, the Squire's family name has been changed from Cobtree to Banks.

17. In this version, Ransley is given the forename Joe.

The Disney empire does not look favourably upon reproduction of stills or posters, and permission has not been given to illustrate their film in this way. However, this unposed shot depicts star Patrick McGoohan with local resident Joe Barnes, during a break in filming (photograph used with kind permission of the Barnes family)

stances surrounding this have fuelled his father's opposition to the press gang. Harry is taken into hiding along with Bates. The pair, however, are captured and taken to Dover Castle. Syn's audacious escape plan involves ambushing the press gang in The Ship (where the smugglers are aided in their work by Mrs Waggetts) and stealing their uniforms. The new 'press gang' arrives at Dover in the dead of night and walks out with all the prisoners, under the noses of both Brackenbury and Pugh. Although Brackenbury recognises Syn, he is sympathetic to his cause and remains quiet – and his actions allow him to get closer to Kate Banks, whose father had previously opposed their love match.

Following the release of the prisoners, Hellspite (Mipps) turns up at the Court House and forces the Squire and Kate to ride to the beach, where the Scarecrow is waiting to ship Harry Banks and Bates over to America, via Holland. The film ends with Syn and the Squire drinking to the health of lovers Kate and Brackenbury and – in a scene reminiscent of the Squire hoping that Bone avoids justice in *Further Adventures* – to the Scarecrow.

Cast

The choice of Patrick McGoohan[18] as Doctor Syn is in some contrast to the earlier George Arliss portrayal, and most critics agree that this was a masterful piece of casting: McGoohan cuts a very plausible figure, with a hint of menace lurking behind his country parson persona. The choice of George Cole as Mipps was also excellent, and Geoffrey Keen plays the curmudgeonly General Pugh well. Sean Scully's character – the young John Banks – lacks

---

18. McGoohan was also keen to have some control over the script, although reports as to his success in this regard are contradictory.

credibility but this is arguably a weakness within the plot, which casts a 14-year-old boy as a major cog in the smuggling operation.[19]

Production issues

There are some further Americanisms that have crept into the film which a British audience may find a little irksome. The Prosecutor, Fragg, pledges to Ransley that – if he turns King's Evidence – 'the *Department of Revenue* will protect you'; and Ransley himself is given one hour to cross the *county line* by the Scarecrow. Some critics have suggested that Mipps's use of 'mum's the word' was not contemporary and that the phrase originated in World War II; there is some evidence, however, that it has been in use since Shakespeare's time. A very minor issue is that the date shown on the 'grave' of Ransley (erected for the benefit of Fragg, as he flees the Marsh) is 17 May 1775, whilst the book settings are at least a year earlier.

The haunting title track by Terry Gilkyson is surprisingly good, although the maniacal Scarecrow laugh was edited out of some reissues. This was due to Disney's concerns that younger audiences might be unduly scared.

Variations and availability

The original production was a three part mini-series completed in 1963. It was re-edited and screened in British cinemas[20] in December the same year (although the screen credits show 1964). In 1964, the mini-series was also run on American television as part of Disney's *Wonderful World of Disney*. It played throughout Europe and Central and South America in 1966; and was again re-edited before its first American cinema release in 1970. The US film was of 129 minutes duration whilst the original UK version ran for only 97 minutes. The Disney Channel has also subsequently re-broadcast original and re-edited versions of both film and mini-series. There was additionally a short 8 mm cine film (*The Mysterious Doctor Syn*) produced, on a 200 ft reel. This was silent and in black and white. Although not that common an occurrence, Disney and some other distributors did sometimes offer such 'spin-off' films for home viewing, in an age that preceded videotape.

Further film re-edits have also been produced. The first – featuring material from all three episodes of the mini-series – was released on VHS in 1980; and a 94-minute film version released in the UK later the same year on the same medium.[21] The condensing of the TV trilogy has led to a lack of clarity in a couple of scenes within the film versions, and it is a shame

---

19. Whilst it can be argued that Jerry Jerk was even younger when inducted into the Night-riders (*Doctor Syn*), he did not assume such a central role.
20. Part of a double bill with *The Sword in the Stone*.
21. The main difference between this and the 97-minute version is that the scene showing the capture of the press gang has been significantly cut.

that the scenario involving the smugglers taking cover when the Dragoons first arrive and the subsequent capture and release of Hadley is completely omitted from the film. Other scenes to be cut include the arrival of the press gang and Mipps 'hamming up' a village idiot persona when first meeting the press gang in the pub.

The three-part television mini-series (which runs to approximately 150 minutes) was very successful – apparently one of the most popular Disney serialisations – and was re-run on the Disney Channel in the United States as recently as August 2001. Each episode is to a degree self-contained and expands the characters, although there is some repetition: notably of a complete scene involving Syn and Mipps providing sanctuary to the American fugitive (this appears in both the first and third episodes). A re-run shown on US television in the 1970s merely omitted the second part without losing any significant continuity. Each episode of the mini-series was prefaced with an introduction by an enthusiastic Walt Disney, who makes some rather alarming claims. He first professes to having a passion for adventure stories that have a 'special appeal' when based upon the lives of 'real people'; and then refers to Syn as 'a real-life Dr Jekyll and Mr Hyde'. In describing the Romney Marsh as being (the area known more widely as) 'the White Cliffs of Dover', he displays an ignorance of the area.

In November 2008, Disney issued for the first time a DVD of *Dr Syn: The Scarecrow of Romney Marsh*. This was a two-CD set, the second of which contains the American serialisation (the full version). It was released as part of the *Disney Treasures* collection, with a run limited to 39,500 copies. The issue fully sold out in three weeks, although in February 2009 the DVD was also made available to members of the Disney Movie Club. Despite the fact that it was available on import only, the re-release was reported in the UK media and the event marked on Romney Marsh. As befits its limited edition status, the CD set attracts very high prices on auction websites, although 'pirated' copies have become increasingly available. The authorised DVD contains two bonus features. The first is a 16-minute documentary: *Dr Syn – The History of the Legend*, which is introduced by Leonard Maltin against a backdrop of Old Romney church. It features Disney historians Brian Sibley and Paul Sigman, comic book artist Bret Blevins and Patrick McGoohan himself. Although this promises much (particularly the interview with McGoohan), it does not add a great deal. The second DVD includes a short (12 minute) feature: *Walt Disney from Burbank to London*, which explores the corporation's film-making in England.

Locations

A very pleasing aspect of the film is that so much was shot in – or close to – its authentic settings. Rye is used for many of the street and village shots and Dover Castle and Camber Sands feature prominently. Also extensively used is Camber Castle – a semi-ruin that exists in the same state today and is open to the public at certain times. This is used for signalling the 'all clear' to smugglers on the beach and is additionally the scene of the rendezvous between Ransley and Fragg. Nearby Castle Water and Rye Harbour also appear. Whilst these locations

Interior of St Clement Church, Old Romney

are just outside the Marsh 'proper',[22] another instantly recognisable location – St Clement Church, Old Romney – is very much part of the fabric of the Marsh. This doubles for St Peter and St Paul, Dymchurch. It was widely reported that St Peter and St Paul was not used because subsequent development would make shooting of a period film difficult. This is not true, however; in many ways it would have been easy to use and presented few shot restrictions. The reality is that shooting would have been hampered by the hustle and bustle of a seaside resort in the summer. St Clement – the archetypal English country church – allowed excellent long-range and panoramic shots and had the added advantage of seclusion. Furthermore, it had sufficient space around it to allow the construction of a highly authentic period 'road' to be used by the stagecoach during filming, which makes a most interesting cameo for those familiar with Old Romney. Internally, the church is also a gem and the unusual example of a fine Minstrels' Gallery appealed to the Disney organisation. Dymchurch's loss was certainly Old Romney's gain as Disney made a much-needed and substantial donation towards

22. Camber Castle is just to the west of Rye, in East Sussex, whereas the coastal resort of Camber is on Romney Marsh (in Kent). When built, the castle was at the end of a spit facing Camber; subsequent land reclamation has significantly changed the landscape.

St Clement Church, Old Romney

the restoration of the church (at the time, essential repair work to the roof had halted through lack of funds). The surviving and rather unusual pink and black colour scheme of the pews dates back to this time. Unfortunately, all the interior scenes – whilst appearing in the mini-series – were cut from the film versions.

The exterior shots of the village pub are not of The Ship at Dymchurch, but of a building in Church Square, Rye. Again, the main film version omits a number of the pub scenes, but the mini-series includes interesting footage of sheep being driven past the building. It also focuses on the inn sign – *The Silent Woman*, depicting a headless lady. This is not a pub to be found within the pages of Thorndike (or even Buchanan), but reflects the way in which the production team genuinely became integrated with the community. Through frequenting the pubs of Rye, the team became aware of a legend surrounding the naming of a local road, Dumbwoman's Lane.[23] The legend has it that the only way to effectively ensure a woman's silence is to remove her head; the production team apparently liked the tale and made a late change to the script to accommodate this 'nod' to local history. Disappointingly, the interior shots of the pub use studio sets.

The dialogue leads the viewer to believe that the closing scene in which the Scarecrow ships Harry Banks and Simon Bates off to Holland depicts St Margaret's Bay. There is a logic to this, as St Margaret's Bay is the closest point to continental Europe (and conse-

---

23. This is a small lane in Winchelsea, less than two miles from Rye (and where comedian Spike Milligan once lived).

quently the traditional starting point for cross-Channel swimming attempts). It was shot, however, at Cliff End[24] (Pett Level), with a number of other scenes using farmland in the vicinity. To confuse the viewer further, the Courthouse sequences have no local connection whatsoever – these were filmed at Iver Grove in Buckinghamshire, a setting frequently used for films of the period (and convenient for Pinewood Studios, where the film was produced).

Related products

As this was a Disney film, there were inevitably some marketing tie-ins and gimmicks to accompany its release. The most obvious of these was a book by Vic Crume, which is discussed in Chapter 3. Far tackier were the giant Scarecrow mannequins ('standees') provided to theatres screening the movie and a boxed Scarecrow mask.

More enduring were a series of Scarecrow comic books, the first released by Gold Key in 1964 – *The Scarecrow of Romney Marsh*. A further two comic books were published the following year under the banner *Walt Disney's The Scarecrow* and the whole series republished in November 1973 – with slight cover changes – to coincide with a US re-release of the film. It is likely that this re-release was also responsible for the Xenophile series of *Doctor Syn* comics, which are abridged retellings of events within the film. The *Twilight Zone* series has also featured Captain Clegg[25] in a 1962 Disney Comic; and Doctor Syn was afforded a role in Volume 2 of a limited series for America's Best Comics entitled *League of Extraordinary Gentlemen*.[26] Some of the Xenophile comics (with only minor changes)[27] have been separately published in Australia.

The soundtrack to the Disney movie was for a time available on a CD – The *Films of Gerard Schurmann* (Cloud Records), which includes the track *Smugglers' Rhapsody*. The theme tune *The Scarecrow of Romney Marsh* by the Wellingtons (lead singer Terry Gilkyson) was additionally released on 45 rpm vinyl (with a 'B' side entitled *Trick or Treat*). Neither of these, however, is still available commercially.

Popularity

There are reports that Disney considered reviving *The Scarecrow of Romney Marsh* in the 1970s and 1980s. This has been confirmed by Bill Cotter, the acknowledged Disney expert and

---

24. This is at the western end of the Royal Military canal, some six miles from Rye.
25. All this character really has in common with the Doctor Syn saga is the name Clegg. Even the setting (sixteenth century) is 'wrong' and the story seems to have more in common with John Carpenter's 1979 film *The Fog*. A boy, lost in fog, becomes transported in time and finds himself in sixteenth-century England and having to crew for Clegg. The only survivor of Clegg's tyranny, he is subsequently returned back to the twentieth century via another fogbank and digs up Clegg's treasure.
26. In which Syn – as Clegg – has a romantic encounter with Fanny Hill!
27. All the comic strip drawings remain the same, but no photos are used alongside.

writer, who has underlined the very high ratings that *The Scarecrow* achieved.[28] The reason why this did not materialise is not clear. Any such revival would have presumably depended upon the availability of Patrick McGoohan and, whilst McGoohan was a very popular and successful actor – fitting perfectly the Disney requirement of a clean-cut family role model – he nevertheless gained a reputation for being a difficult and demanding man. He chose his own work, often with morality issues in mind, and it could be simply that Disney's plans did not fit in with his own. An interesting alternative reason also put forward is that the Scarecrow character was too frightening for some children. Certainly, Disney was obsessed with its family image and – despite the general popularity – would have taken seriously related audience research (as it did in relation to Gilkyson's title song).

Disney has always jealously guarded its exclusivity to Doctor Syn, sometimes going to ridiculous lengths to safeguard its copyright. Whilst this means that no other company is likely to pursue a Syn film, it is not out of the question that Disney will go down this route. Indeed, shortly after the 2008 DVD release it was reported that Disney were planning a remake starring Johnny Depp. This is not as fanciful as it may sound, as Depp was at the time a huge success in Disney's *Pirates of the Caribbean* franchise – a series of films of not dissimilar genre. In the first of the *Pirates* films (*The Curse of the Black Pearl*), Depp's character (Jack Sparrow) is accused of crimes that include 'impersonating a cleric of the Church of England' as well as piracy. Whilst to link the character to Doctor Syn in this way might be dismissed as a wild conspiracy theory, such rejection underestimates the Disney empire. Disney has a record of cross-fertilisation and maximising marketing opportunities and more concrete evidence can be found elsewhere to support this line of thought. As with the marketing for the Syn film, *Pirates of the Caribbean* has spawned a number of spin offs, including comic books. As part of the *Pirates of the Caribbean Disney Adventures* series, a comic was issued in late 2005 entitled *Enter . . . The Scarecrow!* The plotline involved Sparrow being captured and held prisoner aboard the Royal Naval vessel *HMS Achilles*. He encounters Mipps – apparently a former accomplice – who is now serving on the naval vessel. A wild figure on horseback is seen on the cliff above the bay and before long the Scarecrow has effected Sparrow's release; Sparrow gives the Scarecrow the opportunity to join his crew, but the Scarecrow declines as his duty is to protect the people of his beloved Romney Marsh.

In the absence of Patrick McGoohan, Depp would be a popular choice to reprise the role of Syn for a new (and larger audience). The pirate/smuggler theme is one that Disney does well and Depp's character is instantly recognisable (indeed, Jack Sparrow is portrayed at the Day of Syn and receives much more recognition and attention from younger visitors than Syn himself). It is unlikely that any Disney remake of Dr Syn would be anything other than a commercial success. Reliable sources have confirmed that representatives claiming to be from

---

28. It is strange that, whilst this message has consistently been given by the Disney organisation, the DVD release of *Doctor Syn alias the Scarecrow* had by far the lowest issue run of the *Disney Treasures* collection. The fact that it sold out so quickly confirms the interest.

Disney did visit Dymchurch in the winter of 2008/09 to check out possible locations, but nothing has so far come of this.

The League of Extraordinary Gentlemen

A more tenuous appearance is made by the Scarecrow in the 2003 film, *The League of Extraordinary Gentlemen*. This had a strong cast list and there is a scene where Sean Connery's character is summoned, along with numerous other superheroes of the time, to meet the vigilante leader, *M*. Clearly visible behind *M* is a montage of other superheroes, in which the Scarecrow is prominent.

Other media appearances

Dr Syn on stage

Given that Thorndike had originally conceived *Dr Syn* as a play, it was perhaps inevitable that he would take the character to the stage. The stage play, however, has led to much confusion amongst theatre historians. There are numerous conflicting accounts of when this play was performed and for how long it ran and, unfortunately, some prime records were lost during the bombing of London in World War II.

A common contention is that the play was first staged at the Strand Theatre, in late 1923 or early 1924, and that – after a successful London run – it went on to tour in southern England and Wales. Other sources state that the play started in the provinces and then transferred to the West End. There have been claims that the Lyceum was the first to host the play, and a photographic credit of Russell Thorndike playing alongside Alma Taylor is dated January 1925 – at Wyndham's Theatre. Surviving evidence suggests the first performance may have been at the Wyndham, but not until October of that year. It was billed as a play in three acts, featuring the Interlude Players. Surprisingly, playwright Ivan Frith was credited with the dramatisation – and also (for a time) took the part of Mipps.

In 1926–27, the play had runs at both the Strand and Lyceum Theatres, by this time under Thorndike's own management. These timings are confirmed by programmes and by the biographies of those such as accomplished actor Esmond Knight – which record his early appearance in *Doctor Syn*. It is easier to confirm the stagings at venues outside London and these included: the Grand, Swansea (January 1926); Richmond Theatre (1926); Margate Hippodrome (May 1928); Devonshire Park Theatre, Eastbourne (June 1926); the Gaiety Theatre, Hastings (1926);[29] and the Palace Theatre, Westcliff-on-sea (Southend) amongst others. In many cases, programmes at these venues advertise the presence of the full London cast.

---

29. A press cutting of the time states that this production was under the direction of Nelson Knight.

THE MAGAZINE PROGRAMME

Strand Theatre

LONDON

Proprietor · KYRLE BELLEW BOURCHIER
Sole Lessee and Manager · GEORGE GROSSMITH

BY ARRANGEMENT WITH GEORGE GROSSMITH

6D.

NELSON KING *presents*
RUSSELL THORNDIKE
in

"DR. SYN"

A PLAY OF ADVENTURE
adapted
(with the assistance of IVAN FIRTH)
by
RUSSELL THORNDIKE
from his Novel of the same name

Smoking Permitted

The cover of the Strand Theatre production programme

Whatever the sequence of its staging, this was no small-time production: Thorndike wanted everything to be just right for what he saw as his life's major work. This is reflected in some of the actors that he was able to sign up. In addition to Knight, other notable stars included Jane Welsh (as Imogene), Hay Petri and Tom Reynolds. Russell and Sybil had first seen Reynolds playing alongside Henry Irving in New York. This was very soon after the seminal incident at Spartanburg,[30] and Sybil had whispered: 'Russell, there's the living proto-type of your sexton and coffin-maker, Mr Mipps'. Although this episode took place some 20 years earlier, it was not one that Thorndike was to forget, Reynolds subsequently taking the

---

30. See Chapter 1.

STRAND THEATRE

Licensed by the Lord Chamberlain to George Grossmith

EVERY EVENING at 8.30

By arrangement with GEORGE GROSSMITH

NELSON KING

presents

"DR. SYN"

A PLAY OF ADVENTURE

on the Romney Marsh in the County of Kent

Adapted (with the assistance of IVAN FIRTH)

BY

RUSSELL THORNDIKE

From his Novel of the same name

Characters in the order of their appearance :

Town Crier	FRED EMERY
Mr. Mipps (Village Sexton)	TOM REYNOLDS
Mrs. Waggetts (of the "Ship" Inn) ...	LOLA DUNCAN
Mr. Rash	CHARLES DICKENS
"Sally"	GRACE EMERY
A Preventive Man	VAL CUTHBERT
Denis Cobtree	CHARLES HICKMAN
Imogene (Dr. Syn's Ward)	FLORENCE McHUGH
Captain Howard Collyer, R.N.	OSWALD LINGARD
Boatswain	JOHN C. BLAND
Barker (the Bo'sun's Mate)	JOHN BYRON
Spiker	PETER GUERNEY
Si Anthony Cobtree (Squire of Dymchurch)	EDWIN ADELER
Dr. Syn (Vicar of Dymchurch)... ...	RUSSELL THORNDIKE
The Mulatto	CHARLES RAYMOND
Mr. Harding	HAROLD YOUNG

Fishermen, Nightriders, King's Men

THE PLAY PRODUCED BY TOM REYNOLDS

OPERA GLASSES MAY BE HIRED FROM THE THEATRE ATTENDANTS 6d. EACH.

The Strand Theatre production programme: cast list

role at the Strand. Alma Taylor was widely described as 'Great Britain's first true screen star' and also played the part of Imogene. As well as performing in the West End, she took the part to the Grand Theatre, Swansea and others of the provincial venues. The character played by Esmond Knight was Jerry Jerk (he is credited with 'Juvenile lead' at the Strand), although he would have been 20 at the time, significantly older than the character he played.[31] It was also in this play that the young Robert Morley made his acting debut (at Margate).

---

31. Even older than George Moffatt in the 1937 film.

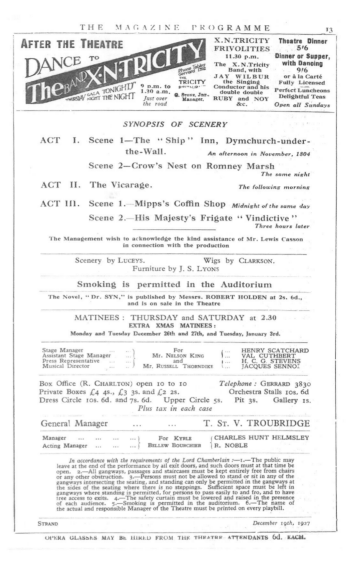

The Strand Theatre production programme: synopsis of scenes (note the 'involvement' of T. St. V. Troubridge as General Manager – see also Chapter 2)

As to be expected, the stage play was very faithful to the original novel although, for the sake of expediency, within a key scene Syn administers his own tattoo.[32] This was an incident which drew much admiration from both audience and cast members as, with his back to the audience, Thorndike apparently managed to convey effectively the sound of sizzling flesh whist simultaneously singing Clegg's shanty!

---

32. A further slight variation was the introduction of some minor new characters, to assist with scene setting. One of these was a Master Woodilands, reflecting the Dymchurch Woodlands family (dairy farmers and fishermen) with whom Thorndike was on friendly terms.

The play, as many of Russell's works, was very well received by the media. Typical was this review by the *Portsmouth Evening News*:

> A splendid reception was accorded 'Dr Syn', which was presented at the Theatre Royal Portsmouth, last night, prior to its production in London.[33] The audience applauded in a manner which proved beyond doubt that the piece was thoroughly enjoyed, and at the close Mr Russell Thorndike, who plays the name part, had to yield to the persistent calls for a speech. London certainly has a treat in store. 'Dr Syn' is a melodrama of land and sea, dealing with some of the most daring smuggling exploits in English history dating back to the 'good old days' of George III. The plot, which is maintained to the end, is laid on the famous Romney marsh, and every detail is presented with deadly accuracy and in keeping with the period. Certain articles are used on the stage for which Mr Thorndike had to search the whole of London to secure, and without which the play would lose much of its effectiveness. To disclose the plot and its sequel would destroy much of the charm of anticipation for those who will undoubtedly avail themselves of the opportunity of seeing the play during the week. It is sufficient to say it teems with romance and mysteries, concluding with the most exciting thrill of all. The acting of Mr Thorndike is superb, and the support he receives from the splendid company, including Miss Alma Taylor, the British 'star', makes 'Dr Syn' one of the finest plays seen in Portsmouth for a long time. The character of the play is such that will appeal to any audience.

In 2001, Marsh Arts Promotions staged a play by J Michael Fields based on the novels, featuring a cast of locals as well as professionals. This included Fields himself, Steven Povey and Ben Barton. Thorndike's son, Dan (by then in his 80s), both narrated and took a number of parts. Given that theatre essentially began in churches, it was doubly fitting that performances should take place in a number of the Marsh churches. The play premiered on 3 August at St Mary-in-the-Marsh and other venues included St Mary's, Rye; St Peter & St Paul, Appledore; and St Nicholas, New Romney. Appropriately, the last performance was in St Peter and St Paul, Dymchurch (on 18 August). The play sold out on each night but the long arm of Disney seems to have imposed a number of copyright constraints: the play was not allowed to be staged other than in the Churches and – regrettably – although performances were filmed, the release of these recordings has not been permitted.

Doctor Syn in Music

An opera, *Doctor Syn*, has also been performed. Commissioned by Kent Opera with funding from the Arts Council of Great Britain, this was specifically written for schools to perform.

---

33. This does not necessarily confirm that the play toured the provinces prior to its West End debut: there may have been a run between London stagings. Unfortunately, the review is undated.

Russell Thorndike and Alma Taylor in *Doctor Syn* (photograph Getty Images)

With libretto by Johanna Platt and music by Adrian Cruft, the opera is for 12 soloists, SATB (soprano, alto, tenor, bass) chorus, piano/electric organ and percussion. The duration (exclusive of intervals) is approximately 1 hour 45 minutes. The work is based upon and true to the original novel and all the principal characters (Syn; Mipps; Pepper; Mrs Waggetts; the Cobtrees; Rash; Jerk; and Collyer) are present. The opera was first performed in 1963 at Norton Knatchbull School in Ashford, and comprises three acts:

Act I
Sunday, the hour of Evensong (The Ship Inn) c 36 minutes
Act II
Scene 1 – Sunday night (outside the schoolmaster's house) c 11 minutes
Scene 2 – Monday, first light (Quayside) c 15 minutes
Scene 3 – Monday evening (Mipps's house) c 16 minutes
Act III
Tuesday afternoon (village square; moving to church interior) c 26 minutes

The work has since been performed at a number of local churches.

More recently (2011), a local musician produced a double CD Album: *Chris Lea's Scarecrow*. This is a 'rock folk romp' based upon the Doctor Syn saga. It comprises music and narrative, both centred on key stories from the Syn novels, but also provides a commentary to the legal and cultural aspects of smuggling of the time. Lea's band comprises: Dave Webb; Joe Whittaker; Stephen Skey; Brian Withstandley; Peter Brooker; Samantha Rush; Peter Bundell; and Jennie Trevillion; and songs from the album have been performed live at The Ship Inn.

Doctor Syn on the Radio

From 2006, the BBC has broadcast a number of adaptations of Thorndike's Syn novels on its BBC7 radio station. The first of these was a 10-part adaptation combining elements of *High Seas* and *Returns*. This initially went out in December 2006 and was repeated in June 2007. Another 10-part adaptation was *The Further Adventures of Doctor Syn*. This was first broadcast in December 2007 and confusingly included events from another novel (*Shadow*). Finally, a six part series – an abridged reading from the original novel *Doctor Syn* – ran in January 2010. Each of these was narrated by Rufus Sewell. Compilation CDs covering all these broadcasts are available on internet auction sites.

5

Activities of Syn:
Lawbreaking on Romney Marsh – the Reality

Smuggling

> 'All Marsh folk has been smugglers since time everlastin'[1]

The act of smuggling has undoubtedly been glamourised and romanticised, particularly with the passage of time. Kipling reveals himself to have been sympathetic to the smugglers, and Charles Lamb came up with the memorable line: 'I like a Smuggler – he is the only honest thief'. To many of the time, smugglers were only indulging in an activity into which they had been forced by the ludicrous and harsh laws of the day. To others they were a desperate band of cut-throats and ne'er-do-wells who enjoyed terrorising the innocent. The reality was as always somewhere in between, although it is doubtful that there were many 'innocents' in and around Romney Marsh.

Romney Marsh has had no monopoly on smuggling, but for more than 700 years was known as the 'Smugglers' Paradise'. It is not hard to see why: a long, safe coastline with accessible beaches, proximity to both London and the continent and a thriving sheep-farming industry combined to provide unmatched opportunities. When John Wesley visited Rye in 1773 he was appalled to see the way in which the law was openly being flouted and begged the locals to 'give up that accursed thing, smuggling'. Predictably, although they flocked to hear his message, they could not bring themselves to do what he asked. For what Wesley and others at the time overlooked was that smuggling was not necessarily a manifestation of greed; as Eve McLaughlin aptly points out: 'honesty was a luxury the average pauper could not afford.[2]

Origins

The word smuggling derives from the Saxon word 'smugan', which means to creep about with secrecy. If it is accepted that smuggling is an inevitable consequence of taxation, it was

---

1. Tom Shoesmith, Kipling's *Dymchurch Flit*.
2. *The Poor Are Always With Us*.

probably Ethelred the Unready in the late tenth century who unwittingly created the activity by imposing a tax on each barrel of liquor landed in the country. In the early thirteenth century, King John placed a prohibitive tax on the export of fleeces, a measure subsequently reinforced by Edward I to finance wars with France. In both cases it is doubtful that much would have been collected, however, for reasons that still existed at the end of the eighteenth century: the lack of any centralised and efficient collection system and the huge advantage of local knowledge weighed heavily in favour of those not disposed to pay their taxes. King John's actions resulted in a flourishing two-way trade with tea, wine, brandy tobacco and other goods being imported in exchange for fleeces, and set the trend for decades to come.

Early on, those on the Marsh involved in the 'wicked trade' were known as *owlers*, the Kentish term for wool smugglers. The word probably derives from the fact that the smuggler's work (as the owl's) is mostly undertaken nocturnally. However, it may also owe something to the owl's call often being used by smugglers to contact each other, or even be a corruption of the word *wool* or *wooler*. As the penalties for smuggling wool reflected its status as the most important, valuable and profitable export, the owlers were acknowledged to be a tougher breed than those involved solely in the running of brandy, tea and tobacco. The stakes were high, the players rougher and more desperate than their counterparts; and the whole was a long way removed from the romantic ideal.

Owling was the mainstay of smuggling activity until – broadly speaking – the end of the seventeenth century. By this time, Britain's foreign policy had led to a series of highly expensive wars. That with Holland in 1688 was a particular catalyst, resulting in swingeing increases in taxation to finance the operation. Taxes on goods continued to rise sharply throughout the eighteenth century, so much so that illegal importation was positively encouraged (although sometimes the objective was to finance the purchase of wool for owling). By 1770, a pound of tea costing 7d (7 old pennies, equivalent to 3 [new] pence) in France could be sold for 5 shillings (25 pence) in this country, and trade in silk and lace was similarly well rewarded[3] (such cargo involved in a rare seizure near Hythe in 1773 was valued at £15,000 – an incredible sum for the day). Accordingly, there was very good money to be made from the free trade. At a time when the average farm labourer could expect to earn only 7–8 shillings (35–40 pence) a week in the summer (and often nothing at all in the winter months), the 10 shillings (50 pence) or so on offer for a night's work with the owlers must have seemed a fortune. Apart from the black market income that resulted, smuggling was also the only practicable means by which many could hope to obtain goods that would have been deemed 'luxury' at the time. Tea was then the national drink – favoured by the lower classes – and some two thirds of the tea imported was done so illegally. Many accordingly took the view that smuggling, rather than being illegal, was providing some sort of public service.

---

3. This is brought out well within *Courageous Exploits*, where Thorndike explains how the risks were financially worthwhile, even if only one cargo out of three was safely landed.

Subsequently, the introduction of the press gang was a further factor in encouraging smuggling. On the one hand, its operation in coastal locations took away a significant part of the able-bodied workforce and in so doing exacerbated the economic hardships of those remaining. On the other, the indiscriminate nature and brutality of the press gangs further blunted morality and removed remaining sympathy for those in authority. Many – if not most – coastal dwellers (up to and including squires and magistrates) were involved in smuggling, although most shunned violence, particularly against officers of the Crown.

Enforcement

Allied to this, there was often very little effective deterrent. Enforcement was always a very difficult business and it was not until 1671 that Customs Officers were afforded sloops to patrol the seas. Even then, they were far too poorly resourced to make any sort of an impact. Some 20,000 packs of wool a year were at this time reaching Calais alone (to put this in perspective, over 150,000 sheep were being grazed on the Marsh). Although the death penalty for smuggling wool was introduced as early as 1662, even this was counter-productive as there was no incentive for the smugglers to be unarmed (it is tempting to speculate that the prevalent view was that the owlers felt that they may as well be hanged for sheep as for lambs). At first, there was no enforcement at all; but, even by the end of the seventeenth century – although Riding Officers were patrolling the shore and surrounding area – there were still less than 50 such officers covering the whole of Kent. There is a record of a William Snipe and two of his crew (John Burwash and George Fuller) being captured with a cargo of fleeces bound for France in 1702, but such successes for the Crown were very few and far between.

When Lydd Riding Officers seized two notorious smugglers near Camber Point after watching them leaving a French smuggling sloop near Dungeness in March 1720, they secured them in chains at the George Inn. The commander of the Rye revenue sloop takes up the story:

> 6 officers with them, 20 fire locks loaded with powder and ball. At 5 on Sunday night 9 men well mounted & as well armed comes up to the house & dismounts from their horses & runs up staires fireing all the way up, & ye officers fired down on them – wounded three officers & got away between ye officers & their Armes & carried away Walter (and) Bigg, & if these 9 men had not carried them off a 100 more was hard by ready to make another attack.

The problems of the lone Riding Officers are accurately portrayed by Thorndike, although even those that were diligent would have known that juries would rarely convict, whatever the evidence. An example of what could happen to a conscientious Riding Officer is provided by the case of one such officer, a Mr Darby. The Customs Officer for Hythe wrote to John Collier, Surveyor General of Riding Officers for Kent:

The George Inn, Lydd

The smugglers have got to such a height of impudence at Lydd, that they have drove Mr Darby and wife and family from their habitation, threatening to murder him if they can catch him . . . All officers in my district are afraid to go out of their houses.

More often, however, the odds were so overwhelming that the authorities simply turned a blind eye. Few Riding Officers and enforcement officials were as diligent as Darby. They were poorly paid, which made them more susceptible to an attractive bribe. Often they would be 'entertained' at a local hostelry when a run was in progress, but other more subtle techniques were also invoked, such as the use of the 'gauger's pocket'.[4] This involved the use of a concealed crack or fissure in a cliff face: in return for his co-operation, the official would find a bag of gold hidden behind a stone placed in the fissure. Others not actually in the pay of the smugglers were reduced to the role of observer, taking notes from a distance. That the authorities were anyway hampered at every turn is not difficult to demonstrate. In the 1680s,

---

4. 'Gauger' being the slang term for an excise official, who would gauge the amount of duty payable on a consignment of liquor.

ten men were caught carrying wool across the Marsh to the shore but the Mayor of Romney gave them bail instead of detaining them. The person who had informed on the miscreants – a William Carter[5] – clearly read between the lines and fled to Lydd where he expressed open surprise at even greater levels of smuggling being undertaken. The locals decided to teach this outsider a lesson and he was chased as far as Guldeford, from where he beat a retreat by ferry.[6] On another occasion, four local men who provided the Mayor of Hythe with information relating to the smuggling of horses from England to France were thrown into gaol for their pains. They also had their papers – which at that time had the status of passports – confiscated, which made life for them very difficult indeed. And in 1692, another Mayor of Hythe (one Julius Deedes) was himself arrested for wool smuggling. This was what would now be described as an 'open and shut case': Deedes had set upon some of the Revenue Officers with a bat. However – and predictably – the local jury decided that the wool was not destined for France but another part of the country and acquitted him.

Periodically, the government of the day made gestures, some more futile than others. It was clear that the problem was most acute in south-east England, for reasons explained above. In 1734 – underlining the significance of the village in smuggling terms – almost all of the Kent Riding Officers were moved to Dymchurch.[7] The local response was swift and the smugglers moved their unofficial headquarters to Lydd, concentrating operations on the beaches of Dungeness, Camber and Littlestone (or what is now known as Romney Sands). Notwithstanding, there was still an attitude of 'untouchability' and many runs took place in broad daylight. An account of the time, submitted by the Romney Riding Officer to Collier sums up the lawlessness:

> Here (at Lydd) they pass to and from the seaside 40 or 50 in a gang in the day time, loaded with tea, brandy and dry goods; that above 200 smugglers mounted were seen one night upon the sea beach there, waiting for the loading of 6 boats, and above 100 were seen to go off, all loaded with Goods.

Nor was Lydd an exception: a report by Thomas Clare, the Hythe Customs Officer, of a visit to the Rose & Crown at Old Romney described the stables as being full of smugglers' horses. He further claimed that in the morning he saw:

> 18 men (armed with brass muskatoons, brass fuzees, and pistols) and one boy, all with brazen faces . . . with 60 horses all loaded with dry goods . . . they were such fellows as dare bid Defiance to all Laws and Government.

---

5. William Carter was an interesting character, in that he attempted to set himself up as a freelance smuggler-catcher.
6. Although Guldeford is now firmly landlocked (the result of reclamation), at this time it was one of a small number of islands.
7. Previously Dymchurch boasted just two Riding Officers and two Dragoons.

The Rose and Crown, Old Romney

Mechanics

The logistics of the 'business' clearly dictated the need for meticulous organisation (particularly as import and export were often both involved), and necessitated strong leadership. Just as the fictional smugglers had their Scarecrow leading his gang of Night-riders, so most smugglers were organised in gangs with firm (if not enlightened) leaders. The gangs themselves comprised core members, supplemented by casual labour on the night of a run. At the head of the smaller operations would be the *investor*, the entrepreneur who put up the funds at personal risk. It was he who lent the money to the captain of a smuggling vessel, and he would be repaid the capital and a proportion of the profits on successful completion of a run.[8] The *captain* would have responsibility for buying the cargo and delivering it to the pre-arranged site(s). With the largest gangs, of course, the activities were self-financed.

Runs would normally take place in a structured fashion. Two or three alternative landing places had to be arranged to mitigate against any unexpected Customs presence, and final responsibility for choice of site would rest with the *lander*. In the event of unwanted attention,

---

8. Predictably, this arrangement could lead to violence between the two in the event of an unsuccessful operation, or dispute over entitlements.

The Woolpack at Brookland, one of the classic smugglers' inns to be found on Romney Marsh

the cargo might be left in the sea – the tubs roped together and anchored at each end with large stones in between and buoys left to mark the spot for later recovery.[9] On receiving an 'all clear' signal from shore (usually conveyed with a *flasher*,[10] as accurately depicted by Thorndike), however, the vessel would approach the shoreline at high tide. *Skirmishing parties* (members of whom were known as *batmen* by dint of the stout cudgels or bats that were the tools of their trade) would stand guard, whilst packaged goods were carried ashore and loaded onto pack horses and carts by the *tub carriers*. The tub carriers would be charged with conveying the contraband either to a final destination or, more commonly, to an interim hiding place. They would often – particularly on the Marsh – be assisted by *guides*, whose local knowledge of the area would be invaluable.[11]

Pubs, churches and farm barns were commonly used as interim hiding places. Barely a pub that predates the twentieth century does not lay some claim to smuggling fame, although some have false walls and hiding places that lend credibility to such assertions. The importance of wool to the region is reflected in the number of inns in the south east that bear the name

9.   A process known as 'crop sowing'.
10. A special lantern featuring a long funnel so that the light could only be seen from the one direction.
11. There was a hierarchy within the smuggling gangs, with those taking the greater risks receiving higher rewards. This is well depicted within *Further Adventures*, where Ransley becomes disgruntled that the Scarecrow pays the landing crews more than those who work the hides.

The Bell Inn at Hythe features widely in smuggling histories

Woolpack. There are two such surviving pubs on Romney Marsh, at Warehorne and at Brookland, and the latter has many confirmed links to the free trade, including that stock-in-trade of any smuggling adventure story – the secret tunnel.[12] At Rye, the Flushing Inn has an underground vault and, not to be outdone, the nearby Mermaid Inn has a bookcase that doubles as a door, a means of ready escape.[13] The Bell Inn at Hythe (which is claimed to date back to 1420) has a revolving cupboard fitted with carved doors, through which a smuggler or refugee from justice could escape. The Bell was fortunate in having a millstream running alongside and smuggled barrels would be floated down the stream. Behind the mill wheel, a tunnel connected the stream to the cellar and this would be opened to divert the casks, which were then retrieved by hoist and stored on ledges carved in the tunnel. In the event of attention from excise officers, the mill-wheel would be set in motion, blocking access to, and identification of, the tunnel entrance. Here, too, recent excavation work revealed the skeleton of a smuggler's pony. At New Romney, the New Inn has concealed chimney recesses to support its claims of involvement in smuggling and at Dymchurch recent renovation work has confirmed that The Ship was regularly used by smugglers. This should be no surprise in view of its location and proximity to the beach.

---

12. Also of interest here is the 'spinning jenny', which is stored between two of the beams on the ceiling of the main bar. Although some say that this is just an ancient pub game, others believe that it was used for dividing up the spoils from a successful run.
13. See Chapter 6.

Snargate church, not unacquainted with the free trade

Thorndike's depiction of Marsh churches being used to store contraband goods relates not only to his central character being a vicar. There is evidence of Brookland Church being used for such purposes and that Snargate church was similarly utilised is confirmed by Reverend Richard Barham.[14] Indeed, Barham is reported as having said that, on a misty day, he could find his way to the church simply by following the smell of tobacco! At Ivychurch, a part of the floor of the north aisle is removable and there is at least one record of so much contraband having been stockpiled that a service had to be cancelled (the vicar being advised in no uncertain terms that official events were 'off'!). Some hiding places were spectacularly imaginative, such as a manorial pond that allegedly could conceal up to 100 barrels of spirit within a cavern carved under water. When any arising furore had died down, goods would be sent on to London by means of a network of contacts, any real danger long gone. Some, of course, stayed where they were (in the local pub) and various hiding places were needed to protect the landlord from inquisitive customs officials, who could identify that such barrels – if kept in the cellar – had not been subject to duty.

---

14. See Chapter 2.

The name of the Flushing Inn at
Rye bears testimony to
smuggling links with the
continent

The pack horses used for transporting contraband were often taken without the permission of the owner. As once again illustrated by Thorndike, some farmers and gentry not actively involved in the free trade would awake to find their horses ungroomed and exhausted, but with a generous gift of spirits, tobacco and lace secreted in the stables. The web of complicity in this way stretched further, with the stable owners potentially incriminated.

The trade that developed with the continent had other side effects and often resulted in strong links being forged between communities in England and mainland Europe (particularly Belgium). As individuals became known, they were afforded free and unhindered passage and in some cases this led to English businesses expanding into Europe. Shipbuilding provided a number of good examples of this, and a particularly flourishing business was established in the Belgian port of Flushing.

Major gangs

The most successful and renowned of the organised smugglers were the Groombridge and Hawkhurst Gangs, whose territories extended well along the south coast. The former was of

The Oak and Ivy public house, headquarters of the Hawkhurst Gang, features on the Smuggers' Trail launched by the Hawkhurst Community Partnership in 2010

longer standing (operating from 1733) whilst records suggest that the Hawkhurst gang first operated some two years later. The fact that both disappeared in the same year (1749) serves to demonstrate that membership was not mutually exclusive. It is the Hawkhurst Gang, operating from the Oak and Ivy public house, that is the better known, partly for the brazen practice of its members drinking with loaded guns and pistols on the tables of no less an establishment than Rye's Mermaid Inn.

The Hawkhurst gang was tightly knit and fiercely loyal to its members, and claimed to be able to assemble 500 mounted and armed men within the hour. But it was also notable for its ability to alienate nearly all those locals not directly involved. A well-documented incident involving the gang occurred in the peaceful and law-abiding Wealden town of Goudhurst. Here, a returning soldier by the name of George Sturt was so appalled at the level of lawlessness which the Hawkhurst gang represented that he formed a militia to defend the village, which enraged its then leader Thomas Kingsmill. Seeing this as an attempt to undermine his authority, Kingsmill launched an attack. This was a hasty response and Kingsmill was found lacking (or, more likely, guilty of complacency). Fierce fighting ensued, centred on the Church of St Mary, but the smugglers were routed and driven from the village, losing three of their number (including Kingsmill's brother, George) in the process. The incident marked a change in fortune for the Hawkhurst Gang, but its final demise was

The village of Goudhurst, which eventually rose up against the tyranny of the smugglers

not for another two years. Its downfall was the result of one of the most infamous episodes in smuggling history but involved only an elite handful of its membership; it also serves to demonstrate that the smuggling operation was far from a parochial one. The Gang had been involved in the successful landing of a cargo (which included no less than two tons of tea) in Dorset, but this had been intercepted before it could be stashed. Seven of the gang (led by Kingsmill and his deputy, William Fairall) teamed up with a Colchester Gang to 'retrieve' the cargo from Customs storage at Poole. In the event, there was little resistance and the majority of the haul was recovered by the Gang without incident. In a public house on the way home, however, a shoemaker (Daniel Chater) recognised one of the smugglers, struck up a conversation and learned of the success of the operation. He was careless with his tongue and subsequently 'persuaded' by a Customs Officer (William Galley) to divulge the full details and to give evidence at Poole. He was duly escorted by Galley and the two stopped at another hostelry where, again, drink loosened tongues. Unfortunately for Chater and Galley, the barmaid was in the pay of the Hawkhurst Gang; a message was relayed and their fate sealed. The notoriety of this incident lies in the appalling treatment meted out to the victims: they were tied back to back on a horse and whipped – in the case of Galley – to death. Chater was still conscious when untied and thrown down a well where the job was finished by a hail of boulders thrown by the Gang.

In the light of this and another incident – where a Gang member was (probably unfairly) accused of stealing, convicted by a kangaroo court and summarily executed – public support waned and the Crown found that people would talk more freely. More importantly, some of the more minor players, such as William Steele and Jacob Pring, turned King's Evidence although another – John Dimer (who had been unwittingly responsible for earlier events through talking to Chater) – was murdered by the gang before he could give evidence. Many of the gang were arrested, including Kingsmill, Fairall, Benjamin Tapner, Richard Perrin and William Jackson. All were subsequently sentenced to death, although Jackson 'cheated' the hangman by suffering a heart attack just after being measured for a gibbet by the blacksmith. The Hawkhurst Gang was now a spent force.

The influence of the Napeolonic Wars

Successive increases in duty saw smuggling generally peak around the 1780s,[15] when a significant reduction in that for tea (which fell from 129% to 12.5%)[16] took effect. On the Marsh itself the Napoleonic Wars, which commenced in 1803, were responsible for an influx of building workers to construct the Royal Military Canal; this also brought a large military presence, which itself impacted upon smuggling. However, a rare success by the Revenue in 1805 in intercepting a lugger aground in Dungeness Bay yielded a 'catch' of 665 casks of brandy, 237 of Geneva, 118 of rum, 119 bags of tobacco, 6 packages of wine and 43 pounds of tea,[17] which gives a good indication of the scale on which smuggling was still then operating. An 1813 report concerning the Rye and Hastings area estimated that between 300,000 and 400,000 gallons of spirits was still entering that area alone each year, whilst other contemporaneous reports suggest that 13 million pounds of tea (over 50% of the nation's consumption) was being illegally imported into England annually.

The Napoleonic Wars provided further opportunities for the smuggler to diversify. Gold guinea coins (value £1.05), for example, could be sold in Paris for the equivalent of £1.50 a piece. While dealing in these items had started before then, the trade gained a new momentum as gold guineas became the preferred currency for Napoleon's troops.[18] Smuggling vessels were also used to carry newspapers and reports from French spies based in England – and even to transport spies back and forth across the Channel. This trade in human cargo had first started in earnest during the Reign of Terror,[19] when aristocrats were desperate to escape France.[20]

Later, the cessation of hostilities with the French in 1815 encouraged legal avenues of trade with the continent. Nevertheless, it remained a time of economic hardship for many, and the large number of fit and active men discharged from the navy (many either unsuited or

---

15. The setting of the Syn saga is fully consistent with this.
16. Through William Pitt the Younger's Commutation Act, 1784.
17. Predictably, the smugglers were not prepared to let this rest, but a joint rescue party from Lydd and Dungeness was foiled by the militia.
18. Gold running is depicted by Thorndike and is a plotline within *Returns*.
19. However, there is evidence of a limited trade in human cargo in the eighteenth century, with agents landing on south coast beaches on spying missions for the exiled James II.
20. An issue accurately mirrored by Thorndike in *Shadow*.

unwilling to undertake agricultural work) swelled the ranks of the smugglers. Against this, the defeat of Napoleon allowed the government the opportunity to concentrate its resources closer to home. Accordingly, the Preventative Service became more appropriately staffed and allied to this was a gradual improvement of roads, which facilitated the movement of troops. The end of the Napoleonic Wars thus heralded a new episode in enforcement. Captain William McCullogh was commander of a Royal Navy ship supporting the revenue service, and he proposed the creation of a unified service to guard the Kent coast, combining shore, in-shore water and off-shore cruiser patrols. In 1816 this came into being under the name Coast Blockade Service, commanded by McCullogh and patrolling the whole coastline between North Foreland and Dungeness. In addition to preventing most unauthorised vessels from reaching shore, parties of 10 sailors were stationed every three miles along the coast, some of whom were in Martello Towers. It was to be a highly successful operation, but a widely unpopular one. With the fervour of a convert (his own father and grandfather had almost certainly been smugglers on a large scale) McCullogh took personally the news of every successful run. He was a strict disciplinarian and his men were to become very familiar with the cat-of-nine-tails; the harsh regime that he created led to some men defecting to the smugglers and others indulging in self-mutilation to escape the service. McCullogh was to become known as 'Flogging Joey' and those who served under him were labelled 'Flogging Joey's Warriors'.[21]

The Blockade really did signal the end of the 'golden age' of smuggling, and local records of poverty and starvation in 1820 suggest that the local economy suffered a severe downturn.[22] With a successful run still netting between £400 and £500, however, many considered the risks to remain worth taking, and the most desperate smugglers formed better-organised gangs and continued to ply their trade. Post-Blockade, therefore, the gangs that were left became even more ruthless. The notorious Aldington Gang was arguably even more depraved than most of its predecessors, with the exception of the Hawkhurst Gang (who must be considered to have been in a league of their own). Any remaining goodwill existing between the smugglers and the more law-abiding but once sympathetic villagers now completely disappeared. The Headquarters of the Aldington Blues (as they were also known, in deference to a penchant for blue tunics) was the Walnut Tree Inn at Aldington, yet another public house still open today.[23] These smugglers might even be seen as pioneers of all-day pub opening as, when the Walnut Tree was shut, they thought nothing of breaking in and stealing whatever food and drink took their fancy.

---

21. *Flogging Joey's Warriors: how the Royal Navy fought the Kent and Sussex smugglers* is one of a number of recommended accounts of smuggling in the South East by John Douch. Douch has also written a good fictional account of smuggling in Romney Marsh and East Kent – *Moonlight Man* – which (like Doctor Syn) is set in the eighteenth century.
22. At this time the Coastal Blockade was employing 6700 officers and men, at a total annual cost of over £500,000.
23. See Chapter 6.

Smugglers injured in the infamous battle of Brookland who were not deemed too ill to move were carried to the nearby Royal Oak Inn (the church and its separate spire – see Chapter 6 – can also be clearly seen)

A large run by the Aldington Blues at Sandgate (just to the north east of the Marsh) in November 1820 was reasonably successful, but the authorities made it clear that they would not countenance any further snub. Accordingly, although a successful landing took place at Camber the following February, the navy pursued its quarry with vigour and this culminated in the infamous Battle of Brookland. On the one hand – with the tub carriers needing to be guarded by armed men – the smugglers could proceed only slowly; offset against this, the Blockade forces were hampered by heavy, wet uniforms and the physical geography of the Marsh. Two midshipmen were wounded and an officer – John Mackenzie – killed one mile from the village of Brookland. Casualties were heavier amongst the smugglers, with four found dead on the road later that morning and at least 16 wounded. This was by far the most appalling casualty list of any Marsh run and the shock experienced across the region was responsible for many of the fringe players ending their connection with the free trade. Nor was the fall-out confined to Romney Marsh; the trial of the captured smugglers took place at the Old Bailey and attracted wide interest. One of the ringleaders (Richard Wraight) was acquitted through lack of evidence, whilst another (Cephas Quested) was sentenced to death and subsequently hanged.[24]

---

24. Although Quested was additionally sentenced to be hung in chains at Brookland, this part of the sentence was never carried out; following the intervention of local magistrate Sir Edward Knatchbull, the corpse was quietly removed and buried at Aldington.

Later events

Although not the death knell for this era of smuggling, the Battle of Brookland was a significant watershed. Quested's successor as leader of the Aldington Blues was George Ransley, and he organised a further successful run at the Warren[25] (between New Romney and St Mary's Bay) in March 1826. Possibly emboldened by this, the gang attempted a further run in July of the same year, at Dover. They were apprehended by a naval patrol, but in the ensuing fight the Quartermaster was killed and other naval officers injured. A huge reward for the time (£500) was sufficient to buy information and many of the gang were arrested. From drug-related profits, Ransley himself had built a cottage at Aldington Frith and this traded as an unofficial public house under the name of the Bourne Tap.[26] It was here that he was arrested by a party of Coastal Blockade officers and Bow Street Runners. The death penalty was not imposed, partly for the reason that it was impossible to ascertain who had fired the fatal shot. Ransley was instead transported to Van Diemen's Land (Tasmania), where he was to end his days; his descendants and those of other Marsh smugglers are still to be found there.[27] Many of the Ransley family were involved in smuggling, including George's two cousins James and William, whose excesses earned them the sobriquet 'Roaring Ransleys'.[28] The name Ransley will be familiar to students of Thorndike's novels: his was the character in *Further Adventures* of whom the Scarecrow made an example (but who received a slightly more sympathetic ending from Walt Disney).

This incident marked the end of the Aldingon Blues, but another, which took place earlier the same year and also involved George Ransley, further demonstrates that the balance of power between smugglers and enforcers was shifting:

> A large party of smugglers had assembled in the neighbourhood of Dymchurch, and a boat laden (as is supposed) with tubs of spirits, being observed to approach the shore nearly opposite to Dymchurch, the smugglers instantly commenced cheering, and rushed upon the coast, threatening defiance to the sentinels of the blockade; who perceiving an overwhelming force, gave the alarm, when, a party of marines coming to their assistance, a general firing took place. The smugglers retreated into the marshes,

---

25. The Warren does not appear on all current maps but a pub of the same name alongside the A259 designates the western boundary of the area. There was for a time a racecourse on this site, which is depicted on the inn sign.
26. Such unlicensed drinking premises were widespread and colloquially known as 'blind pigs'.
27. Although hanging was still the norm for acts of severe violence, increasingly at this time smugglers were sentenced to transportation (arguably an indication that the authorities felt that they had broken the back of freetrading). Because many of the smugglers were experienced sailors, they were of great value on the outward journey and were often commandeered to assist on the passage back, securing their freedom. Thus, many such miscreants found themselves back in their homeland not many months after being sentenced to penal servitude for life!
28. Both were hanged for highway robbery and attempted murder in 1800.

followed by the blockade-men, and, from their knowledge of the ground, were indebted for their ultimate escape. We regret to state two of the blockade seamen were wounded; one severely in the arm, which must cause amputation, and the other in the face, by slug shots. There can be no doubt, but that some of the smugglers must have been wounded, if not killed; one of their muskets was picked up loaded – abandoned, no doubt, by the bearer of it, on account of wounds. The boat, with her cargo, was obliged to put to sea again, without effecting a landing, and notwithstanding the vigilance of Lieutenants Westbrook, Mudge and McLeod, who were afloat in their galleys on the spot, from the darkness of the night, effected its escape.[29]

That is not to say that officials had become incorruptible. It was still possible to bypass the authorities, and a newspaper article of 1833 (a copy of which was held by a recent licensee of Dymchurch's Ship Inn) demonstrates how this was frequently done. The article includes a statement from an elderly resident by the name of Dale:

> My uncle, father and grandfather were all smugglers. When my father expected anything in he would invite mounted officers down at Dymchurch into the Ship Inn to play cards and stand them drinks, he played for guinea points and took care to lose. While this was going on, the goods would be run all safe.

But smugglers were generally having to become smarter, too, to outwit the authorities. At around the same time a Rye fishing smack, the *Isis,* was found to have been built with a double skin, used to ferry contraband secreted in the space between the skins. This practice became increasingly widespread and is again accurately referenced within the Syn novels. Vessels found to be involved in such practice would be sawn in two, to prevent any recurrence and act as a deterrent. An illustration of how meticulous some of the smuggling operators could be is provided by the capture of a lugger, *The Four Brothers* in 1823.[30] Whilst not strictly a Romney Marsh vessel (the crew were mostly from nearby Folkestone), this was one of many which fell into the Government net following redeployment of forces after the defeat of Napoleon. It was spotted by a naval cutter, which gave chase and ultimately captured the crew. Although an official was killed, the main relevance of this episode lies in the fact that the smugglers were deemed by the jury to be foreign and therefore carrying foreign cargo. This highlights a prevalent practice of the time of male children being christened in more than one country (frequently Holland being used to provide the dual nationality) to allow just such outcomes.

After 1831, taxes on many imported goods were abolished[31] and in 1853 the Customs Service underwent wholesale reform, which improved efficiency. These two events combined to

---

29. From the *Cinque Ports Herald.*
30. *Courageous Exploits* features a fishing vessel the *Four Sisters*; this may be an oblique reference, although vessel names did often reflect family ownership.
31. At this time, too, the Coast Blockade became absorbed into the Coastguard Service, which had itself only come into being some nine years earlier.

Vessels that had been seized and sawn in two by the authorities would often be pressed into service as storage huts by fisherman – as demonstrated by this exhibit on the Stade at Hastings

impact further on smuggling activities, but there still remained decent margins for those prepared to take greater risks. In 1877, some 300 pounds of tea was washed ashore at Hythe and Sandgate (as a result of which the master of the *Wasp* – a vessel that had run aground at Hythe – was arrested and imprisoned).

As recently as 1932, a new Revenue Officer appointed to Littlestone reported – after a fortnight's investigation – that the coast between Dymchurch and Dungeness 'positively reeked with smuggling' and that he considered New Romney and Lydd nothing more than 'a nest of contraband runners'. He further considered that there were few residents not directly or indirectly concerned with smuggling, suggesting that Tom Shoesmith's perceptions remained valid at this time.

Other Marsh Links and Incidents

Although most histories of the area and of smuggling itself concentrate on the major gangs already discussed, there were many other smugglers and incidents of note. The Stanford Gang was of some significant size; whilst it was not in the same league as the Aldington or Hawkhurst Gang, landings requiring up to 50 packhorses are on record. More minor gangs –

some involving only the odd fishing vessel – were no real threat to the large gangs and consequently were allowed to operate with little interference. In the mid-eighteenth century, in addition to the Stanford Gang, the Howe and Grays and Bowers Gangs are also recorded as being active on the Marsh – mainly in the Dengemarsh area. Individual smugglers mentioned in reports of the time included Arthur Gray and Robert Fuller (who were both subsequently hanged for their misdeeds) and George Betts (who hailed from Rye and may be the inspiration for the smuggler of the same name in *Further Adventures*).

In addition to boasting the Cathedral of the Marsh, Lydd holds a prominent position in smuggling lore and in true tradition the village hostelry – the George Inn – was at its hub. It was here that Coastal Blockade Officer John Mackenzie died following a wound sustained during the aforementioned Battle of Brookland. A regular patron of the George was George Walker, a known smuggler who was to meet his end in what were rather unfortunate circumstances. Forced to change a landing because of rough weather, Walker and his crew ran into a Coastguard patrol sheltering from the worsening weather. After a struggle, Walker and two of his colleagues were arrested and subsequently tried, found guilty and sentenced to four years on a man-of-war. Whilst being escorted to the gaol, a large crowd secured Walker's release. After hiding in the churchyard, he was flushed out and 'murdered' in the eyes of many by a revenue officer (Lieutenant Peatt), who ran him through with a sword. His body is buried in Lydd Churchyard, with the following epitaph:

Let it be known that I am clay,
A base man took my life away,
Yet freely do I him forgive
And hope in heaven we both shall live

Buried in the same churchyard is Francis Sisley (1748–1808), great-grandfather of artist Alfred Sisley, but himself a very active local smuggler. He originally hailed from Ivychurch but moved to a large house and extravagant lifestyle in Lydd, funded by his smuggling exploits. Never afraid to diversify, he variously dealt in gold guineas, silks and laces but his shrewdest move was to realise the importance of having a trustworthy contact on the other side of the channel. Consequently, he installed his son, Thomas, in France to oversee his interests. It was to be a mutually beneficial act, with Thomas becoming a wealthy and prosperous merchant.

In 1744 another Lydd resident, John Southerden, was amongst a gang of about 50 smugglers stumbled upon by Dymchurch Riding Officers Solomon Sparks and Richard Drake. This incident took place at Brockman's Barn (the site of which is now occupied by the Grand Redoubt near Hythe). Southerden was the only one captured, and had no goods or firearms on him. This was an unlikely scenario to say the least – no charges could subsequently be brought against him – and there was much speculation that he had allowed himself to be captured so that he might try and effect the release of a cutter that had itself been seized from the Stanford Gang and which was impounded at Dover. Southerden himself was a character of great interest; he kept a 12-oar galley at Folkestone, which was used to make

The ruins of All Saints Church, Hope, a well-known smugglers' rendezvous

frequent trips across the Channel, principally for the purpose of smuggling gold guineas – an act of treason. Paradoxically, he was also reputed to be a government spy. Because he was so well known in both England and France, he could move freely, and passed details of information gleaned on the strength and positioning of the French fleet to the Admiralty. Again, parallels with the activities of both Southerden and Sisley can be found within the plot of *Shadow*.

As discussed in Chapter 1, there is no direct evidence of smuggling parsons on Romney Marsh, but a fair few clergymen had what could be described as 'working arrangements' with the smugglers. It cannot be assumed that every time a church was used as a hide by the smugglers that it was with approval; however, a generous gift (the 'brandy for the parson, baccy for the clerk')[32] would usually assure silence. If not, underlying threats would do the trick. In many ways the predicament of the clergy would have been similar to that of the landed classes, whose horses would unwittingly be used on a run: they would be handsomely 'rewarded' and compliance was healthy for all concerned. Clearly, Richard Barham turned a blind eye, but to what extent this was attributable to sympathy, fear or pragmatism is open to conjecture. Many communities were dependent on the smuggling trade to maintain any sort of a life, and there would have been a certain moral dilemma for any parson considering blowing the whistle. The disused and ruined All Saints Church at Hope, near New Romney, was a regular meeting place for smugglers until Preventive Officer Charles Rolfe, hiding in one of the walls, overheard and managed to disrupt plans for a forthcoming run. This incident forms the basis of an incident within the Walt Disney Film.

---

32. From Kipling's *Smuggler's Song*.

Also worthy of note is Ralph Papworth Hougham, the Brookland surgeon. Whilst not a smuggler himself, he would often be called out at night to attend both wounded smugglers and Blockaders. Where the former were concerned, he would be led blindfolded on his horse to the wounded men, so as to be unable to divulge details if subsequently pressed by the authorities. A special wallet to fit into his greatcoat pocket was designed and made to contain medicines and instruments. He had a son – George – who followed in his footsteps and also became a surgeon.

Smuggling today

Whilst smuggling continues – the cargoes the modern staples of alcohol, tobacco and drugs (but increasingly also humans) – the questionable romance has long gone. It is doubtful whether future generations will look back fondly on the days of White Van Man taking the ferry over to France every weekend to stock up on cheap alcohol and cigarettes over and above his personal needs. Nevertheless, tales do crop up from time to time that raise a chuckle – or at least an eyebrow. The late Hope & Anchor public house at Dengemarsh had a significant reputation, perhaps inevitable with its seashore (beach!) location. A post-war tale told by Michael Mirams in *Bygone Kent* recalls the visit of a stranger to the inn who, having imbibed and gained the locals' trust, locked the door and declared himself to be a Customs Officer. A search revealed pouches of tobacco hidden behind pictures on the wall and the landlord was subsequently fined. Even more recently (in the 1970s and prior to more organ-ised and commercial human trafficking), an Asian family was landed one winter's night on the beach at St Mary's Bay. Three days later the police were called to interview a group of people who had been sitting patiently on the platform of the Romney Hythe & Dymchurch Railway. They had after all only been following instructions: to head for the nearest railway station and await a train to London . . .

The highwayman

In similar vein, the 'profession' of the highwayman has been embellished and romanticised over the years. One of the central characters of the Syn saga is 'Gentleman James' Bone, who oozes charm, displays chivalry and achieves great riches through regularly holding up the Dover Stagecoach. In reality, the world of the highwayman was a desperate, seedy one, fraught with great danger. Whilst – as portrayed by Thorndike – there was some limited evidence of drivers being in league with highwaymen, there were few desperadoes who would chance their arm against the very real danger of the coachman's blunderbuss; and even fewer operated alongside other criminals. Most highwaymen ploughed a lonely furrow and earned slender pickings from assaults on sole travellers. To be caught inevitably resulted in the noose.

Films based on legendary highwaymen such as Dick Turpin (in reality a character with few if any redeeming qualities) may give the impression that the country was awash with highwaymen, but whilst there were some opportunists there are few records of individuals in the south east who earned their living by this means. In East Sussex in 1796, Richard Russel earned a degree of fame by becoming possibly the youngest highwayman on record by robbing the Hurst Green Mail when aged only 13; and in Tunbridge Wells Gabriel Tomkins – who combined highway robbery with the more legitimate profession of Customs Officer – was sent to the gallows in 1750. The site of the former town gibbet at Rye is alleged to be haunted by the ghost of a highwayman who swung for his misdemeanours and after many days was cut down and buried beneath the gallows. It is sometimes reported that a highwayman by the name of *Black Rob(b)in* operated in the Canterbury area at the turn of the nineteenth century, but this would appear to be based on the existence of a pub of this name at nearby Barham. This overlooks, however, that *black robin* is an old Kentish term for a highwayman.

Worthy of note is Lady Katherine Ferrers, who lived between 1634 and 1660. It is alleged that this well-bred woman tired of her pampered existence and turned to a life of crime, becoming possibly Britain's first highwaywoman and terrorising travellers in Hertfordshire. Others have disputed whether this was in fact the case, but the relevance to this account is that some commentators have linked the manner of her death – escaping whilst mortally injured and dying on reaching home – to that befalling both Cobtree daughters. There is no evidence, however, that Thorndike drew on this particular source.

Much further afield, but also of interest to students of Syn is Cannards Grave, to the south of Shepton Mallet in Somerset, where the ghost of seventeenth century publican Giles (Tom) Cannard is said to walk. Cannard was a real-life ne'er do well who regularly robbed those of his patrons that had the misfortune to stay overnight, and who arguably became the last man in England to be hanged for sheep stealing. A startling claim (made on the Shepton Mallet Town Council website) is that he was also a highwayman who may have been 'in league with the notorious Dr Syn, the Scarecrow of Romney Marsh (immortalised in the 1962 Disney film by Patrick McGoohan)'. It is interesting that a real character can be linked with a fictional one in this way, particularly when there is no evidence to support Cannard ever having left the west country! In reality this is an example of a town council trying to cash in on another legend – the compiler clearly unaware that Syn was not a genuine historical figure.

6

The Land of Syn:
Thorndike's Marsh – Then and Now

Romney Marsh

> . . . she's a queer sort of a corner, is Romney Marsh[1]

The term *Romney Marsh* is something of a misnomer. Strictly speaking, it is an area of just 24,000 acres: a triangle with Appledore, Hythe and New Romney at its vertices; and with boundaries delineated by the Royal Military Canal, the English Channel and the Rhee Wall.[2] Very rarely, however, is this definition applied. The term is more generically used to denote the larger area comprising additionally Walland (essentially Lydd to the Kent ditch) and Denge (Lydd and Dungeness) Marshes; and also embracing Broomhill and South Brook Levels.[3] This area is some 46,000 acres in total and akin to a slice of cake in shape. It is effectively an island bounded by the sea to the south and east, and now by the Royal Military Canal (RMC) to the west and north. Some sources additionally include the coastal plain extending west of Rye to Fairlight (encompassing Rye Harbour, Winchelsea Beach and Pett Level); this would appear to have some legitimacy in terms of the similarity of geography, and due to the fact that the RMC begins (or ends!) at Pett Level.

Romney Marsh has for long captivated many people from all walks of life. In addition to Thorndike and his literary and thespian contemporaries who would flock down at weekends, a great many artists have also been attracted to the area. Prominent amongst these are John Piper and Paul Nash. More recently, Derek Jarman came to Dungeness to make a film, bought a cottage and spent the rest of his short life there. Thorndike, almost evangelical in his championing of Romney Marsh, himself influenced others to come to the area, both directly and indirectly. These included fellow actor Donald Sinden. Sinden (who played Captain Hook

---

1. Septimus Mipps, *Doctor Syn*.
2. The Rhee Wall runs for 7.5 miles between Appledore and New Romney. Built originally to reconnect the Rother to the harbour at Romney, it consisted of two parallel earth banks some 50 metres apart and remains can still be seen alongside the A259 road.
3. Thorndike recognises this within the novels, particularly *Courageous Exploits* and the Prologue in *High Seas*.

to Thorndike's Smee in Peter Pan at London's Scala Theatre) writes[4] of his time as a neighbour in Chelsea. 'Author Russell Thorndike . . . told me of the magic of Dymchurch and the Marsh so, at his instigation, in 1954 . . . I bought the house in which I still live.' TV presenter and gastronome Loyd Grossman never met Thorndike, but has often told how his love of the Doctor Syn books has resulted in him becoming a frequent visitor. There is no simple way to summarise its charms, although Piper came close when he described it as '97% atmosphere'. Puck[5] rather neatly refers to the Marsh as 'she' or 'her'.

In the same way that no book on smuggling can refrain from quoting from Kipling's *Smuggler's Song*, so no volume on Romney Marsh is allowed to omit the saying: 'the world is divided into five continents – Europe, Asia, Africa, America and Romney Marsh'. Although spoken by various characters within the Syn saga, the words were originally Barham's. A common variation is that the Marsh is 'the fifth quarter of the globe' and other terms include 'the eighth wonder of the world'. Regardless of how it is described, the Marsh has clearly long had a reputation of being – if not unique – very different from the norm. Part of the ongoing attraction is that it is relatively unspoilt by man. True, the bulk of Dungeness power stations would undoubtedly – and rightly – be described as a monstrous carbuncle by certain sections of the Royal family, but even these fail to destroy the landscape. When viewed from above (from the top of the old lighthouse) against the huge shingle expanse of the Ness, the landscape seems only to mock man's attempts to reshape nature. And, at night, the power stations shed an eerie and ghostly light that has a magical quality of its own.

The individuality of the Marsh is reinforced by the fact that it is only a 90-minute journey by train from the heart of London, making the contrasts very poignant. It has many moods and yet can be so benign. Choose a summer's day and look down over the Marsh from Lympne Castle or the Isle of Oxney[6] to get the full benefit of its charms. Winter storms can be fierce – try walking along Littlestone beach or Greatstone dunes in the middle of winter to really appreciate its atmosphere. Much of the housing development on the Marsh in recent times has been of the bungaloid variety, and most of this concentrated on the coastal belt; accordingly, on vast parts of the Marsh today there is little light pollution as there are few buildings. The sea mist can roll in quickly and, in such conditions and when surrounded by dykes and the call of the oystercatcher, curlew or owl, it is really not difficult to imagine the smugglers' paradise of days gone by or to appreciate the qualities that so captivated Thorndike.

---

4. In a foreword to *Life on Marsh* by Andy Holyer and Niko Miaoulis.
5. Kipling's *Puck of Pook's Hill*.
6. A view also admired in literature by the eponymous hero of H G Wells's *Kipps*.

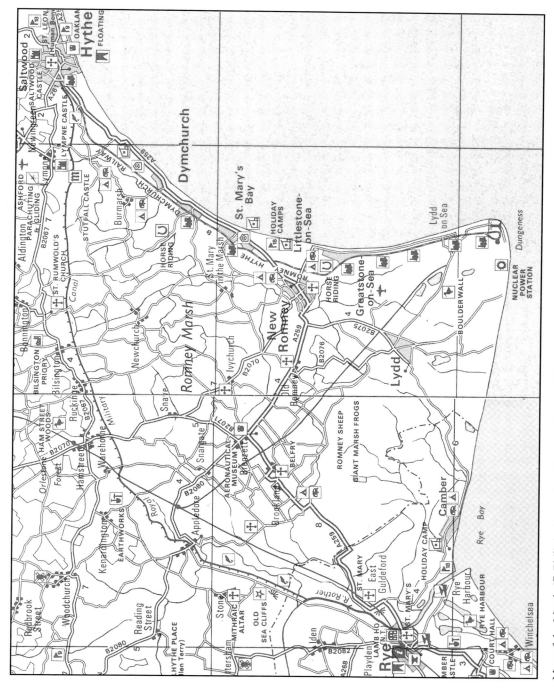

Map of the Marsh (© Philip's; Reproduced by permission of Ordnance Survey on behalf of HMSO. © Crown copyright 100043101. All rights reserved.)

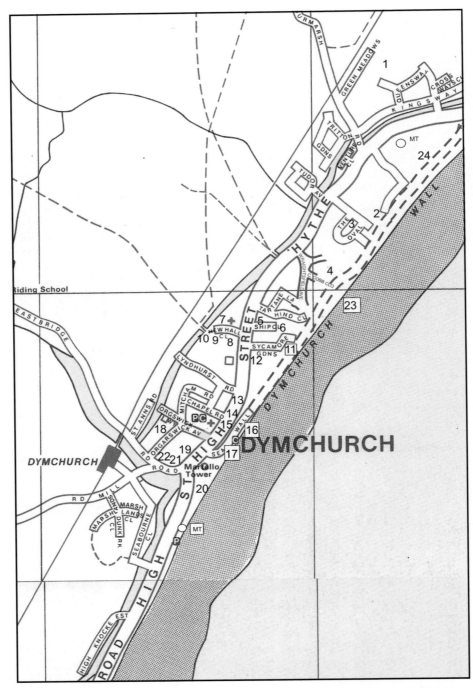

Street plan of Dymchurch (© Philip's; Reproduced by permission of Ordnance Survey on behalf of HMSO. © Crown copyright 100043101. All rights reserved.)

Key to street plan of Dymchurch

1   Site of former gypsy encampment

2   Site of Wraight's Boat Yard

3   No. 1 The Oval (formerly Maxstoke)

4   Charles Cobb Close

5   The Ship Inn

6   Mister Mipps' Dining Room

7   St Peter & St Paul Church

8   War Memorial (former gallows site)

9   New Hall Museum

10 Old Rectory, the former vicarage (now a nursing home)

11 Newington House (now Sea House), Russell Thorndike's home for many years

12 Sycamore House (former home of Edith Nesbit)

13 Thorndyke (sic) Cottage

14 City of London Inn

15 Donnie Thorndike's properties in Marine Terrace

16 Royal British Legion Club

17 Site of Boathouse Cottage

18 Village Hall (venue for Art of Syn – see Chapter 7)

19 Dormers, High Street (holiday cottage; former guest house and private dwelling used by Russell Thorndike)

20 Ocean Inn

21 Old Tree Cottage (Mipps's house)

22 Dr Syn's Guest House

23 Sea Wall

24 Approximate line of former main road (dashed)

Villages and localities on and around the Marsh

Dymchurch

Any tour of the Land of Syn can only really start at Dymchurch, which arguably became the spiritual home of the Thorndike family. While Russell was still young, his mother Donnie bought two former coastguard cottages in the village. These were numbers 3 and 4 Marine Terrace,[7] along from the City of London public house. These houses back on to the sea wall and Russell would undertake much of his early writing (including the first Syn novel) in Boat-house Cottage[8] on the wall. He would later perform his own sketches at the Royal British Legion Club. This formed a very neat and small triangle, the buildings being within 50 yards of each other.

Later, Russell would rent or stay in numerous properties within the village which included, at various times, Dormers (in the High Street) and Maxstoke (in The Oval). Most significantly, in the 1930s, he rented a larger house in Sycamore Gardens,[9] which looked out to sea, and which provided an excellent home for his growing family during school holidays. Dymchurch – affectionately known as 'Dym' in the family – also became a great favourite with all the Thorndike and Casson children. Sybil's son John Casson recalls bathing in the sea and stuffing himself with large fresh sticky buns from Smith's the Baker's on such family occasions, and writes fondly of 'long summer holidays of sand castles, picnics and kites'.

Dymchurch was also the permanent residence, of course, of both Doctor Syn and his fac-totum, Septimus Mipps. It features in all the novels and in only one (*High Seas*) is the bulk of the action set outside the village. Thorndike was by no means the first and certainly not the last to write of Dymchurch; indeed, it is extraordinary that a village that nowadays is so very ordinary has had so much written about it, in addition to playing host to so many literary fig-ures and artists. Kipling's works include the celebrated *Dymchurch Flit, The Dykes* (which fea-tures Dymchurch Wall) and – of course – *The Smuggler's Song*.[10] Barham refers to Dymchurch within the *Ingoldsby Legends* and Ford Madox Hueffer (Ford)'s poems include *The Peddlar leaves the Bar Parlour at Dymchurch*. Another work of note is by a little known Victorian poet, John Davison (who achieved a level of posthumous fame when he ended his life by calming walk-ing, fully clothed, into the sea). His poem, *In Romney Marsh* recalls a time at Dymchurch when telephone wires were still a novelty.

---

7. Number 3 later acquired the name *St Joan*, reflecting the play that George Bernard Shaw wrote for Sybil, and which really established her as a star.
8. Or Lifeboat House, a rather grandiose name for what was essentially an upturned boat.
9. This was Newington House, which has subsequently been renamed Sea House. Some sources advise that it was also known as Camber House at one time, but it has not been possible to verify this.
10. From which the classic line: *Watch the wall my Darling while the Gentlemen go by* is a specific refer-ence to both Dymchurch Wall and smuggling.

Although the Arcade was destroyed by a WWII bomb, Marine Terrace still stands. The houses have been renumbered, however. The central property in these pictures (front and back views) owned by Donnie Thorndike was formerly No. 3 Marine Terrace, but was later named 'St Joan'. At the time of writing it is a barber's shop

Russell's mother Donnie at the window of 'St Joan' (Thorndike family collection)

The site of the former Boathouse Cottage, long gone

As already established, Dymchurch was also in real life of major significance in the smuggling trade – although there is little verifiable record of the activity during the period in which Thorndike's books are set. Part of the reason for this was the futile attempts of the authorities to reduce smuggling on the Marsh, which they tried to achieve by concentrating their scarce resources on Dymchurch in the eighteenth century (as described in Chapter 5). Dymchurch, however, was a natural base for smuggling, boasting the advantage of being in the middle of the long open beach running between Hythe and Romney.

Dymchurch has historically held great administrative significance, stretching back to the thirteenth century. At that time, the Kent and Sussex coast was subjected to a number of violent storms, and it was evident that only a combination of the sea walls along the Dymchurch stretch and the man-made dykes (ditches) behind had saved the Marsh from being recaptured by the sea. There was concern in the coastal communities that action by the authorities was needed to allow quick decisions to be made in the event of future flooding and, as a result, Henry III granted a Royal Charter giving the right of self-government – with unique Administrative and Judicial powers, which were at the outset vested in the 23 Lords of the Manors of Romney Marsh.[11] These Lords were more commonly known as Lords of the Level, a level being the self-contained area used for the purpose of land drainage. In the constant battle against the sea, the Lords thus had powers to raise local taxes to pay for the upkeep of flood defences.

---

11. The powers of the Lords were eroded by subsequent Government legislation, although the Lords still meet annually to hold the Grand Lathe.

The Royal British Legion Club. Older residents still fondly recall the performances that Russell Thorndike would deliver here at Christmas and Easter

The former Newington House, one time home of Russell and his family

At one time the village was more widely known as Dymchurch-under-the-wall (the village itself – as well as much of the Marsh – is below sea level at high tide), and this is reflected in the Syn saga. There are many references to the wall within the novels, and the oft-quoted entreaty to 'Serve God: Honour the King, but first maintain the wall' has long been the slogan of the Marsh and highlights how crucial the wall has been to the continued existence of the

Dymchurch Wall then and now. The upper picture is from 1928 (© The Francis
Frith Collection); the lower picture is the same view in 2012

area.[12] Early defence barriers were crude and simple and often breached, and it was only during the reign of Henry VIII that a more robust structure was introduced. This took the form
of a sloping earth bank into which wooden hop poles were driven; the spaces were filled with
bundles of blackthorn which was (wrongly) thought to be impervious to sea-water. Main-
tenance of the wall relied heavily on the availability of blackthorn, and it was made compulsory for everyone in the area to grow thorn trees. Failure to do so, or the cutting of trees
except with express permission, resulted in swingeing fines. Before long, a tax known as a scot

---

12. The issue of the sea wall receives most prominence within *Amazing Quest*. It is afforded even
    greater significance in Buchanan's novel.

was levied to finance the upkeep of the wall. Those who lived on the higher land and were thus exempt were deemed to 'get off scot free', an expression which has survived into modern culture. There are reports of breaches of the wall during the 18th century at times of storms and exceptional high tides, but it nevertheless (and surprisingly) stood for over two hundred years, and even recent borings by archaeologists have confirmed traces of blackthorn. But by the beginning of the 19th century it was clear that to combat the continual erosion and harness improved engineering techniques, a new and more solid construction was required. To this end, John Rennie[13] was engaged. Work on the project started in 1803, although the current three-mile concave concrete structure is the product of its rebuilding in 1847, major repairs following severe storm damage in 1953 and further enhancements in 2010.

Madox Ford described Dymchurch as being: 'small and white and very still nestling beneath the shadow of the sea wall, it is quiet as quiet can be' (this at the end of the Napoleonic Wars); Edith Nesbit spoke of it as being 'then quite secluded, and almost unknown to the outside world' of her first visit in 1893 (only shortly before Thorndike became acquainted); and Marsh historian Anne Roper writes similarly. An interesting if long-winded account of Dymchurch in the 1930s (relative to the time in which the Syn saga is set) is provided in the Preface to the little-known volume *The Scarecrow Rides* ('In which the visitor puts back the clock and listens in beneath the Rookery'):

> Anyone visiting that thriving holiday resort of Dymchurch Sands today would be hard put to it to recognise the obscure village that it was in the days of Dr Syn. However, if you will take the trouble, the mental trouble only, which will not disturb the peace, obliterate the bungalows which spring up like mushrooms in the fertile Romney marsh, remove the obsolete wheel-less railway carriages which give camping shelter to so many happy families during the season, and pack up the enterprising little railroad whose express engines scream their way with such import across the Marsh, although one of them bears the name of Doctor Syn. Having done all this, you must then mentally demolish the telegraph posts, loud speakers, electric lights and telephones, motor caravans, aeroplanes, 'buses and the 'Bus station. Then, down in your imagination with the teashops innumerable, leaving only those houses of call that are licensed to sell Beers, Wines, Spirits and Tobacco. Ruthlessly use a spiritual pickaxe upon every building that is not fashioned of mellow Queen Anne brick, Kentish rag and ship's timber. Rip off all the concertina lines of corrugated iron and laboriously hang red tiles in its stead. Work your thoughts, and without asking permissions from the Ecclesiastical Commissioners, knock down the modern rectory and restore the white-washed, rambling parsonage with its red-tiled roof, and in order not to tread upon the corns of sainted rectors dead and gone, re-christen it The Vicarage. Having done all this, sit down and rest upon the mounting block at the road entrance of Sycamore Gardens, which you will now find transformed into a

---

13. Famed for building a number of the better known London bridges.

rough meadow, a farmstead and barn behind your back, and let your eyes survey the old church and the Tudor building of New Hall, then as now, the Court House of Dymchurch and headquarters of the Lord of the Level. One thing more is left for this our thoughtful restoration. Since you have hypnotised yourself back into a period with Trafalgar yet unfought, and Pitt's Martello Towers not erected, you must replace the stately Memorial of the War in our time with the grim symbol of Justice which preceded it upon that very sight – a gaunt and creaking gallows, and you may tell yourself that the skeleton which swings there in the sea breeze was in its living flesh a sheep stealer; a crime unspeakable and unpardonable in the summing-up of Dymchurch magistrates.

This account suggests that relatively little has altered since but does demonstrate that major change occurred between the late 1890s and the 1930s, the very time that Thorndike became a regular visitor. This followed the passing of legislation toward the end of the nineteenth century, which resulted in responsibility for roads being passed to the County in 1888. A new road was commissioned, which the current A259 follows and which was responsible for much of the subsequent development. Also, around this time (in 1906), the windmill was demolished.[14] More recently, parts of the village suffered bomb damage in a raid in August 1940.

Arguably, with its abundance of touristy shops, fast food outlets and an amusement park, which sits incongruously within the village, Dymchurch is now little different from many small seaside resorts throughout the country. But for a student of Doctor Syn this matters little and, if Dymchurch is the place to commence a tour, then the specific location must be The Ship Inn. Unless you have actually parked in its car park, this will also give you an opportunity to walk along Dymchurch Wall. Weather permitting, you should have fine views both out to sea and north across the Marsh towards Aldington. One of the first things that you will notice about the pub is that it is 'back to front' in that it backs onto the main road. Within Dymchurch, the pub is not unique in this: the aforementioned construction of the new road around the turn of the nineteenth century cut the village in two; the original road from Hythe ran right under the sea wall, into the forecourt of The Ship and then back along the sea wall.[15] The Ship claims to date back to the 16th century, although there is also a reference to an inn on this site in a survey conducted in 1452. It once had a chimney breast with a recess used for storage, now sadly gone; however, this, a sliding wall panel and a number of other places of concealment, indelibly link it to the smuggling trade. Unfortunately, numerous renovations and changes to the building preclude confirmation that there was once a tunnel connecting to the local churchyard. There is little officially documented of eighteenth- and early

---

14. The mill had been built in 1829 and continued working until 1882. Photographs of the village in the late nineteenth century and at the turn of the twentieth century are dominated by the mill situated – naturally enough – in Mill Lane.

15. See photographs in Chapter 2.

The Ocean Inn

ninteenth-century smuggling at the inn, although there are some nineteenth-century references to the Ship as the Smugglers Inn.[16] The Ship in the early nineteenth century was very much the largest inn or hotel in the area and offered many other services including open and closed carriages for hire, a charabanc service to New Romney and Hythe, a bowling green, quoits and a lawn tennis court. As was the practice of the day, it was often used for holding coroner's courts.

The Syn novels feature three pubs in Dymchurch – the Ocean and the City of London being the other two. At the time they were set, however, there was probably only The Ship and one other (the Rose Inn).[17] The Rose Inn may have been a 'beer shop' rather than a tavern and may have evolved into the Ocean or the Good Intent; it does not appear to be until the 1830s that there were three pubs serving the village. The Ocean and City of London are close to each other and still in business today. The latter – which features heavily in *Returns* (initially under the name Sea Wall Tavern) – was for a time home to the Night Riders Motorcycle Group and, although closed for a while, reopened in 2010 as a Sports Bar. Both have some interesting Syn memorabilia and are fully involved in Day of Syn celebrations.

---

16. Walter J C Murray's history *Romney Marsh* is one source that refers to it as such.
17. See also Chapter 2.

The City of London Inn

Coastally, the scene has changed somewhat from Syn's day: in addition to the current sea wall, the Martello towers post-date him. The Napoleonic War with France started shortly after Syn's death and the towers – there were originally four of these constructed at Dymchurch – formed part of the defences against Napoleon. Three now remain in Dymchurch (Nos 23, 24 and 25), one of which is owned by English Heritage and another by Shepway District Council. Number 23 – the northernmost of the Dymchurch towers – was on the market at the turn of the 21st century, with an asking price of £250,000.

Whilst in Dymchurch, a visit to the church of St Peter and St Paul is a must, although sadly – due to the threat of vandalism – it is no longer open to the public at all times. The church itself has changed slightly since Syn's day, with the former taller steepled tower having been replaced during alterations in the 1820s. Inside you will find not only a tablet recording Russell Thorndike's association with the village, but also dedications to Rev Charles Cobb[18] and Francis Rogers, a local Customs Riding Officer who served for 15 years (this is sited in the centre of the Chancel). In the churchyard, don't forget to seek out the tombstones of Solomon Pepper[19] and smuggler Charles Keely (killed in a skirmish with blockade men in 1825).[20] On

---

18. Cobb was the rector who effected the rescue from the *Courrier de Dieppe* and probably provided the inspiration for the character Rev. Bolden in *Returns* – see Chapter 2. He is also commemorated at the northern end of the village, where you will find Charles Cobb Close.
19. See chapter 2.
20. Ironically, the officer who fired the fatal shot – Richard Morgan – was himself shot dead by smugglers the following year.

The church of St Peter and St Paul

leaving the churchyard, you will see the New Hall,[21] administrative home of the Lords of the Levels, which also contains a complete 18th century Court Room and a tiny gaol. This is open to the public as a museum on occasion and well worth a visit; you will need to check in advance the days that it is open – although the Day of Syn is always a good bet. Also in New Hall Close, look out for the Old Rectory, which is now a care home. Some sources have suggested that Sycamore House[22] rather than the Old Rectory may have been the model for Syn's vicarage. Sycamore House was certainly well known to Thorndike through the family connection with Edith Nesbit and it was at one time also used as the vicarage. Both buildings display the attributes that Thorndike describes, being very close to the Court House, near to the sea and overlooking the Marsh. However, records suggest that Sycamore House was not used for this purpose until after the first Syn novel had been written. On the balance of probabilities, it is likely that the Old Rectory was the setting for Syn's vicarage.

---

21. From historical records it does not appear that the Squire made his family home at the New Hall; but it is a fine building and worthy of the status that Thorndike bestows upon it.
22. See photograph in Chapter 2.

New Hall

The Old Rectory, New Hall Close

War Memorial, New Hall Close, site of the village gallows

Although the village gallows has now been removed, a fitting reminder can be seen directly opposite, at the Ship Inn

Finally, before leaving New Hall Close, note the location of the Dymchurch War Memorial. This was the site of the village gallows – clearly visible from both the Ship and the church, as faithfully recorded within the novels.

Old Tree Cottage, Mill Road

There are numerous other reminders within the village of the author and his novels. In addition to the aforementioned public houses, Mr Mipps' Licensed Restaurant/Dining Room in Ship Close and Doctor Syn's Guest House in Mill Road are well-established businesses. Both are situated off the main road and so retain character more in keeping with a bygone age. Accommodation at the latter reflects characters from the Syn novels, including the Mr Mipps, Mrs Waggetts and Captain Clegg rooms. Next door to the guest house is a listed eighteenth century cottage. This is Old Tree Cottage – Mipps's coffin shop of the same name. There have been some more transient establishments – such as the Scarecrow Café, which did good business on the main road for a short period. No doubt, others may come and go. In addition to the church plaque, the author himself is commemorated by a cottage in the village which is named Thorndyke (one assumes that this was the intention of the owner, despite the misspelling!).

Aldington and Aldington Knoll

Aldington and Aldington Knoll feature heavily within the Syn novels. Situated on the northern boundary of the Marsh, the area is inextricably linked with smuggling, chiefly through the Ransleys and their headquarters, the Walnut Tree Inn. Whilst Thorndike moves the Ransley

Doctor Syn's Guest House

Mr Mipps' Licensed Restaurant

family to a different part of the Marsh, he has another smuggling desperado (Grinsley, who is killed in *Returns*) based at Aldington, and the Walnut Tree also features. The pub remains today, the quintessential English smuggling inn of the period, with a smugglers' spyhole in the main door, through which its clientele can still command a good view of the whole Marsh.

Walnut Tree Inn, Aldington

Although only 95 metres above sea level, the grassy mound that is Aldington Knoll is prominent as it is the highest point on the Marsh border. This is a Roman Barrow which has long served as a landmark for sailors. Any such natural feature has obvious uses as a signalling and look-out point for smugglers, and the Walnut Tree has a window built specifically to observe the Knoll, to and from which messages would be passed. There are no historical indications that smugglers regularly fired beacons to signal the start of a run, however. The reality was that even the under-resourced authorities would have been wise to the significance of the regular construction of huge bonfires. Occasionally, though, small fires would be built at very short notice to alert smuggling vessels that the authorities were nearby and that it was no longer safe to land a cargo. The Knoll does appear to have been cut into at one point (only really evident in winter, once foliage has died down) and, although it would be tempting to believe that this is due to Farmer Finn or his ilk attempting to level it, the damage reflects wartime use – the Knoll being used in WWII as an occupation-post. It is claimed that the towers of 36 churches can be seen from the top of the Knoll and, although it would take a day of almost unprecedented clarity to confirm the fact, the view for the lover of Romney Marsh is well worth the journey. Prior to Thorndike, Richard Barham used the Knoll as a setting for black magic in *The Leech of Folkestone*.

Aldington Knoll

Aldington Knoll is not easy to find, and signposting is poor. It is best approached from the B2067 road, and the Ordnance Survey grid reference is TR071353/TR0710335300. Nearby (part of the hamlet of Court at Street) can be found the ruins of a chapel dedicated to the Holy Maid of Kent.[23]

Dungeness

Dungeness features in most of the novels, often as the scene of runs. This is a fascinating part of the Marsh – if not a separate continent within a continent, then certainly the largest shingle expanse in Europe. Although more stable now due to the artificial actions of man (lorry loads of shingle have long been transported daily to combat the effects of longshore drift and thus protect the power stations), in the mid-nineteenth century it was expanding at the rate of 50 feet each year.

Arguably romantic, the 'Ness – isolated and exposed – is one of the most dangerous spots for Channel shipping. Its magic and charm may not be apparent to all, but the range of habitats and fauna that such an apparently bleak landscape accommodates is truly incredible. The scene that Thorndike would have viewed at the turn of the twentieth century has seen much change in the subsequent years although, perversely, it remains instantly recognisable. This is

---

23. See Chapter 2.

the enduring quality of Dungeness – man may try and mould it but cannot destroy its soul. Clearly, the power stations were not around at the turn of the twentieth century, although Thorndike would have witnessed their early development. Only one lighthouse was then in place, but neither of those that stand sentinel there today: the old black lighthouse (now in private ownership and accessible to the public and well worth the visit) did not come into being until 1904. The more modern Trinity House Tower now in use – which is in part a response to the shifting shingle that forms the 'Ness and in part results from the impact of the power stations – was built in 1960 and is chronologically the fifth of the Dungeness lights. Otherwise, the *ad hoc* scattering of shacks and fishermen's cottages may have been added to over the years, but to no great extent.

There would have been a railway line when Thorndike first visited, but not that belonging to the Romney Hythe & Dymchurch Railway (whose Dungeness extension opened in 1928). To those not steeped in the history of the area, a trip back in time to the late nineteenth or early twentieth century would reveal a most incredible scene, and one that reflects an equally unlikely story, which could have been written by Thorndike himself. For Dungeness was – back in the 1870s – seen as the new gateway to Europe, with a number of schemes casting the 'Ness as a new steamer terminal. As unlikely as this may seem today, there was some inherent logic to the idea: a deep natural harbour allied – through the provision of a link to Le Treport (a fishing and holiday town with a direct rail line to Paris) – to the potential for the shortest and quickest link between the French and English capitals. In anticipation, a line from Appledore was laid and the Dungeness section opened in 1881 (although this was initially limited to freight traffic). The dream never materialised and the railway was realigned in 1937 in an attempt to capture anticipated traffic deriving from the developing resorts of Greatstone and Lydd-on-sea.[24] Evidence of the former line, Dungeness station buildings (and platform) can still be clearly seen.

The typography of the 'Ness has always lent itself to smuggling, for the advantages to the smuggler were many. The long shingle beach afforded natural cover for the burying of tubs, and was also very unattractive to those required to police it. Preventive cover was for long extremely limited and local knowledge and skill in traversing the vast expanse of shingle was invaluable: movement over this terrain was far easier for the locals, versed in the use of 'baxters' than for the preventive man, however diligent and motivated. The Britannia Inn was for a short time in the late twentieth century known as the Smugglers before reverting back to its original name, whilst the now defunct Hope and Anchor features in smuggling lore.[25] In addition to smuggling, Dungeness has associations with the darker practice of wrecking. As late as 1630 there are records of locals luring a Spanish vessel onto the beach, murdering the crew and making off with its cargo of spirits.

---

24. This venture was similarly unsuccessful.
25. See Chapter 5.

Old and New Romney

Thorndike found the history of the Marsh fascinating, and with good cause. Nowhere is it more dramatic than Romney, although curiously neither Old nor New Romney features prominently within his novels. New Romney was once the major Cinque Port, but a huge and violent storm in 1287 changed its status for ever. The mouth of the River Rother (then known as the Limen) became completely blocked, and the river itself diverted to Rye. New Romney carried on as a port for a short time, with a canal being cut to rejoin it to the main river near Appledore. This soon silted up, however, and its residents had to accept that Romney would never again recapture its former prominence.

Every local guide worth its salt will point out the irony of New Romney dating back to 1140. The prefixes 'Old' and 'New' relate to the fact that, due to reclamation and silting, the natural harbour moved eastward. Prior to this time, Old Romney was the more important settlement. Now it is a very sleepy village, easily missed if travelling the main road at speed. For those with an interest in Romney Marsh, smuggling or Doctor Syn, however, a visit is a must. Although the area is not unused to exaggeration, the claim of St Clement to be 'the loveliest church in the world' has foundation. Surrounded by sheep and with the obligatory single yew tree standing sentinel in the graveyard, it is the quintessential Marsh church. It is also the church used by Disney in *Doctor Syn alias the Scarecrow*. The fact that the church is still standing – as well as the unusual colour scheme within – is in no small part due to the Walt Disney Corporation.[26] Along the southern edge of the A259, the line of the former Rhee Wall is clearly visible, bearing testament to the skills of the original engineers. Also at Old Romney is the Rose & Crown public house. A pleasant enough hostelry in its own right, this is featured in smuggling history, and there are records retained by the landlord that bear this out.[27]

Despite its decline, New Romney for many years remained the centre of commercial activity for the Marsh and at the turn of the twentieth century – when sheep farming was at its height – had great prominence as a market town. Busy in the tourist season, it has not changed greatly in recent years. This is borne out in the film *The Loves of Joanna Godden*,[28] much of which was shot in New Romney and shows the town as Thorndike would have known it.

In New Romney High Street, the Ship Inn – with authentic links to smuggling – still stands and has retained much of its character. It features in *Doctor Syn Returns*.

Littlestone

Littlestone rates a number of mentions within the novels, often as the site of landings. In *Amazing Quest*, it is at Littlestone that Syn and the Welshman, Jones, are buried up to their necks; and in *Doctor Syn*, Jerk constructs his gallows near Littlestone Point.

---

26. See Chapter 4.
27. See also Chapter 5
28. 1947 film adaptation of Sheila Kaye-Smith's classic novel.

The development of Littlestone went hand in hand with the decline of New Romney. New Romney had been operating as a port at the head of a pool, marked by the Little and Great stones on the north and south heads respectively. But, in tandem with the Rhee Wall canal, the pool also silted up until it reached the stage where New Romney was no longer viable as a port, and hence a causeway was built across the pool. In time, Littlestone developed an extensive flat shingle and sand beach and became a much-favoured spot for the landing of cargo, as reflected in four of the seven Syn books. Littlestone started to develop as a resort at around the time of Thorndike's birth. As a result of the sea receding and the seawall containing natural erosion, Littlestone now has a very attractive and broad green frontage as well as a good beach. As with Dungeness, however, the area never fully developed as envisaged and plans for a state-of-the-art pier did not materialise. The impressive water tower, which dominates the skyline and is still known by some locals as 'the folly', bears further testimony to the optimism of the time. The tower was privately built in the 1890s and would have been known to Thorndike. In his time, there was still a gap between Littlestone and Greatstone. The latter is not mentioned by name in the books for the good reason that there was no settlement there to speak of prior to the twentieth century.

The strange structure that can now be seen just off the coast at low tide certainly post-dates Syn. It is a section of Mulberry Harbour, towed out to Dunkirk to assist in the D-Day Landings in WWII – this part clearly never made it but presents an interesting seamark. A latter day parallel with the Syn saga may be found in the fact that one of the Great Train Robbers laid low in Littlestone in the 1960s. The perception that this would be a quiet place to hide belies the earlier dream of a vibrant resort, although it was not as remote as Jimmy White had hoped – he was arrested after being spotted by a local resident.

Botolph's Bridge

Botolph's Bridge is the scene of duels between Raikes and Brackenbury/Raikes and the Scarecrow in *Further Adventures* and also earns a mention in *Amazing Quest*. This is another very small Marsh settlement little changed since the time of both Thorndike and Syn. There has never been any major development here, although it formerly had greater significance as a crossing point over the series of sewers (ditches) that criss-cross the Marsh (particularly for those trying to reach Burmarsh). Nestling at the foot of the Hythe Hills and alongside the Royal Military Canal, the hamlet can fairly be described as picturesque. The most notable building is the public house of the same name, which has a very distinctive inn sign showing a body being carried over a river by a number of ghostly figures. Disappointingly, this is not a depiction of Night-riders, but an illustration of the legend surrounding St Botolph.

Brookland

Although the village itself is tiny, the name of Brookland is well known. This can be attributed to two factors: as the site of the infamous Battle of Brookland;[29] and for a church that shuns convention by having its steeple not mounted, but set alongside. There are a number of legends surrounding the peculiar architecture of St Augustine's Church, which would do justice to the storytelling of Thorndike himself. Popular are that the steeple jumped off the church in shock after a couple turned up to get married without having to (i.e. without the bride being pregnant) and that, when drawing up the plans, the architect drew the spire alongside the church as he only had a small piece of paper; the builder then constructed it as drawn. The reality is less interesting: the Marsh geology would not support the full weight of the structure and bells, which necessitated the action taken. The Church is also mentioned by Kipling as one of the strange sights of the Marsh.[30]

The village has not withstood the march of time, having been cut in two by the straightening of the main A259 road in the name of progress. As a consequence, however, what was once the main street of the village is now bereft of traffic and has reverted to how it would have looked in Thorndike's time (the only significant difference being that the slaughterhouse – which stood next to the church – has long been demolished).

The Royal Oak,[31] one of Brookland's two current public houses, features in both *Courageous Exploits* and *Amazing Quest*. Disappointingly, its other – the Woolpack – is not so mentioned within the saga. The Brookland Woolpack[32] is an unspoilt, atmospheric gem, which has *bona fide* smuggling credentials and contains a number of smuggling relics: it is commended to anyone with a love of the Marsh, an interest in smuggling or a yearning for a simpler, quieter way of life. This fifteenth century inn also featured in the aforementioned Sheila Kaye-Smith novel *The Loves of Joanna Godden*, and heavily so in the film version. Its interior further appears in an Ealing Comedy, *Green Grow the Rushes*,[33] which is centred around smuggling. In the High Street, look out for Pear Tree House, home of Dr Hougham (Thorndike's 'model' for Dr Sennacherib Pepper) between 1813 and 1859. For those of a romantic or curious disposition, a riddle surrounding the death of Hougham's son is also of interest – it has been claimed that Kipling's poem *I met a maid on the Brookland Road* contains clues to the answer (the maid being a ghost connected with the episode).

As part of a visit to Brookland, a detour to Fairfield Church is recommended. To describe Fairfield as a village would be a gross exaggeration: it comprises just a couple of farm build-

---

29. See Chapter 5.
30. In *Puck of Pook's Hill*.
31. For a short period early in the twentyfirst century, the Royal Oak was renamed the *Yew and Ewe*, before reverting to its original name.
32. See photograph in Chapter 5.
33. A 1951 film starring Richard Burton and Honor Blackman. It contains much interesting footage of Romney Marsh, including scenes shot at Littlestone, New Romney and Rye.

Pear Tree House, High Street, Brookland

ings in addition to the church. However, St Thomas à Beckett Church is one of the symbols of the Marsh – standing remote amongst the fields and on occasions completely surrounded by water. There are tales (contemporaneous with Thorndike) of the vicar and congregation arriving by boat: a Syn-esque scene if ever there was one. There are a number of references to a 'Fair Field' within the Syn saga, but it is not clear if the current day Fairfield is the pertinent location as there are numerous such sites on the Marsh (at New Romney, Dymchurch and near to Dungeness). The church does feature, however, on the back cover of the 1972 Arrow edition of *Doctor Syn Returns*.[34]

Burmarsh

Often mistaken for Burwash (the erstwhile home of Rudyard Kipling), this village in the frequently bypassed northern part of the Marsh rates mention in a number of the novels. On most occasions it is the Shepherd and Crook public house that is the focus of attention, and this is another pub that survives today (complete with some limited Syn adornment and memorabilia). This hostelry was also the venue for a number of services in the late nineteenth century, when the church of All Saints was closed for renovation. The rather obvious 1980s

---

34. See photograph in Chapter 2.

Road sign, Burmarsh

housing development precludes any claim to the village remaining untouched, but it otherwise retains a rustic air. The only thoroughfare on the Marsh that commemorates the author – Thorndike Road – connects the village to the Dymchurch Road.

Hythe

One of the original Cinque Ports, Hythe is a pleasant seaside town on the eastern boundary of the Marsh. Like New Romney, its previous importance faded when it lost its harbour due to infilling (the result of longshore drift and south-west gales in this case). Still a sizeable town, Hythe's main claims to fame are St Leonard's crypt (home to a vast collection of skulls), that it is a terminus of the Romney Hythe & Dymchurch Railway (RH&DR) and that it is the venue for the unusual Venetian summer Fayre (centred on the Royal Military Canal).

Considering its size and historical importance, it is surprising that Hythe (like New Romney) does not feature more prominently in the Syn novels. Occasionally, trips are made to Hythe by Mipps and in *Courageous Exploits* the town provides employment for apprentice cooper George Lee and his girlfriend Polly Henley. The latter works at the Red Lion Inn, which is where the London stagecoach stops. It is the coaching inn stop that is the source of most of the coverage afforded to Hythe by Thorndike, and the Red Lion is one of a number of hostelries regularly visited by Mipps. The Red Lion survives and, even if this ceases to be the case, its location – Red Lion Square – will live on.

Lydd

Home to the Syn dynasty and not to be confused with the coastal bungaloid development of Lydd-on-sea (which significantly postdates the period of Thorndike's writing), Lydd was a centre of smuggling and for a time the headquarters of the Marsh operation. It boasts the Cathedral of the Marsh, the colossal All Saints Church, which is totally out of proportion to the size of the community it serves. This does not indicate that the settlement was once much larger than now: it rather reflects the practice of building a new church to give thanks when a new parcel of land was reclaimed from the sea. Its churchyard testifies to Lydd's past, with graves including those of George Walker and Francis Sisley.[35]

There is more documented evidence of the free trade in Lydd than in Dymchurch or any other Marsh settlement. The George Inn, in particular, is steeped in smuggling history.[36] Lydd would have been a rather quaint and cosy village back in the eighteenth and nineteenth centuries, and the centrepiece then – as now – was the vast green known as the Rype. Although much of the Marsh has remained untouched, the same cannot be said of Lydd, which has benefited or suffered (depending on your point of view) from the attentions of two significant employers, the power companies at Dungeness and the Army. Whilst the power stations were not part of the Marsh that Thorndike knew as a boy, the military presence was (and to a far greater extent than now).

Lympne

Lympne (pronounced 'Lim') was the fictional home of Sir Henry Pembury, when it claimed a strategic importance on the northern hills bordering the Marsh. It is today fairly sleepy, but plays host to Howlett's, the wildlife park established by the late John Aspinall. It also boasts a fine castle open to the public. This is worth a visit if only for the spectacular views it boasts of the Marsh. Lympne undoubtedly has *bona fide* links to smuggling, and the castle includes a four-poster bed once used to hide contraband. Near the castle are the old Roman steps, which are the backdrop to a key scene within *Shadow*.

Rye

Rye – 'across the ditch in Sussex' – is unarguably the jewel in the crown of East Sussex, with character oozing from every pore. W J C Murray in his seminal work *Romney Marsh* describes the town as 'the gateway to Old England, the Marsh and to the past'. Rye is also rich in smuggling history, with the Mermaid Inn (the aforementioned haunt of the notorious Hawkhurst Gang) very much to the fore. The Flushing Inn in Market Street was another smugglers' hang-out, whilst the Traders Passage between Watchbell and Mermaid Streets was used to alert smugglers to the presence of customs men.

There are frequent references to Rye within the Syn novels, particularly to the Mermaid Inn – a regular retreat for Dr Syn and also the temporary headquarters of Tappitt, McCallum and Merry for their ill-fated attempt to destroy Syn in *Returns*. Tappitt was indeed

35. See Chapter 5.
36. See also Chapter 5.

The Mermaid Inn Rye (picture courtesy Judith Blincow, the Mermaid Inn)

arrested in its bar. The Mermaid remains the hotel of choice for the discerning visitor and is one of the few establishments in Rye that advertises its Syn connections, boasting the Doctor Syn Bedchamber.[37] This has a bookcase (clearly seen on the left of the photograph on page 134) that doubles as a door to a secret passageway leading to the bar. Clearly linked with smuggling, this arrangement now serves a more legitimate purpose as a fire escape, with privacy for occupants preserved by way of a bolt on the inside. Watchbell Street also features in the *Doctor Syn* novel and those familiar with the Walt Disney dramatisation will recognise a number of buildings and locations around Church Square. The town is a very good base for those setting out to tour the Marsh and for those of a literary bent; Henry James lived in Lamb House and Rye is featured in fiction more even than Dymchurch. Alongside Thorndike's books, E F Benson (*Mapp and Lucia*),[38] Rumer Godden and Patric

37. Both the Mermaid Inn and Dr Syn's bedchamber feature in the 1968 Timi Yuro film *Interlude*. The sequence lasts around four minutes, beginning at 48:20.

38. Within the *Mapp and Lucia* books the name *Tilling* – taken from the name of the river – is substituted for Rye.

Doctor Syn's Bedchamber, with the concealed door, in the Mermaid Inn Rye (picture courtesy Judith Blincow, the Mermaid Inn)

Dickinson have all set novels here. Beatrix Potter also weaves Rye into one of her stories (*The Tale of the Faithful Dove*). More recently, the children's works of Malcolm Saville and Christopher Ryan (the *Captain Pugwash*[39] books and cartoons) have been based in and around the town.

There is a Dr Syn self-catering complex in Rye and, from time to time, some of the local potters (Rye hosts a number of such enterprises) offer items that bear the Syn name or reference to the legend. The two Tourist Information Centres at times hold literature relating to Dr Syn and staff are invariably knowledgeable on the subject.

St Mary's and Jesson

Jesson Flats and Jesson Beach (mentioned in both *Returns* and *Shadow*) may cause some puzzlement to readers as they do not appear on current maps. The name Jesson refers to the area bounded by Dymchurch and Littlestone, but now known as St Mary's Bay. The name –

---

39. In the *Pugwash* books, the town goes by the name of *Sinkport*(!) – Rye being one of the ancient Cinque Ports.

Traders Passage, Rye

possibly a contraction of Jefferstone[40] – is still occasionally used by locals, although mostly in relation to the former holiday camp. Development before the twentieth century was sparse and, where Thorndike refers to Jesson within the Syn novels, it would have been little changed from the era of which he was writing.

Thorndike's use of the name Jesson for St Mary's Bay clearly indicates that St Mary's – used in two of his novels – refers to the inland settlement of St Mary-in-the Marsh. St Mary-in-the-Marsh has changed little over the centuries. Today it remains a genteel Marsh village, with a charming church and an equally acceptable village pub (the Star). There is little housing but there is a very good example of a preserved lookers' hut nearby. Many visitors are attracted to the churchyard, where the grave of Thorndike's friend and mentor – Edith Nesbitt – is to be found.

Warehorne

Warehorne rates occasional mention in the Syn novels and more frequently in histories of smuggling. It is on record that, one one occasion, a cargo of smuggled goods was brought

---

40. Jefferstone Lane still runs through the middle of the St Mary's Bay and also gives its name to the station on the RH&DR. There are, however, alternative theories as to the derivation of the name.

from Dymchurch to Warehorne, for repackaging into smaller quantities for onward transportation. Being on a hill above the Marsh, the village provided a good look-out point and opportunities to escape the excise men. Richard Barham, who was rector here and at Snargate, confirms that the church was used by smugglers and there are reliable reports of three tunnels converging there. One of these – inevitably – connected with the local pub (the Woolpack).

Dover

Although some distance from Romney Marsh, Dover's position has long made it a highly important location both in terms of defence of the realm and for the smuggling of goods from (and to) mainland Europe. Reflecting its strategic prominence, the large hill above the town has hosted an Iron Age fort and a Roman lighthouse (which still stands and can be seen today). William the Conqueror built a formidable castle, although the current very imposing structure has its origins in work started by Henry II in the twelfth century.

From the Conquest right up until 1958, troops were continuously garrisoned at Dover Castle, an aspect that Thorndike explores in a number of the Syn novels. Similarly, the press gangs did often operate from the castle and take advantage of prisoners who were held there. The castle was justifiably considered a safer place of confinement than local lock-ups, so high-profile prisoners were often incarcerated there, although it did not play host to many smugglers prior to the nineteenth century. This was to change when the castle underwent massive rebuilding during the Napoleonic Wars and at their end, when tunnels (constructed to house a greater number of troops) were partly converted and used by the Coast Blockade, specifically to combat smuggling.

Dover Castle

Other villages/localities

Of other places featured in the Syn saga, Bonnington is worthy of note and has changed little since the eighteenth century. It is not so much a village as a linear development on the road from Aldington, and a few of the Aldington smugglers had their roots here. Within *Returns*, a landing is effected at Knockholt Beach, which does not exist today and of which there is no trace on modern maps. It is likely that this refers to a local name for a stretch of the beach between Dymchurch and what was then Jesson, now known as High Knocke.

Although not featuring in the novels, the village of Ruckinge is of interest. This was the home village of many of the Ransley family, and the grave of the two brothers convicted of highway robbery and hanged on nearby Penenden Heath in 1800 can be found in the churchyard.

Fishing connections

The Marsh has traditionally been associated with two legitimate occupations: sheep farming and fishing – both of which have financed smuggling enterprises. Fishing is a regular backdrop to Thorndike's Syn novels, but some of the terminology may not be obvious to all

Preserved herring hang, Tarts Lane

readers. Kettle, keddle or kiddle trapnet fishing was for a long time a mainstay of the Marsh fishing community, and photographs of Dymchurch in the 1930s often depict this activity. The practice continued until quite recently and, while there are small pockets of this left today, EC legislation has effectively sounded its death-knell. The term is believed to derive from the sight of the fish desperately thrashing in the nets as the tide recedes, leaving them trapped in a diminishing pool of water – resembling the effect of a kettle boiling. The main fishing family in Dymchurch was for years the Henleys, but there were several other kettle-net specialists including the Southerdens, Tarts, Gilletts, Freathys, Blacklocks, Smithers and Paines. The main catch of this type of fishing would be mackerel (but not exclusively so). In many fishyards there would be a curing house, known locally as a 'herring hang'. This was a tall building typically only some 8–10 square feet in floor area. The Henley Herring Hang is featured in *Amazing Quest* (particularly as the site where Syn and Jones are buried on the beach up to their necks). The location is depicted as being close to Littlestone Beach; whilst there is no such building shown on maps of the period, there was an area of Dymchurch Beach that was known locally as the 'Herring Hang' and that was indeed used by smugglers as a landing place in the early part of the eighteenth century – although Thorndike does not reference this. There is only one good remaining example of a traditional hang on Romney Marsh: this is at Tarts Yard[41] in Lydd (to the rear of Skinner Road) and is now the subject of a preservation order. Note that this is significantly larger than the norm.

41. Grid reference TR045220510.

7

The Legacy of Syn

Any member of the library service in the area, Dymchurch shopkeeper or publican will confirm that interest remains very much alive today. One of the most frequently asked questions is: 'where is Doctor Syn buried?'. A number of visitors have expressed irritation that they have been unable to find his burial plot in the Dymchurch cemetery and others complain that his name has been omitted from the list of past vicars![1] An internet search under 'Syn' will produce countless website references, almost as many of American origin (where the Disney film captured imaginations) as British.

A tour of the Marsh villages and environs may identify further references and reminders, some obvious and some less so. Most certainly amongst the former is Syn Cottage at Newchurch; whilst others such as the cottage at Dungeness named Imogene are more open to conjecture. Further afield, Groombridge Place – a moated Manor house in the village of Groombridge, near Tonbridge – would seem to be an unlikely venue to have an association, but its Halloween Evening held in the Enchanted Forest is sometimes hosted by 'the infamous smuggler Dr Syn and his evil companion Megilante'.

As with all legends, there is a tendency to stretch and misuse. In the mid-1990s, this author was amused during a tour of St Clements Caves at Hastings to be told by the guide that a huge figure carved into the rock (and previously described by other guides as a sculpture of Napoleon) was actually that of Doctor Syn, 'a real-life eighteenth-century parson who was infamous for his smuggling exploits in the Hastings area'. Perhaps Mipps was right and those pesky smugglers really were Sussex men after all!

Tourism

The local Tourist board was not quick to jump on the bandwagon, but has recently actively marketed the area as 'The Land of Syn'. The area has understandably (for reasons of geography) long been popular with cyclists and a series of cycle routes produced by Shepway Council includes one entitled 'On the Trail of Doctor Syn'. In 2011, the Catford Cycling Club

---

1. Beware of some websites that contain 'doctored' lists, which include the name Christopher Syn!

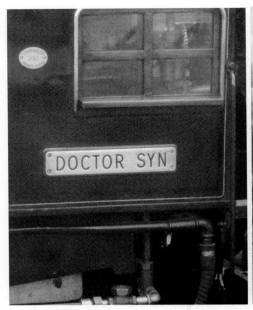 

The RH&DR locomotive No 10, Doctor Syn

– regular visitors to the Marsh – promoted their annual tour under the banner: 'Dr Syn's Tour of the Marshes'. A pack of footpath walks also references Thorndike's leading character. For a time, the single-track railway line between Ashford and Hastings was marketed as 'the Marsh Link', complete with distinctive Scarecrow logo.

A staple of the local tourist industry is, of course, the Romney, Hythe and Dymchurch Light Railway (RH&DR) – the best known attraction on Romney Marsh and responsible for bringing many visitors to the area. For some, a journey behind the sleek black Canadian Pacific locomotive number 10 *Doctor Syn* is their introduction to the legend, which the railway in turn helps to promote. This locomotive made a well-publicised trip to Waterloo Station in January 1948, where it was displayed as part of a campaign to promote the Southern Railway Servants Orphanage fund.

In addition to having run special named trains such as *The Scarecrow*, the RH&DR Association for a number of years included The Scarecrow as a regular contributor to its journal, under a column 'From the last Coach'.

Day of Syn

The most prominent single tourism-inspired initiative is the celebrated Day of Syn. Building on the interest arising from the Hammer and Disney films, this came into being in 1964,[2]

---

2. Prior to this, the parochial church council had organised an annual fete with a smuggling theme, but on a very small scale.

An early outing for the Day of Syn Society (members depicted 'flying the flag' at an event in Ramsgate)

orchestrated by the then vicar of Dymchurch – the Reverend Ron Meredith – as a fundraiser for church roof repairs. For the inaugural event, Russell Thorndike presented the church with a written document authorising the use of the title *Day of Syn*. A star guest was the actress Jill Curzon, who had played Katherine Banks in the Disney film released earlier that year. This first *Day of Syn* was such a great success that another was undertaken by the Church the following year and this also went well. By 1966, however, the event was becoming too large for the Parochial Church Council and a committee, additionally involving other local organisations, was established. This committee decided to make the *Day of Syn* a bi-annual event, with the established pageant joined by a fete at the local recreation ground, where charities would run sideshows and stalls.

The *Day of Syn* continues to be held every two years and falls on the August Bank Holiday weekend when the year is even. The main events are on the Monday and start (usually) at 10 am in The Ship Inn car park, which fills up with red-coated dragoons and striped-shirted sailors, who mingle through the village alongside entertainers in period dress. Mipps, the press gang and of course Syn/The Scarecrow (in early years played by the vicar of Dymchurch) all take part. During the day various scenes from the novels are re-enacted, including the escape of a smuggler from custody, a prisoner taken from the gaol at the New Hall, a duel, the press-gang in action and a firing squad performing its grim and noisy duty in the garden of the Ocean Inn. The centrepiece is the beach landing of a 'cargo' and a skirmish between the

Old meets new: Dr Syn leads the procession from the beach to the Recreation ground, crossing the RH&DR (picture credit: Kentish Express PD1072516)

smugglers and authorities,[3] which involves the use of authentic cannon and cutlasses. The finale sees the Scarecrow lead his gang through the village to the mammoth fete at the Recreation Ground. The standard of acting is good (some professional actors take part) and footage has appeared on a number of television programmes. At one time, a mummers play was also re-enacted at the three village pubs, but this has in recent years been replaced by Morris dancing at each of these locations. This is a wonderful community event, with large numbers involved, and has now expanded to include events on the other two days of the holiday weekend – one of which is sometimes a Sunday Evensong at the church.[4] The RH&DR is also heavily involved, with their locomotive Number 10 in some years patrolling the Dymchurch sidings. The *Day of Syn* is billed as the largest free festival in south-east England. In 2012, an art exhibition – 'The Art of Syn' – was introduced. Held in the Village Hall,[5] the event was officially opened by Russell's granddaughter, Nina, who also judged a competition for the best painting.

The event made national headlines in 2008 when, after 44 years, the title character was forced to dismount and lead Gehenna through the streets and across the beach. Whilst this was billed by the media as another example of *health and safety gone mad*, the reality was that the insurers had increased the premium to take account of the risks of a rider on horseback to a level that the organising committee just could not afford. The revised arrangements have

---

3.   The timing of this is dictated by the tide, and the sequence of other events varies accordingly.
4.   On occasion, this service is accompanied by a violin, à la Rash.
5.   Off Orgarswick Road. See the map in Chapter 6.

Scenes from the Day of Syn in 2010 (author's photographs) and 2012 (photographs David Penfold)

unfortunately detracted from the spectacle. Despite this setback, the event greatly benefits local charities as well as the tourist economy. In an age where the fabric of society is chang-

Russell Thorndike's son, Dan, pulls a pint of Scarecrow Ale at The Ship (photograph courtesy of The Ship Inn)

ing, it also serves to unite the community in a way arguably reminiscent of the smuggling of which Thorndike wrote. In 2001 (one of the intervening years) a Gallows Day was staged, which centred on the New Hall and the church. A Scarecrow (bearing a facsimile of the Disney mask) was hung from the gallows and the old town lock-up was opened to the public. This was also a success and, such is the popularity of the *Day of Syn* that the time may not be far off when there is an annual celebration.

The Ship Inn, Dymchurch

In 2009, The Ship Inn was taken over and refurbished by local entrepreneur and self-styled 'megalithic engineer, silversmith and purveyor of fish and chips' Niko Miaoulis. Miaoulis is a great champion of Romney Marsh[6] and he developed a Doctor Syn theme/shrine at his pub. With some justification, Miaoulis claimed to have one of the largest collections of Dr Syn memorabilia in the world. Whilst Miaoulis and The Ship parted company in December 2010, the new owners have maintained the theme. Here you can buy Dr Syn posters, post

---

6. Miaoulis has also co-written (with Andy Holyer) *Life on Marsh (a journey through the mysteries and magic of the 'fifth continent')*; and has jointly presented the *Niko and Terry the Scarecrow* show with Terry Anthony on Romney Marsh FM.

One of the endearing and unique knitted Scarecrow characters sold at The Ship (this additionally contains chocolates!)

cards, mugs, t-shirts and key rings, as well as Scarecrow rock. One of the two restaurants is named 'Scarecrows' (the other is 'the Fifth Quarter'). On occasion you can buy Scarecrow Ale[7] over the bar, and enjoy a drink while studying the impressive collection of Dr Syn film posters and paintings that adorn the walls..

Syn in art

There are a number of individuals whose work and passion highlight the Syn legend. One such was Andrew Newell Wyeth. Living between 1917 and 2008, Wyeth was part of a highly significant American family of artists and inventors. Such was his popularity that he was commonly known as the 'Painter of the People'. What is less well known is that he counted *Dr Syn alias the Scarecrow* amongst his favourite films. He frequently introduced subjects of personal interest into his paintings, and his 1981 'self-portrait' is a rather bizarre and disturbing work. It depicts a half-dressed skeleton sitting in a wooden chair within the tower of a lighthouse rented by his wife on Southern Island, Maine. The tower itself is fitted out as Horatio Nelson's quarters on board *HMS Victory*. It is entitled *Doctor Syn*.

Local artist Terry Anthony has painted many pictures depicting Dr Syn and related themes. He holds regular exhibitions (*Syn at the Grand*) at the Grand Hotel on the Leas at Folkestone and has his own Dr Syn Gallery and café at Hythe. He was also commissioned by Disney to

---

7. Brewed by the Nelson Brewery at Chatham Dockyard.

produce the artwork to accompany the 2008 DVD release *Dr Syn: The Scarecrow of Romney Marsh*. His work has been championed by the likes of comedian Vic Reeves and been showcased in Spartanburg, the 'birthplace' of Doctor Syn.

Other artists worthy of note include Dee Taylor, who has exhibited at The Ship Inn, and Paul Draper, who formerly ran the *Syn Art Gallery* in the unlikely location of Pershore, Worcestershire.

Syn in modern music

Rather surprisingly, Gerard Schurmann's *The Scarecrow of Romney Marsh* was covered by heavy metal outfit Madd Hunter and released via the Youtube website in 2000. This track is set to footage of the Disney mini-series.

Other musicians have also recorded tracks that they claim to have been inspired or influenced by Russell Thorndike's work. Probably the most prominent of these is by the renowned recording artist, author and journalist Paul Roland. His early work has been favourably compared to that of Marc Bolan and the first track on his 1990 Album *Masque* is entitled: *Dr Syn is Riding Again*. Led Zeppelin's film *The Song Remains the Same* allegedly incorporates interpreted elements of the Doctor Syn saga within the 'No Quarter' fantasy sequence (bassist John Paul Jones reportedly being inspired by Thorndike's work).

Closer to home, a resident of Dymchurch (self-styled 'Man o' the Marsh') who goes by the stage name of Jayl, is a poet, songwriter and rock performer who – like many others – was smitten by the Doctor Syn books when a young man. His stage act often involves him dressing up as the Scarecrow and his television and promotional work has featured numerous Marsh venues. Jayl's publishing company is Scarecrow Records and his brother William Lowdell – also a performer – goes by the stage name of Jimmie Bone(!).

Another musical connection is provided by an R&B Band in East Anglia that has performed under the name *Doctor Syn*. This was founded in 1996 by Dave Basham (with the name additionally reflecting his previous interest in *Pirates* and *Doctor Feelgood*).

Dr Syn at sea

Whilst you are unlikely to encounter Captain Clegg on his sloop deck, you could still meet *Dr Syn* patrolling English coastal and inland waters. This is in the form of a 16-foot Wayfarer yacht owned by Mike Bull, a Marsh exile currently living in the north of England – and a self-confessed fan of Syn. This has been used as a training vessel in the past but is often to be found attending Wayfarer events and re-unions. Regular updates on voyages and escapades are posted on line.

The Scarecrow of the South

A rather unlikely news story broke in June 2009 when it was announced that plans were in place to erect a giant sculpture in the style of the Angel of the North and the proposed Gateway to the South.[8] This was to take the form of a 100-foot tall statue of 'The Scarecrow of Romney Marsh'.

Whilst some locals dismissed this as a (very!) late April Fool story, it became the lead item on the local BBC television news and was followed up by some of the national media. The proposed site was Haguelands Farm (home to the maize maze next to the RH&DR near Dymchurch). The estimated cost was quoted as being £1m, with partial funding to be sought from the European Union. The proposal also included a £300k revamp of one of the Martello Towers at Dymchurch to house a Visitor Centre and Museum of the Marsh; the two sites would be linked by the RHDR (and marketing would promote the link). The scheme allegedly had the backing of – amongst others – leading London theatre producer Marc Sinden.[9] A spokesman for Shepway District Council initially advised that no approach had been made with regard to planning permission, although later newspaper reports claimed that a 'blueprint' had been sent to the Council. At the time of writing nothing has come of this, although local newspapers report from time to time that the project has not been shelved. Reports are far from consistent, however, and by February 2010 the size of the proposed sculpture had risen to 160 feet!

Cynics could argue (with some justification) that the proposal was at least in part a publicity stunt to promote a number of local businesses and interests. The idea – most fittingly – was conceived in the bar of The Ship, which had only formally re-opened the previous month; and no doubt the timing of the publicity was very helpful to the re-establishment of the hostelry (landlord Niko Miaoulis was interviewed by press and TV). Whatever the realities, the debate that this has stimulated can only be good for the area and the establishment of the giant wind farm at nearby Little Cheyne Court means that planning permission may not now be as difficult to obtain as it once would.

Syn in the Future

The 'new wave' of Doctor Syn proponents have not always seen eye-to-eye with the 'old guard', who have complained that the former have used the Syn name and the *Day of Syn* to publicise their own work. This has sparked some interesting correspondence in the local newspapers, but serves to underline that people still care – passionately – about Thorndike's

---

8. aka the White Horse at Ebbsfleet.
9. Local resident and son of actor Donald Sinden, friend of the Thorndike family. Russell presented him with a full set of the Syn novels when he was a young boy.

creation and demonstrates what he means to the residents of Dymchurch and Romney Marsh. Few authors have created such an enduring legend as Dr Syn. The character has captured the imagination of many and focused world attention on a proud village in a small corner of south-east England. Furthermore, there is no sign of interest abating, as demonstrated by the huge attendances at the *Day of Syn*. Another 'barometer' is provided by Shepway Rural Partnership's shrewd move (in the autumn of 2008) in launching the *Dr Syn Writing Project* (subtitled *The Scarecrow Rides Again*). This involved 12 local schools taking part in a cross-curricular approach that involved ICT, Art, History and Literacy. Local authors and members of the *Day of Syn* Society were involved, smuggling history imparted and artefacts displayed. Dr Syn himself even put in an appearance at Dymchurch churchyard! The event clearly went down well with the pupils and they created their own graphic novels. All involved pronounced the venture a great success and the Shepway authorities indicate that they are keen to repeat the exercise. It is fitting that Syn shoud be introduced to a new generation and that Thorndike's memory is perpetuated in this way. Tales of smuggling, particularly when set in the special and unique surroundings of Romney Marsh, remain attractive to many more than a century after Doctor Syn was conceived. All the evidence shows that Syn is alive and well – and likely to remain so far into the future.

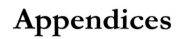

Appendices

Appendices

Appendix 1

Russell Thorndike Filmography

Macbeth 1922
Thorndike plays the title role, alongside sister Sybil as Lady Macbeth. These portrayals are also included in the 1922 compilation *Tense Moments from Great Plays*.

It's Never too Late to Mend 1922
Drama: Thorndike takes the lead role (Squire Meadows).

A Christmas Carol/Old Scrooge 1923
Thorndike plays the title role of Scrooge.

Wonder Women of the World: Henrietta Maria; or the Queen of Sorrow 1923
Historical drama with Thorndike playing Charles I.

The Bells 1923
Based on the play by Leopold Lewis, which centres on the role of a hypnotist. Thorndike's character is Mathias.

The Fair Maid of Perth 1923
Adventure film in which Thorndike plays the lead male part of Dwining.[1]

The School for Scandal 1923
Based on the Richard Sheridan play. Thorndike takes the part of Sir Peter Teakle.

The Audacious Mr Squire 1923
Comedy based on Sydney Bowkett's play of the same name. Thorndike plays Harry Smallwood.

---

1. During filming in Ashdown Forest, Russell tripped in a rabbit hole and fell onto his sword, suffering significant facial injury. Typically, he insisted on carrying on, but subsequently fainted. The incident was reported in the national press, and it was some time before he could resume work.

The Dream of Eugene Aram 1923

Film based on the poem by Thomas Hood, in which Thorndike plays the part of a murderer (the lead role).

Wonder Women of the World: Lucrezia Borgia; (aka Plaything of Power 1923)

Historical drama; Thorndike plays Cesare Borgia.

The Test 1923 (Drama)

The Sins of a Father 1923

Drama in which Thorndike plays character de Bourbonne.

Love in an Attic 1923

Film following the staging of a play, in which Thorndike is the producer.

Heartstrings 1923

A romance based on the novel *A Manchester Marriage* by Elizabeth Gaskell. A sailor who is presumed dead returns home to find his wife has remarried for the sake of their crippled child. Thorndike plays the part of Tom Openshaw.

Human Desires 1924

The story of an underworld cabaret singer's rise to fame and affluence and a man's discovery that not all the wealth in the world will buy a woman's love. Thorndike's character is Paul Perot.

Miriam Rozella 1924

A poor young woman employed as a companion to a titled lady is accused of theft and tempted by an older Casanova. Thorndike plays the part of Crewe Slevens.

Love's Bargain 1925

A wronged woman tries to commit suicide by jumping into the river. She is rescued by a legionnaire with whom she subsequently falls in love.

A Shot in the Dark 1933

A whodunnit/thriller involving an apparent suicide which is not as it first seems. Thorndike plays a drug-addicted doctor (Dr Stuart).

The Roof 1933

Crime/comedy thriller in which jewels left in trust with a lawyer are stolen. Thorndike's character is Clive Bristow.

Puppets of Fate 1933 (aka Wolves of the Underworld 1935)

The story of an escaped convict who blackmails a murderous doctor into helping him. Thorndike plays Dr Orton Munroe.

Whispering Tongues 1934

Crime film with a central character who bears a close resemblance to Raffles. Thorndike plays the part of Fenwick.

Fiddlers Three 1934

Story involving British soldiers caught in a thunderstorm at Stonehenge where a flash of lightning transports them back to the Imperial Rome of the Emperor Nero. Comedy musical starring comedy heavyweight Tommy Trinder. Thorndike is cast as a high priest.

Fame 1936

Comedy. The story of an inefficient shopworker with aspirations, who wins a newspaper competition to play the part of Oliver Cromwell in a film. Thorndike plays a judge.

Henry V 1944

Directed by Laurence Olivier, who takes the lead role. Strong cast includes Robert Newton. Thorndike plays the Duke of Bourbon.

Caesar & Cleopatra 1946

Thorndike plays a harpist's master. Cast includes Vivien Leigh and Stewart Granger.

A Midsummer Night's Dream 1946

TV movie in which Thorndike plays the character Quince.

Hamlet 1948

Directed by Laurence Olivier, who again also stars. Thorndike plays a priest.

Richard III 1955

Another all-star cast, which includes Laurence Olivier and John Gielgud. Thorndike once more takes the role of a priest.

Appendix 2

Russell Thorndike Bibliography

Fiction/historical novels

Doctor Syn saga
See Appendix 3

The Slype
A murder mystery novel set in Dullchester (Rochester), The Slype being a passageway within the Precincts of Rochester Cathedral. The plot involves clergy and references Mipps and other characters from the Syn saga. (Holden 1927)

The Vandekkers
An adventure set in the eighteenth century. A young Dutchman travels to the West Indies to avenge two murders and rescue a damsel in distress. Some parallels with Doctor Syn. (Appleton & Co., New York 1930)

Devil in the Belfry/Herod's Peal
A detective novel, with shades of Dickens' *Edwin Drood* and *Bleak House*. Dullchester features again, as do some of the characters from *The Slype*. (Butterworth 1931; Dial Press 1932)

The Water Witch
This is referred to erroneously as *The Watch Witch* by some sources. (Butterworth 1932, Arrow 1953)

The Forbidden Room
(Dial Press 1933)

Jet and Ivory
(Rich & Cowan 1934)

Show House Sold
(Rich 1941)

The House of Jeffreys

A detective novel, also written as a play in three acts. Central character is Georgina Jeffreys, a descendant of the infamous Hanging Judge Jeffreys. (Rich & Cowan 1943)

Master of the Macabre

A collection of ghost stories. (Rich & Cowan 1946)

Oliver Twist

The classic Dickens tale retold by Thorndike for children (a small card book with illustrations from the *Cineguild* film). (Raphael Tuck and Sons 1948)

Little Dorrit

Another Dickens tale retold for a younger audience. (Raphael Tuck & Sons – date unknown)

The First Englishman

An historical fiction/romance that has Hereward the Wake as a central character. (Rich & Cowan 1949; White Lion 1971)

Non-Fiction

Sybil Thorndike

An early biography of his sister. Some sources have pointed out inaccuracies/exaggerations in the accounts of their childhood. (Butterworth 1929; subsequently republished by Eyre & Spottiswoode 1941 and Rockliff 1950)

Children of the Garter

Subtitled: *Being the Memoirs of a Windsor Castle Choirboy during the last years of Queen Victoria.* Thorndike draws on his own experiences as a choirboy. An historical record, which includes photographs of the Royal Family. (Rich & Cowan 1937)

A Wanderer with Shakespeare

A commentary on Shakespeare. (Rich & Cowan 1939) A re-typed edition was published on-line in January 2010.

In the Steps of Shakespeare

Essentially an update and extension of *A Wanderer with Shakespeare*. Book compares the Elizabethan settings of Shakespeare's work with mid-nineteenth century England. This and *A Wanderer with Shakespeare* confirmed Thorndike as an authority on Shakespeare. (Rich & Cowan 1948; 1950)

Books in collaboration with others

Lilian Baylis

A biography written jointly with sister Sybil. (Chapman & Hall 1938)

Six Against the Yard

A collaborative work by six authors (a series of short individual novels by leading novelists of the day). Thorndike's contribution is entitled: *The Strange Death of Major Scallion*. (Selwyn & Blount 1936)

Plays

(excluding Grand Guignol 'playlets' written with Reginald Arkell)

Saul:[2] a Historical Tragedy in Five Acts, Depicting the Life and Death of King Saul (1906)

The Sausage String's Romance or A New Cut Harlequinade (c. 1913)

Doctor Syn (c. 1923)

---

2.   For which Sybil Thorndike composed the musical accompaniment.

Appendix 3

Canonical Syn Novels – Publication Details

This excludes Book Club editions.

Doctor Syn on the High Seas (aka The Adventures of Captain Clegg)

Rich & Cowan Ltd 1936; Arrow editions 1959, 1963, 1966, 1972; Romney Publishing 2010.

Copyright Hutchinson & Co. 1936

20 chapters; 153 pages (Arrow editions)

Dedicated to the memory of John Buchan

The Return of Doctor Syn

Rich & Cowan Ltd 1935, 1938; Arrow editions 1959; 1964; 1966; and 1972. Romney Publishing 2011.

Copyright Hutchinson & Co. 1935

17 chapters; 178 pages (Arrow editions)

The Further Adventures of Doctor Syn

Rich & Cowan Ltd 1936, 1949; Arrow editions 1959, 1963, 1966, 1972; Romney Publishing 2012.

Copyright Hutchinson & Co. 1936

20 chapters; 152 pages (Arrow editions)

Dedicated to J H Crane[3]

The Courageous Exploits of Doctor Syn

Rich & Cowan Ltd 1939; Arrow editions 1959, 1964, 1966, 1972.

Copyright details unknown

15 chapters; 250 pages (Arrow editions)

Dedicated to Charles Braybrooke[4]

---

3.   A publisher with Rich & Cowan.
4.   A family friend, believed to be in the publishing field.

The Amazing Quest of Doctor Syn

Rich & Cowan Ltd 1938; Arrow editions 1964, 1966, 1972.

Copyright details unknown

8 chapters; 184 pages (Arrow editions)

Dedicated to George Arliss[5]

The Shadow of Doctor Syn

Rich & Cowan Ltd 1944; Arrow editions 1964, 1966, 1972.

Copyright details unknown

24 chapters; 188 pages (Arrow editions)

Dedicated to Emma Treckman[6]

Doctor Syn

Doubleday, Page & Company (US) 1915; Thomas Nelson 1915; Rich & Cowan Ltd 1915; Jonathan Cape Lock 1933, 1959; Arrow editions 1964, 1966, 1972. Wildside Press (US) 2004;[7] New Romney Bookshop 2008; Romney Publishing 2010.

Copyright Hutchinson & Co. 1915

40 chapters; 210 pages (Arrow editions)

The Scarecrow Rides

Dial Press (US) 1935.

See Chapter 3.

Note: at the time of writing, re-typed versions of most of the volumes can be found on the internet and reprints are starting to appear from various different sources. The titles of some reprints are misleading.

---

5. The acclaimed actor, who took the title role in the 1937 *Doctor Syn* film.
6. An actress whom Thorndike met at Windsor Theatre and who was mentored by him. Despite this, her career was short-lived.
7. This edition perpetuates the mistake in the first edition, by spelling the author's name as Thorndyke.

Appendix 4

The Scarecrow Rides – Chapter Titles

Highlighted, italicised titles are those that also appear within *Doctor Syn Returns*.

Preface: In Which the Visitor to Dymchurch Puts Back the Clock and Listens Beneath the Rookery[8]

Chapter 1:   Why Two Sour-Faced Men Braved the Storm

Chapter 2:   Meg Fears for her Husband

Chapter 3:   *The Wreck of the Brig on Dymchurch Wall*

Chapter 4:   The Wooden Devil

Chapter 5:   The Death of the Sea-Captain

Chapter 6:   The Survivor Takes the Whip-Hand

Chapter 7:   The Sea-Chest

Chapter 8:   *Doctor Syn Returns*

Chapter 9:   Doctor Syn Takes Leave of Himself

Chapter 10:   Doctor Syn Makes Preparations

Chapter 11:   The New Doctor Syn Appears in Breakfast

Chapter 12:   Doctor Syn Occupies the Pulpit

Chapter 13:   Doctor Syn Delivers an Ultimatum

Chapter 14:   Mr Merry Confronts Three Merry Blades

Chapter 15:   Meg's Tavern Becomes "The City of London"

Chapter 16:   Doctor Syn Sees Danger in Charlotte Cobtree

Chapter 17:   *Mr Mipps Appears*

Chapter 18:   The Housekeeper Objects

Chapter 19:   Doctor Syn and Mister Mipps

Chapter 20:   *The Death of the Riding Officer*

Chapter 21:   Grinsley Posted for Murder

Chapter 22:   *The Secret of the Figure-Head*

---

8.   This is reproduced within Chapter 6.

Appendix 5

Doctor Syn on the High Seas – Plot Synopsis

Setting: 1754–1775

The novel begins with a useful piece of scene setting: a Prologue introducing the Syns of Lydd. This establishes that there are only two living descendants – Christopher and his uncle Solomon – of the Syn family that once held great prominence on Romney Marsh. The subsequent decline has been due to a combination of Marsh ague and Jacobite fervour (a number of the family having been killed fighting for the Jacobite cause). There is also a very early introduction to Septimus Mipps as a smuggler hiding from the Customs. He threatens Syn with a blunderbuss in the belief that the latter is a Customs Officer on his case.

Syn's life as the youngest don at Oxford is touched upon, and he journeys back to Oxford to escort a Spanish lady and her daughter (acquaintances of Sir Henry Pembury) on business following the death of the lady's husband. Syn and the daughter (Imogene) fall in love but have to contend with the other party to this business – one 'Bully' Tappitt – who wants both his own wicked way with Imogene and her share of the estate. Tappitt kidnaps her mother to try and force the daughter's hand.

Bully Tappitt is the uncle of one Nicholas Tappitt, an Englishman abroad (trading in Spain) and former suitor of Imogene. Nicholas returns to England to perform a role in the settlement of the estate and he and Syn initially form a close friendship. Bully Tappitt's actions lead to a sword fight with Syn which the latter is clearly winning when – by arrangement – a farmer whose daughter has been 'ruined' by Tappitt is allowed to finish the job with a shotgun. Syn and Imogene wed, but Imogene feigns illness when it is time for Syn to return to Romney Marsh to take up his position as vicar of Dymchurch (the previous incumbent having conveniently been looking to retire). The plan is for Imogene to rejoin Syn on her return to full health, and Nicholas Tappitt – whilst secretly wooing Imogene – keeps Syn updated on her progress. By this time, however, Imogene is missing the Spanish sun and is depressed by the thought of returning to Romney Marsh with its 'flying mists'. Tappitt also plays on the dullness of being a parson's wife.

Imogene decides to elope to Europe with Tappitt and plucks up the courage to write to Syn to advise that she will not be joining him in Dymchurch. Syn sprouts a vivid white lock in his raven hair and takes to the bottle. In a dramatic moment when Tappitt's ship rounds Rye

Bay, the moonlight affords him a view of Syn watching the scene from Dymchurch Wall. Having won the lady, however, Tappitt becomes drunk and abusive toward her. Syn swears vengeance and vows to follow him to the ends of the earth. So begins the Odyssey of Revenge: Syn plans well and installs at his own expense a married parson to act as curate in Dymchurch. He learns Spanish from a prisoner on parole in Sandgate, and arranges with his uncle Solomon a bankers' system by which to draw monies abroad.

Syn sails to Amsterdam, and then reships for Spain, but on arrival at San Sebastian finds that his quarry has left for Lisbon that very morning. Syn waits, but on his return, Tappitt sees his adversary waiting on the harbourside and flees. The relentless pursuit now begins in earnest. After a year, a shipping agent advises that Tappitt's ship is posted amongst the lost; Syn refuses to believe this and subsequently learns that Tappitt has in fact changed vessels in Charleston. He now goes by the name of 'Black Nick', and has a child in tow.

The hunt moves to the Americas and Syn sails for Boston, but his ship is intercepted by pirates. The captain exhibits cowardice in the face of the enemy and demeans himself in Syn's eyes. For this, Syn shoots him dead and then challenges the pirate captain to a duel. He kills a pirate who tries to trip him up during the fight and then contrives to finish the duel in the sea. For dramatic effect sharks arrive on the scene and then a further pirate who enters the water is found to be . . . Mipps! Mipps honours a bargain struck earlier on Romney Marsh; Syn is welcomed on board the pirate vessel and is embraced by the crew. The pirates elect that Syn and Mipps should jointly lead them, and Syn introduces a more efficient and ruthless regime.

This chapter of piracy is only short lived, however, because Syn has not relinquished his quest. In preparation for careening, the ship anchors off St John's River mouth whilst Syn and Mipps undertake a spying mission further up the creek. Unbeknown to Syn, Mipps has sabotaged the ship, which explodes when their own boat is just out of range. By this time, Mipps has sworn to assist Syn in carrying out his quest and they journey on, via Charleston and New York, to Albany. Here they 'learn', through the Governor, of the destruction of their ship. Alarmingly, the telegram imparting this news also advises that there was a survivor, a mulatto temporarily struck dumb through the shock of the ordeal. To cover their own tracks, Syn and Mipps concoct a story that they have embarked upon a mission to preach to the Redskins but have failed to return.

The pair do now travel into Red Indian territory, having heard that Tappitt has set out by canoe to trade with the Indian tribes. Their guide is ambushed by a rival tribe; Syn and Mipps intervene with pistols to rescue him but find him already dead and instead save another Redskin (Shuhshuhgah). During a series of events that culminate in the sworn friendship of Shuhshuhgah and the two Englishmen being made blood brothers of his tribe, Shuhshuhgah's wounds attract the interest of a large horse-fly. Shuhshuhgah removes the fly, and releases it in the direction of some cattle, which promptly panic and cause a diversion that allows Shuhshuhgah's tribe to rout their opponents. The local name for this fly is the 'Clegg'.

The story continues apace, with Tappitt buying a whaling vessel in the mistaken belief that Syn will be put off the scent. As a result of various indiscretions through drink, Syn is able to track him down, and resolves to follow him by himself buying into a whaling ship. Shuhshuh-gah is still with the pair and recommends that they travel initially to Nantucket – where the biggest and fastest whalers are to be found. Syn purchases a share in such a vessel and returns to sea with both Shuhshuhgah and Mipps (as ship's carpenter). During this time, Syn acquires and learns to expertly handle a harpoon. He narrowly misses a confrontation with Tappitt, who nevertheless hears of Syn's presence and is terrified. We learn at this point that Tappitt is himself considering a future in piracy.

Syn walks into the Staunch Brotherhood Inn in Santiago and announces himself as Captain Clegg. Stretching coincidental credibility, when he demands to see the finest rooms, he finds them to be taken by one Nicholas Tappitt, his wife and child. Tappitt is now fully engaged in privateering, and has a forthcoming commission to escort a couple of treasure ships. Syn boldly commandeers Tappitt's ship and Tappitt flees, leaving his son and Imogene in a convent. Syn loots the treasure ships, sinking one with the probable loss of all on board. He now changes the name of the vessel to *Imogene* and generally runs wild, holding both Santiago and Havana to ransom amongst other excesses.

Syn stages a meeting with Tappitt and a planter – McCallum – whose treasure ships it is that he has looted. Syn is in turn ambushed but rescued by Shuhshuhgah, who displays impeccable timing. Events culminate in Syn hanging the Governor of Havana from the Docks (a reversal of events that the Governor had planned) and the party then returns to Santiago, where for good measure their Governor is also hanged. Following this incident, Syn gets horrendously drunk – for possibly the first time in his life – and commands Mipps and the Chinese cook to tattoo his forearm. The tattoo is a highly distinctive depiction of a man walking the plank, with a shark beneath. When sober, Syn realises that he can now forever be identified as Clegg and curses his own stupidity – it is the only regret that he ever expresses.

The next 12 years of piracy (from 1763) are quickly covered, but it emerges that the only case of dissent amongst Clegg's crew occurs when the crew protest that the ship is haunted by a devil who claims that their captain had once blown up his ship. This 'devil' further claims that Clegg will do it again and insists that he must be marooned. Clegg refuses to believe that this is a ghost and demands to see the mutineer. When the mulatto is brought to face him, Syn is enraged and ties him to the mast. Shuhshuhgah cuts out the unfortunate mulatto's tongue and removes his ears; the mulatto is then marooned on a coral reef where the tide rises fathoms deep and sharks abound. The ship's Chinese cook begs that Syn should reconsider; Syn's response is to break his back with a marline spike and hurl him overboard. The mulatto is seen to rise in the sky and follow the ship.

Towards the end of book, Syn and Mipps plan their futures. When they later meet up again in Boston, Syn muses: 'so all that is left to me is Romney Marsh and quiet years'. And then prophetically: 'but will the past rise up against me even there?' This would be a good point at which to end, but the book then neatly segues into the trip back home to England, and the events with which *Doctor Syn Returns* commences.

Appendix 6

Doctor Syn Returns – Plot Synopsis

Setting: 1775–1776

This story commences in November 1775, a seamless continuation of *Doctor Syn on the High Seas*. There is a wild storm off Dymchurch and the *City of London* flounders, catches fire and is wrecked in the bay. The attempted rescue by the stout citizens of Dymchurch accounts for two of their own, including – fortuitously for some – the vicar. The only two survivors, washed up on the beach, are Christopher Syn and the Ship's Captain.

This number is soon to be halved as a local ne'erdowell (Merry) murders the Captain and then tries unsuccessfully to mete out the same fate to Syn, as the latter lies exhausted on the sand. Syn, however, has witnessed the slaying of the captain and uses this knowledge to exert a hold over Merry. In typical Thorndike style, Syn turns up at the Court House just as the local dignatories are discussing him (in the context of the loss of another vicar). Syn is immediately re-installed in the vicarage, but not before he has had the chance to take a shine to the Squire's eldest daughter, Charlotte Cobtree. News of a new Vicar of Dymchurch reaches Mipps's ears, and he returns home, promptly to be engaged as sexton, undertaker, verger, bell-pull and clerk. Syn solemnly warns him against engaging once more in illegal activity.

The murder of a Riding Officer is a significant event. The killer, Grinsley, escapes in clothes taken from a scarecrow and this incident plants a seed in Syn's mind. It is when the Dragoons are out searching for Grinsley that, from Aldington Knoll, a landing is sighted. The Dragoons suspect that Grinsley might be heading for France, and intercept the landing; the captured smugglers include Mipps, who manages to escape without his face having been seen and alerts Syn. Syn embarks on a mission to save his parishioners, and the scarecrow notion takes hold. The plan starts incongruously, with Syn heading out across the Marsh on a pony to visit the sick Mother Handaway. On the way, he passes the Dragoons and notices many of his flock amongst the captured smugglers. He then approaches local gipsies to buy both a wild black horse and an oath of silence.

The real sickness with Mother Handaway is in her mind: she believes herself to be a witch and fortunately is amenable to the idea that Syn is none other than Satan, with Mipps his earthly messenger. This visit secures stabling for Syn's horse, and he next rides in rags back to the beach; in his new Scarecrow persona he taunts the Dragoons with the claim that he is

Grinsley. This creates a diversion that allows the smugglers to escape. As it subsequently transpires that Grinsley had been killed by this time, the idea is born that the Scarecrow has supernatural qualities.

Having lost no time in seducing Charlotte Cobtree, Syn is in the company of her and Merry when he meets the highwayman Jimmie Bone for the first time, in pursuit of business. Following one of Thorndike's character morality traits, Bone declares that he would never rob a clergyman but tries to lift a string of pearls off Charlotte. These are the highly valuable pearls carried by the late captain of the *City of London*, which were earlier presented to Charlotte by Syn on her twentyfirst birthday (and also coveted by Merry). Syn challenges Bone to a strange duel – his knife skills against Bone's shooting – and wins a guinea. He further challenges the highwayman to a fist fight for the pearls; inevitably the older man wins, but mutual respect is a more significant outcome.

In a novel full of action and complicated plot development, Nicholas Tappitt now turns up at the Mermaid Inn in Rye with Imogene (who gives birth to a daughter there) and the planter McCallum. The two men are supposedly involved with English traitors in London supplying France with gold, but there is a more significant agenda to unmask Clegg to the authorities. In conjunction with the former activity they double-cross their contacts and make arrangements for Bone to rob the stage coach on their behalf. Merry by this time has found work in the Mermaid and in his new employ pays Tappitt and McCallum (now respectively masquerading as Colonel Delacourt and Captain Vicosa) great attention. The reaction of Tappitt on seeing Clegg and his carpenter turning up at the Mermaid in the guise of the Dean of the Peculiars and his sexton can be imagined, and he lies low. Merry learns with glee of the past exploits of Syn, against whom he bears a huge grudge. A bond between Merry and the others is soon formed and, on learning of Merry's desires towards Meg Clouder, the planter undertakes to travel to Dymchurch, woo the said Meg and marry her. The unlikely next step is for the planter to then ditch her, leaving Merry to pick up the pieces and take her on the rebound. The first part goes according to plan.

Syn, meanwhile, is busy planning the largest run ever seen on Romney Marsh amid rumours that the mysterious Scarecrow is in reality Jimmie Bone. An amendment to the plan involves the Scarecrow 'holding up' Bone to demonstrate that this is not the case and, so that this act may be witnessed, Syn 'leaks' certain information about the run. 'Death to the Scarecrow' soon becomes the clarion call of the authorities, and the Scarecrow in turn takes every opportunity to bate his pursuers: barrels of liquor are left for the Dragoons, who cannot keep up with the locals when it comes to crossing the Marshes; and 'yokels' delight in leading them down false paths. Syn preaches vehemently against the wicked ways of the smugglers, and even forms a band of vigilantes to counter them. Mipps passes the message for all smugglers to enrol, and the authorities are impressed that no less than 150 locals sign up! These are divided into three parties, each led by one of the Upton brothers (firm disciples of the Scarecrow). Charlotte, meanwhile, buys some old clothes off Mipps.

By this time, McCallum has realised that Bone is not the Scarecrow and that – in all probability – Syn is. When another run is planned, McCallum learns that the instruction is that only the Scarecrow may fire the beacon at Aldington Knoll. He also knows that Charlotte Cobtree is in love with Syn and writes to her to tell her what she already knows (i.e. that Syn, Clegg and the Scarecrow are the same). He demands the pearls from the *City of London* in return for his silence. Charlotte learns that the letter was delivered by Merry, who has deceived his sponsors by holding it back until it is too late for her to act. Charlotte ventures out on her horse to warn Syn, pretending to be the wife of the new Sandgate Riding Officer when challenged by Faunce (the Captain of Dragoons). Underneath her shawl, however, she is dressed in Mipps's rags.

When the London coach that Bone is contracted to hold up is delayed, Charlotte rides off to fire the beacon (in her rags she will pass as the Scarecrow). However, the triumvirate of Tappitt, Merry and McCallum are lying in wait for the Scarecrow and three fatal shots are fired. Charlotte survives long enough to be carried back to Mother Handaway's, but Syn loses his mind. As Charlotte is dying, she 'confesses' to being the Scarecrow, to save Syn's neck. Back with the smugglers, Colonel Troubridge believes that, with the aid of the volunteers, he has captured the ringleaders. The Upton brothers, however, inform him that they have escaped and advise that the miscreants are all Sussex men.

Through trading with his tribe the Red Indian, Shuhshuhgah, has learnt that Tappitt and McCallum are venturing to England either to unmask Syn as Clegg or to kill him themselves. As Syn and Mipps are blood brothers to the tribe, he has a duty to warn them, and now turns up on the scene. Syn is distraught at Charlotte's death and, seeing this, Shuhshuhgah removes a fragment of Syn's brain in a delicate operation with a sharp knife(!). This has the effect of relieving the suffering and installing a lust for revenge in its place.

The time has now come for McCallum to hand over Meg to Merry. This he does when blind drunk, and stumbles and knocks himself unconscious – whereupon Meg runs to the vicarage and relates her sob story. Syn, Mipps and Shuhshuhgah solve her little problem in a particularly gory manner which involves first securing the red bearded planter to the floor and then utilises cockroaches, poison, a jar of molasses and a pickle cork. This is a highly original way of writing a character out of a book and ingeniously leaves no hint of suspicion. Merry is the next to die, after being caught by Syn and Mipps trying to rob Charlotte Cobtree's grave of the pearls, which have been buried with her. Knocked unconscious after being surprised in the act, he is then revived and tricked into donning Syn's clothes in order to effect an escape. On leaving the vicarage he is shot dead by Tappitt who has been stalking the vicar and mistakes him for Syn.

The murder of Merry is traced to Tappitt, who is now widely believed to be the Scarecrow (the circumstances of Charlotte's death and her dying claims not being widely known). A Preventive man is killed by Tappitt as he tries to make the arrest in the Mermaid but Tappitt is in turn overpowered by three Rye constables. Syn now ventures to Rye with Mipps and

Shushuhgah, but first visits Imogene, who has asked to see him. She is dying and tells him that her son (last heard of in *High Seas*) is actually Syn's and not Tappitt's. Syn grants her forgiveness and she dies in his arms after he has promised to look after her daughter.

In his official capacity, Syn visits Nicholas Tappitt in the Rye lock-up. Syn's ingenuity has stretched to arriving on crutches, to which he has strapped a couple of swords and a surreal duel takes place in Tappitt's cell. When Syn finally achieves the upper hand, Tappitt commits a foul after grabbing a crutch. Syn recovers and eventually corners his old adversary. Tappitt, however, trades what is left of his life for the child he loves: Tappitt will go to the hangman as Clegg, whilst Syn will look after his daughter. This is a clever piece of negotiation by Syn, as he has already undertaken to his late former wife to do just that. Syn subsequently visits Tappitt on a daily basis, officially exhorting him to repent, but essentially to get him to sign the confession to his being Clegg. Tappitt thus goes to the scaffold, unrepentant and basking in the reflected glory of his adversary. He is buried in unconsecrated ground, near the Kent border.

Appendix 7

The Further Adventures of Doctor Syn –
Plot Synopsis

Setting: 1776–1777[9]

This volume opens with a Lympne-bound stagecoach carrying the Archbishop of Canterbury and two known foes of the Scarecrow, Troubridge and Faunce. The latter two have both been promoted (to General and Major, respectively) since our last acquaintance. The coachman throws a stick bearing a coded message into the grounds of a farmhouse, details of the next run by the Scarecrow. On what is an eventful journey, the coach is then held up by the notorious highwayman, Jimmie Bone. He takes Faunce's sabretache, which contains details of plans to catch the Scarecrow, and informs Syn that news of the forthcoming run has been leaked and that a full regiment of Dragoons is to be moved from Canterbury to Dover Castle to counter it. Syn makes out that he has touched the conscience of the Highwayman and rides to Dover to meet Troubridge and return his possessions and papers. In return, he earns the confidence of Troubridge and gains clues as to both his plans and the identity of an informant.

The Scarecrow thus rides knowingly into Troubridges's trap, and is captured and confined in Dover Castle. Mipps effects his rescue in a pre-arranged manner, which involves plying the sentry with drink, performing a recently-perfected rope trick with Syn and then insisting that the prisoner has escaped between the bars of the window – which have already been noted as being wide apart. Syn has his vicar's robes on underneath and, as the clothes of the Scarecrow are caught by the wind, there are many witnesses to his 'escape' in this way. The supernatural powers of the Scarecrow are thus reinforced.

What appears to be a failed love match between Kate, the daughter of the Squire of Lympne Sir Henry Pembury, and a Cornet of Dragoons (Brackenbury) results in an unusual wager being struck: should Brackenbury capture the Scarecrow, Pembury will allow him the hand of his daughter in marriage. Syn's sympathy for the lovers means that for a second time he allows himself to be caught; again, his unveiling is delayed, which facilitates his escape. He

---

9. The action begins in November 1776, but this is the only time that a date is given. The nature of events and narrative would indicate a continuation to at least early 1777.

later impresses upon Pembury that Brackenbury kept his side of the bargain and that he must now do the same.

A stranger next enters the Marsh and is accosted by Mipps in The Ship Inn. His name is Fragg – a Customs Officer (although he does not declare his occupation) – who has business with Brazlett, a farmer on the Burmarsh road. Mipps follows him and finds that Brazlett is preparing to sell a list of confirmed smugglers for the incredible sum of 1500 guineas (500 from the Customs, 500 from Troubridge as a measure of his thirst for revenge and a further 500 guineas from the Customs if he appears in the witness box). Mipps learns that Fragg is to take this list to Dover in the morning and also that his own name is on it (he has been rightly identified as the Scarecrow's lieutenant). The following morning, however, the Customs Officer's body is found by the sluice gates, a salutary lesson to strangers venturing out in unknown surroundings whilst drunk!

The underlying reason for Brazlett's betrayal is his intention to start a new life in London, and the good vicar arranges a leaving party for him in the tithe barn as part of the New Year's Eve celebrations. The whole village attends, but the event is hijacked by the Scarecrow who makes an example of the traitor – by hanging him in his armchair.

News of another attempted betrayal reaches Syn, who in his daytime guise is administering to a sick grandmother by the name of Ransley at Bonnington. He learns from her that her son and grandsons are plotting against the Scarecrow, and intend to divert a number of tubs to an unauthorised hide. Syn alerts the Dragoons so as to allow the capture of Ransley and his fellow dissenters, in possession of 200 barrels. At the subsequent trial presided over by the Warden of the Cinque Ports, it seems it is an open and shut case until Syn expounds a theory that the Scarecrow is too clever to be tricked in this way. Has anyone actually checked the contents of the barrels? The answer is obviously no and, when they are checked, the tubs are found to contain dirty water and so the Bonnington smugglers are acquitted. Through this action and others Syn identifies himself in the eyes of the locals as a fierce opponent of the Scarecrow, who is seen to issue threats against him.

At sea, the exploits of a French privateer – Delacroix – are causing embarrassment to General Troubridge's twin brother. Things get interesting when he intercepts two of the Scarecrow's luggers and seizes their cargos. The Scarecrow takes to the seas, teaches the Frenchman a lesson and daringly hands him over to Admiral Troubridge on his own vessel. An incident closer to home now occurs when a local blackguard – Craigen – murders his brother-in-law and his brother to gain the boat that the three men previously jointly owned. The Scarecrow becomes involved when Craigen tries to pin the deed on him and – needless to say – ensures that justice is summarily served.

A Bow Street runner – Jerry Hunt – next comes onto the scene, looking to apprehend Jimmie Bone. Syn tells him that he is sure that Bone has fled to France, and the pair instead discuss the reward on offer for capture of the Scarecrow. Meanwhile, the apparent ongoing 'baiting' of the Scarecrow by Syn continues, with the result that the vicar is kidnapped. Hunt becomes suspicious and masquerades as a dying smuggler seeking an audience with Dr Syn so that he may repent. Through a mirror, he sees Syn change from wild rags into vicar's clothes and it seems that the game is up. With the aid of Bone once again standing in for the Scarecrow, however, Syn persuades him that he has got the wrong end of the stick. After ritual humiliation by the Scarecrow, Hunt returns to London with his tail firmly between his legs.

The next visitors to Dymchurch are the press gang, but they are thwarted by the deviousness of the locals. Things come to a head when a villager is taken by what is seen to be foul play, and three of his family are similarly captured when they try to intervene. Enter the Scarecrow on behalf of an enraged populace, who turns the tables and ensures that – in the words of Thorndike's own chapter heading – the press gang is well and truly 'pressed'. Finally, Thorndike introduces some horse-rustlers, the Tankerton Brothers. They are captured by the Scarecrow and turned over to the authorities. After they have been sentenced to death, the Scarecrow demonstrates who really controls the Marsh by abducting them and invoking his own brand of justice.

Appendix 8

The Courageous Exploits of Doctor Syn – Plot Synopsis

Setting: 1781

The story opens in March 1781, in Old Tree Cottage (Mipps's coffin shop). A squadron of Dragoons is in town, in response to a plea from the Preventive Officer; and there is local consternation at the news that these forces are to be further augmented by the Royal Navy,[10] under the command of a Captain Blain. A new character – Percy, the water carrier for the village – is introduced. To prevent undue spillage, Mipps carves a set of floats for his buckets, but these soon become a rather obvious form of code for passing the Scarecrow's messages in the face of a heavily-resourced enemy.

Fred Hart – fisherman and smuggler – goes missing and his boat is later found, stoved in. It is assumed that he has perished at sea, whereas the reality is that he has been taken prisoner by Blain. Under torture, he turns informant. Despite his reputation for being the village idiot, Percy has realised the significance of the floats he carries and overhears the sailors discussing information received. Hart has disclosed details of the evening's run and Percy seizes the initiative by changing his floats, thus preventing a disaster. Hart has by this time been transferred to the Guard Ship and the Night-riders have to ambush the sailors and steal their uniforms to effect a dramatic rescue. During this escapade, Syn impersonates Blain. Although he is recognized at one point, the mission is successful, and the Scarecrow's flag is flown from the Guard Ship. Syn exiles Hart to France, where other traitors are kept under guard and used to load the Scarecrow's fleet.

Great excitement ensues with the visit to Romney Marsh of the Prince of Wales, who is invited to ride with the hunt. The hunt follows the night of a run and so the gentry find that their horses are too tired for the purpose. This does not apply to the Prince's mount, which has been excluded from the smuggling operation, and the heir to the throne soon finds himself riding alone behind the pack, moving in for a kill. He is denied only by the arrival of the Scarecrow, who outrides him, but this is a small price for the Prince to pay for the kudos of meeting the phantom of Romney Marsh. The Prince infuriates the local gentry by compelling

---

10. This accurately reflects the historical reality.

171

them to drink a toast to the arch-villain, and also pledges that, if the Scarecrow is ever caught, he, the Prince, will personally ensure that the Scarecrow does not hang. The Prince separately promises Syn that he will use his influence to secure a promotion any time Syn fancies a move away from Dymchurch.

News reaches Syn via Mipps and an onion seller(!) of mutiny in France, with the prisoners barricaded within their castle dungeons. Syn arranges a reason to be absent from his parish and journeys to France, where we are introduced to his lieutenant across the channel, Duloge. Syn immediately grasps that Hart has imparted news of the reward currently on offer for the capture of the Scarecrow and that the real reason for the mutiny is to disguise the fact that one of their number has broken out and is making for the Admiralty in London. The traitor who was chosen for the task is Handgrove, the longest-serving of the prisoners. Syn re-crosses the Channel in pursuit but the day's advantage that Handgrove has secured means that he cannot be caught prior to reaching London. Accordingly, Syn has to intercept him at the Admiralty and once there tricks him into a carriage 'for his own safety'. The carriage diverts to the Mitre Inn, the landlord of which is a member of the Scarecrow's gang.

Syn, Mipps and his Night-riders now return to France. En route they fire on and disable a British Revenue cutter. The sound of gunshots is heard in France; the Scarecrow's other prisoners thus have good reason to believe that Handgrove has been successful and that the navy is now coming to their rescue. Their hopes are seemingly realised when they see the landing party dressed in naval uniform. Volunteers are asked to form a firing squad to execute the Scarecrow, but when his mask is subsequently removed there is horror at the discovery that it is in fact Handgrove they have shot and that the Scarecrow has triumphed once again. In order to send a similar message to would-be traitors back home, Handgrove's body is brought back across the Channel and hung from the Dymchurch gibbet. Syn meanwhile continues to receive 'threats' for his preaching against the ubiquitous Scarecrow.

The story next switches to London, specifically the Buck's Club in St James. A young man, Sir Harry Sales, foolishly undertakes a bet for one thousand guineas that he is not in position to honour. Syn happens to be in the Club at the time and the other party to the bet (a Major Culland) suggests that the reward on offer for capture of the Scarecrow would present a good opportunity to settle the debt. His friends agree to assist Sales in the task and a further bet is struck to unmask the Scarecrow in their Club. Independently, Culland also decides to journey to Romney Marsh to try his own hand. Sales's 'dandy sleuths' are tipped off as to the night of a run and, believing they have captured their quarry, whisk him back to the Buck's Club to claim their reward. When 'the Scarecrow' is unmasked, he turns out to be a very dishevelled Culland.

At Christmas, Doctor Syn lays on traditional entertainment with his troop of mummers. The chief object of ridicule is, of course, the Scarecrow. For the performance at Lympne Castle, the Scarecrow 'kidnaps' the actor playing his part and fills the role so expertly that nobody notices the switch until such time that Syn goes missing. Syn and the actor are then found lashed to a tree (Jimmie Bone having once again assumed a stand-in role).

Another new character – Old Katie – a seventy-year-old independent smuggler, is now introduced. She is the only retail smuggler left on the Marsh, and is both tolerated and protected by the Scarecrow. Although her smuggling is small scale, she is apprehended by Blain and proceeds to knock out his bosun with a left hook before 'confessing' to being the Scarecrow. She is tried and, pleading guilty, is inevitably sentenced to death before Syn arranges to call in one of the two favours promised by the Prince of Wales.

Aldington Knoll – a very useful landmark for the smugglers – is next the centre of attention. The landowner wishes to level it, to improve farming yields, but the locals – who know of its significance and anyway fear upsetting the Scarecrow – hide behind the legend that any tampering with the Knoll will attract bad luck, and refuse to have any involvement. There is just one exception: a brute of a man and slaughterman by the name of Knarler. Syn goes along with the work to the point where the chalk face on the seaward side is fully exposed (thus providing an even better landmark) and then contrives for Blain to shoot him, in a tried and trusted plot development, which involves the victim being mistaken for the Scarecrow.

Blain's interest turns to the cooperage at Hythe, where his spies tell him that Mipps has been a regular recent visitor. He threatens young cooper George Lee with the press gang, and Lee divulges that the order placed by Mipps is for special barrels which, whilst facilitating their rolling, also provide space to hide an illegal cargo. The alleged purpose of the barrels is to transport bones (for fertiliser) from the continent, but Blain has suspicions that the real purpose may be the concealment of tobacco. This much is correct, and signals a new enterprise of Syn's. Mipps, however, learns of Blain's intentions and the plan is changed, with the tobacco instead being concealed in ships' ropes and landed under the noses of the authorities.

Despite having once more been outmanoeuvred, the Captain feels that he is getting very close to the Scarecrow and appears to taunt Syn with the news. He has long harboured suspicions of Mipps, but now puts a 'tail' on Syn, allegedly for his own protection. In desperation, Syn ventures once more to London to see the Prince of Wales and begs that he honours his second promise. Although the promise clearly referred to Syn's own promotion, he asks that the Prince adheres to its letter and as a result Blain is promoted to the command of *HMS Crocodile* – the ship on which he was born. Such is Blain's contempt for the Dragoons in general – and Major Faunce in particular – that he does not even contemplate sharing his knowledge and Mipps and Syn are once again left to toast each other and reprise Clegg's shanty.

Appendix 9

The Amazing Quest of Doctor Syn –
Plot Synopsis

Setting: summer 1790[11]

The tale begins with the smugglers out on the Marsh on horseback. An excise man (George Plattman) has infiltrated the group and taken the place of one of the Night-riders. He is, however, identified by the Scarecrow – who shoots him. The other Night-riders all then in turn fire into the body so that they too are implicated. The body is dumped over the Sussex border.

A visitor – David Jones – who has business with Syn but who keeps it very much from the rest of the village, arrives from Wales. After an amateurish attempt to hold Syn at gunpoint (later revealed to be part of a plan to force Syn to Wales, where he was to be murdered by one Tarroc Dolgenny), he tells Syn of the existence of a tontine,[12] by which Syn and Jones are the only surviving claimants of a sum in the region of £75,000. Dolgenny's intention – after killing Syn – is to marry Jones's niece (Ann Sudden) and then kill Jones, thus acquiring the fortune for himself.

Syn arranges for Jimmie Bone to once more double for the Scarecrow on a forthcoming run, so that Jones might witness the proceedings, but a spanner is thrown into the works with the capture of Bone by the Hythe Revenue Officer. Bone is held in the Dymchurch cells, where an initial attempt at rescue by Syn is thwarted; Bone's release thus has to be delayed until he is being transported to Dover. This is ultimately effected by the Scarecrow and his smugglers, who also take Jones and an officious Revenue Officer captive. Jones, however, is soon released and journeys back to Dymchurch on foot, where he finds the Revenue man swinging from the gallows and Doctor Syn once more ensconced in his study.

---

11. The narrative states 1780, but this is most likely a typographical error that has been perpetuated – see Chapter 2.
12. A scheme (named after the Italian banker who originated the system) under which the share of each subscriber who dies is transferred to surviving members until such time the whole investment and income is realised by the last survivor. Occasionally – as here – this could span generations.

Having been instructed by the Squire to remove the body, which the Scarecrow wished to remain *in situ* as a warning to his enemies, the beadle is now in fear of his life – a fear cruelly played upon by Mipps. Syn once more rails against the smuggler from the pulpit and is soon taken captive by his 'enemy'. This time he is in the company of Jones (determined to see the Night-riders at first hand) and it seems that their number is well and truly up when the pair are buried up to their necks on Littlestone beach with the incoming tide lapping against their chins. A gruesome outcome is only avoided by the 'coincidental' entrance of Mipps, allegedly on a routine fishing expedition.

Bone is spirited away to France until the fuss surrounding his escape has died down. At the Court-House hearing into the death of the Hythe Revenue Officer, Tarroc Dolgenny makes his first appearance – as an observer. He buttonholes his old adversary Jones and gives him the news that his brother is dead, the victim of a terrible accident. Jones suspects foul play, particularly as Dolgenny advises him that Jones's niece has now consented to marry him. It transpires that Dolgenny is himself a master smuggler, controlling operations on the north Wales coast. After just a brief perusal of the Dymchurch great and good, he concludes that only Syn would be capable of heading such an efficient smuggling enterprise. Being greatly interested in the prize for capture of the Scarecrow (now standing at a thousand guineas), he privately confronts Syn with his theory. In return for Dolgenny's admission that he in fact murdered Jones' brother, Syn freely confesses to being the Scarecrow and – even more audaciously – to being Clegg (who it transpires was one of Dolgenny's boyhood heroes). Although this could have been used against him, the ever-faithful Mipps is secreted behind a curtain and has witnessed Dolgenny's own confession. Dolgenny then puts a proposal to Syn and Mipps that they should join forces and go buccaneering.

Syn determines to get the better of Dolgenny to prove that he is the greater tactician, to rescue Jones' niece from the peril she is clearly in and to further her love match with a young Customs Officer. Syn thus outwardly agrees to throw in his lot with Dolgenny and he, Jones and Mipps thus travel to Wales – but speed is of the essence if they are to get there before Dolgenny. With this in mind, Syn arranges for Dolgenny to be detained at Lympne (after significantly overstating the beauty of Pembury's spinster daughters). Rather than being annoyed at the reality, however, Dolgenny amuses himself by winning large sums at cards and is in no rush to leave Romney Marsh.

Syn audaciously commandeers Dolgenny's coach and valet, Pedro. He demonstrates that he has Dolgenny's authority by use of the latter's signet ring, which he has obtained by deception. Pedro realises that this is a ruse, but despises his master and warms to the English vicar, who speaks his own Spanish language so fluently. *En route* to Wales, the journey is enlivened by the apprehension of their coach by two inept highwaymen. Syn inevitably sends them packing, but not before he has recovered the valuables of Jones, who is travelling under his own steam and is just ahead of them! Once in Wales, Syn continues the deception that he is acting for Dolgenny and, in an action-packed finale, first arranges for the Welshman's assets to be transferred to his own ships. He then searches for evidence of the murder of Jones's brother by Dolgenny, who – on his belated return – realises that he has been completely duped. Dolgenny murders Jones by cutting the rope from which he is suspended whilst searching the cliff face, in the mistaken belief that it is Syn at the other end. This act unwittingly hands the proceeds of the tontine to the Vicar of Dymchurch. Syn presides over the marriage of Ann Sudden to her Customs Officer lover and promptly decides to bestow half the tontine on the couple. Finally, he takes on Dolgenny in a sword duel to the death. There can be only one outcome.

Appendix 10

The Shadow of Doctor Syn – Plot Synopsis

Setting: summer 1793

The Reign of Terror is in full flow across the Channel when this novel begins. Tales of this and the exploits of Romney Marsh's Scarecrow are the common currency in the clubs of London. In one such club – Crockfords – the young Lord Cullingford is persuaded by his mentor Bully Foulkes to rashly gamble away what very little is left of his erstwhile fortune. In the club at the time are an unlikely triumvirate: Syn, the manager of the Drury Lane Theatre (Kemble) and the playwright Sheridan. In a scarcely fresh scenario Cullingford, in drink, mistakenly wagers more than he can afford. Amidst talk of the reward on offer for capture of the Scarecrow, he determines to follow the course of others and to venture to Romney Marsh. The humanitarian Syn is identified as a potential ally, particularly after Foulkes – worsted in a battle of words with Syn – vows to return himself with the Scarecrow within ten days. When Syn returns to Dymchurch, he is accompanied in the Dover coach by Foulkes and one Agatha Gordon, aunt of Lady Cobtree. However, Bone (by arrangement) is lying in wait at Slippery Sam's and pounces at the bottom of Quarry Hill. Foulkes is humiliated (losing his boots and his wallet, which contains Cullingford's IOU), whilst Agatha Gordon is charmed and subsequently has her valuables returned by the chivalrous highwayman.

Back in Dymchurch it emerges that a new detachment of Dragoons has arrived, headed by a Major Faunce (the younger brother of Syn's old adversary). The plot hots up when it emerges that Cicely Cobtree has disappeared, seemingly without trace. Cullingford's quest appears to end when he is captured by the Night-riders and regains consciousness in time to witness a kangaroo court sentencing a couple of miscreants to exile in France. Steeling himself for death, he is surprised to find a benevolent Scarecrow not only reprieving him, but also handing him Foulkes's IOU. Cullingford calls on Doctor Syn to advise him that events on the Marsh have given him a new sense of purpose, and that he has determined to join the army.

A by-now ritual hanging by the Scarecrow results in a body being found swinging from the Dymchurch gallows. The Beadle is again terrified by Mipps's assertion that he himself will be punished by the Scarecrow for removing the corpse (continuing a theme first developed in *Amazing Quest*). At the inquest the impotent Squire, in the absence of any practical means of ending the smuggling within his jurisdiction, doubles the reward for capturing the Scarecrow by making 1000 guineas of his own available.

Two barrels mysteriously turn up on the vicarage doorstep marked for the attention of the Parson and Squire, with the compliments of the Scarecrow. The Squire is visibly annoyed when Major Faunce appears on the scene and it seems that he must forsake his booty. At this time, Faunce is beginning to have his suspicions about Syn, and keeps him watched. When Syn has left, however, Faunce and Cobtree – with Mipps's assistance – open the barrels only to find that they contain the persons of Maria and Cicely Cobtree. It transpires that the disappearance of Cicely was down to a mission to save her sister (married to a Frenchman) from the atrocities of the French Revolution. That she was successful owed much to the figure of l'Epouvantail,[13] an awesome figure naked from the waist up and sporting a tattoo of a shark on his arm. With dramatic timing, the said Scarecrow now appears on the scene and Faunce and his Sergeant are forced to take the place of the Cobtree daughters as the barrels are repacked and forwarded to the Revenue Officer at Sandgate. This is the prelude to the seduction of Cicely by Syn. In a worryingly short time he has confirmed his true identity as both pirate and smuggler to another – the youngest – of Tony Cobtree's daughters.

It is now the turn of Foulkes – unaware that Cullingford has stolen a march on him – to try to capture the elusive Scarecrow. Syn offers to stand as Foulkes's second in order to facilitate a duel between the two. Foulkes for his part imparts the information that he has dealings with the Frenchman Barsard, although Syn has already had an inkling of this through a note that Bone had found stitched into Foulkes' wallet. Foulkes also indicates that he may have information to link the Scarecrow to Clegg. Syn plans to journey to France to confront Robespierre, but in the meantime has to prepare for Agatha Gordon's 80th birthday party – a seemingly simple task complicated by Agatha inviting the Scarecrow and by Syn's wish to see her happy.

A dramatic change of scene takes place as Syn surfaces in France for his meeting with Robespierre – and soon has the Frenchman eating out of the palm of his hand. Robespierre is convinced that they are working for the same ideals and Syn tricks him into granting papers that effectively provide him with unhampered access to the French ports in defiance of the blockade that has disrupted all other shipping movement. This is successfully put to the test on the homeward journey when the Scarecrow brings six of Robespierre's spies back across the Channel. For good measure, *en route* he also dismasts the Sandgate Revenue Cutter. On reaching English soil, the Frenchmen are unwittingly imprisoned in the Dymchurch Court House cells and the beleaguered beadle (victim of his fondness for alcohol) once more makes a disturbing discovery when he sobers up the following morning.

At Agatha Gordon's party there is much talk of the French prisoners, and the prestige that will be due to the Squire when they are handed over to the authorities. It also emerges (via Maria Cobtree) that Barsard has arrived in Hythe to meet up with his colleagues. The high spot of the party, however, is when the Scarecrow (Bone once again deputising) honours his commitment and demands his dance with Aunt Agatha. Furthermore, he commands Syn to

---

13. French for *Scarecrow.*

join them and Cicely Cobtree in a foursome reel. A neat twist is provided by Agatha knowing the identity of the Scarecrow and Clegg as well as the fact that it is Bone wearing the Scarecrow's rags; hence she requests that her consort roll up his sleeve and prove for once and for all whether or not he is Clegg. The lack of tattoo therefore further clouds the identity issue.

Another twist is that Barsard and Foulkes are actually one, a deduction already made by Syn. Foulkes is escorted by Syn onto the Marsh for the promised showdown – an arranged duel with the Scarecrow. Outrageously, having shown Foulkes his tattooed arm, the Scarecrow removes his mask to reveal himself as Syn. Syn manoeuvres the fight onto the Sluice Gates, where Foulkes flings his burning torch at his adversary. Syn responds by driving his sword through Foulkes' neck.

The Scarecrow advises the Squire by letter that the body of a seventh French spy (Barsard) can be found in the sluice mud: he encloses Robespierre's dossier on him, drawing the distinction between a rogue/scoundrel/rascal/smuggler on the one-hand and the unacceptability of a traitor on the other. Hyde, the Sandgate Revenue Officer, is now involved once more; he has been spying on Syn, who has let down his guard in the presence of Cicely. Syn is instructed to journey to the Court House, where a guard of Dragoons has been prepared. Syn, however, contrives to take his trusty dice box with him, which contains a nauseous chemical liquid secreted in its false bottom. Hyde lies in wait in the vicarage hoping to trap more of the Scarecrow's gang and is surprised when Cicely turns up, dressed in the Scarecrow's rags. Hyde has to re-think but concludes that she, rather than Syn, must be the smuggling mastermind and – not trusting to the efficacy of Dymchurch law – resolves to kill her for the reward. Cicely manages to turn the tables and escape, but Hyde fires at the retreating figure on horseback and scores a lucky hit. Although fatally injured, Cicely manages to reach Aldington Knoll and fire the beacon. She is then assisted by Mipps, but dies in the arms of Syn at the vicarage.

Syn reacts badly to the death of Cicely, and the news is conveyed to the village that the Squire's daughter has met her end in a riding accident. His sanity is saved this time through the actions of Agatha Gordon, who shows him Cicely's diary. It emerges from this that Cicely knew the truth of her sister Charlotte's death in what was also supposedly a hunting mishap.[14] In the final scene the inevitable Clegg shanty is sung by four voices for the first time: those of Syn, Mipps, Bone – and Agatha Gordon.

---

14. *Doctor Syn Returns.*

Appendix 11

Doctor Syn – Plot Synopsis

Setting: (probably) 1793[15]

Schoolboy Jerry Jerk is a central figure in his main appearance in the saga and is soon inducted into the smuggling enterprise. His adversary is Rash, the village schoolmaster, whom Jerk dearly wishes to see hanged (preferably by himself: he nurtures the dream of becoming a hangman). Rash himself tries to woo Imogene, the barmaid of The Ship Inn, but she has eyes only for the Squire's son, Denis Cobtree.

Captain Collyer – Coast Agent and Commissioner – arrives in Dymchurch at the head of the King's Men[16] to investigate the smuggling known to be rife on the Marsh and proves to be a potent threat. One of his men is a curious loner, a mulatto with no ears or tongue. His presence appears to strike terror into Syn, a reaction noted by Collyer. We learn that the mulatto formerly served under Captain Clegg. The plot thickens when the mulatto goes missing and Clegg's harpoon is stolen from its resting place above Syn's fireplace (the harpoon was allegedly presented to Syn after he attended the hanging of 'Clegg').

Collyer initially suspects the Squire of being behind the local smuggling activity but also harbours doubts as to Syn and is convinced of Mipps's involvement. Doctor Pepper – who by dint of spending time on the Marsh visiting sick patients has seen too much – is murdered by Rash and the mulatto is widely suspected of the crime. The murder of Pepper, however, has been witnessed by Collyer – and separately by Jerk, who confides in the vicar. Syn tries to persuade Jerk that it was no more than a dream, but then buys his silence with two crowns, which Jerk uses to commission Mipps to construct him a gallows.

Partly to force Imogene's hand, Rash threatens to turn King's Evidence against his fellow smugglers and a fight between Rash and Syn ensues in the vicarage. This culminates in Rash being injured, an incident also witnessed by Collyer who is watching through the shutters. Syn, however, advises Collyer that the incident and injury to Rash are both down to the escaped mulatto. Syn spends the night away from the vicarage and Rash is guarded by Collyer's men. They are overpowered and Rash's 'disappearance' is arranged by the smugglers.

---

15. See Chapter 2.
16. Sailors.

After he has himself been kidnapped and humiliated by the smugglers, Collyer closes in on the ringleaders. His suspicions of Mipps have hardened and, after Mipps has entertained him in his coffin shop, he realises that the coffins may hold the key to the smuggling operation. In anticipation of imminent arrests, Collyer instructs an attorney (Whyllie) to prepare prison space and then holds Denis Cobtree for the press gang against the production of Rash. Jerk overhears two locals discussing that there is a body swinging from his gallows and congratulates himself on constructing such a realistic dummy. The laugh is on Jerk, however, when he and Imogene discover that the dummy has been replaced by more macabre fruit – ironically, the body of Rash. Denis Cobtree is rescued by means of a plan that involves Syn, Imogene and the attorney's wife. Mrs Whyllie is keen to settle an old score with the pompous Head of the press gang; she relishes her task and subsequently formally adopts Imogene as her own daughter.

Collyer arranges for a decoy to stand in for Syn and springs a trap which confirms his suspicions that Syn is really Clegg. The stage is set for a showdown in church between Syn and Collyer, in front of the whole village. Syn has spread the word that he is to leave Dymchurch on a mission to convert the heathen (a plot device also used in *High Seas*), although he advises the Squire that his real purpose is to recover England's treasure. (The premise is that Tappitt – as Clegg – divulged its whereabouts to Syn on the gallows and that Syn wants to present the booty to Imogene. This is a scenario that finds great favour with the Squire, given that his son intends to marry the girl.) The village church is packed to give Syn a suitable send-off. Collyer, however, is in the congregation and the game is up when Syn spots the warrant for his arrest protruding from his pocket. From the pulpit, Syn publicly admits to his past and dual lives and to the fact that the man hanged at Rye as Clegg was one of his own crew. He also admits to arranging Pepper's murder. Uncharacteristically, he threatens to turn King's Evidence if not aided, and his parishioners/fellow smugglers create a diversion. The sailors ransack The Ship in the belief that Syn and Mipps may be hiding there; they aren't, but the sailors are enraged to find the pub packed with smuggled goods and take their frustration out on Mrs Waggetts, who is hanged from her own inn sign. It seems that Syn may have survived when the sailor Morgan Waters is murdered in a case of mistaken identity (not for the first time, he is disguised as the parson). Whilst this episode buys the real Syn time and an opportunity to take to the sea, a maroon is fired that identifies his whereabouts and the seamen pursue and board his vessel. When it seems that capture is inevitable, Syn is murdered with his (Clegg's) own harpoon and the mulatto bursts from the cabin in an incident that confirms his supernatural credentials. In deference, Collyer allows Syn a burial at sea (what he would have wanted) and, in his death, the words of Clegg's ditty come to life.[17] With the death of Christopher, the charismatic Syn dynasty probably also ends.[18]

17. See Appendix 13.

18. Syn did have a son – also named Christopher – although the two never met. Syn believes that he has been murdered by Tappitt but Tappitt claimed that he had been abducted by friendly Red Indians. This is the central tenet of the novel by Chris George (see Chapter 3).

The death of Syn spells the end of wool running on Romney Marsh. The Squire finds much money secreted in the vicarage; as this is deemed to be part of Syn's estate, it all passes to Imogene, who marries Denis. Mipps ends up in a Chinese monastery in Penang(!), but this is not the last to be heard of him as his exploits resurface in *The Shpe*. We are told that the rest of Dymchurch's inhabitants fare less well, as few survive the forthcoming war with France.

Appendix 12

Index of Names Appearing within the Canonical Novels

Key

Vol. 1: *Doctor Syn on the High Seas*
Vol. 2: *Doctor Syn Returns*
Vol. 3: *The Further Adventures of Doctor Syn*
Vol. 4: *The Courageous Exploits of Doctor Syn*
Vol. 5: *The Amazing Quest of Doctor Syn*
Vol. 6: *The Shadow of Doctor Syn*
Vol. 7: *Doctor Syn*

Entries shown in italics relate to real-life historical figures, families or establishments.

Characters

Adam, Robert – (alluded to) Vol. 6. Credited with designing and supervising the building of Syn's vicarage. *Well-known 18th century architect (best known for designing Syon House).*

Almago, Imogene – Vols 1 and 7. Daughter of wealthy south American based in Madrid and claimed by Syn to be an Incan princess. Meets Sir Henry Pembury whilst he is on a government mission and visits him with mother after death of father. Marries Syn but elopes with Nicholas Tappitt. With Tappitt, ventures around the world being pursued by Syn. Finally returns with Tappitt to Rye, where she dies in Syn's arms. Has four children – the first (a boy) is Syn's. The rest are girls; the first of whom died of black fever in Charleston at age of four; the next died at birth; the remaining one is Imogene (Tappitt).

Archbishop of Canterbury – Vols 3 and 4. Brief appearances, which include his coach being held up by Bone (whilst travelling with Troubridge and Faunce).

Awford – Vol. 2. Landlord of the Walnut Tree Inn, and friend to the smuggling fraternity.

Barsard – Vol. 6. Alias of Foulkes. Aide of Robespierre. It would appear that this character (and name) is closely modelled on a Dickens figure (Solomon Pross, aka John Basard, an informer and spy) in *A Tale of Two Cities* (which is largely set in the French Revolution).

Betts, George – Vol. 3. Smuggler, used as conduit for Mipps in The Ship Inn (their over-heard conversation gives rise to the Tankerton brothers stealing horses). *Local name, with links to notorious Rye smugglers.*

Black – Vol. 3. Family who own farm to which Syn is sent by Scarecrow to minister to dying man after former has been 'kidnapped'.

'Black Satan' – Vol. 1. Captain of the pirate ship *Pit of Sulphur*.

Blain, Capt. – Vol. 4. Detailed from Guard Ship at Dover to augment Dragoons and break up Night-riders. Lost eye in skirmish with the French.

'Blue Heron' – *see* Shuhshuhgah.

Bolden, Parson – Vol. 2. Young vicar of Dymchurch who dies in unsuccessful attempt to rescue the passengers and crew of *City of London*. *Character based upon Charles Cobb, former rector of Dymchurch.*

Bone, James/Jimmie ('Gentleman James') – Vols 2, 3, 4, 5 and 6. Notorious highwayman who conducts his business on the Dover road. Stables his horse with Mother Handaway. Wins sympathy of Squire by escorting him to his dying daughter (Charlotte). One of the Scarecrow's Night-riders (Beelzebub). Frequently stands in for the Scarecrow and is at various times believed by many to be him.

Brackenbury, Philip – Vols 3 and 4. Cornet (subsequently Lieutenant) of Dragoons. Marries Kate Pembury after Syn assists him in capture of Scarecrow (forename attributed by Buchanan).

Brackenbury, Robert – Vol. 3. Father of Cornet of Dragoons; attended Oxford University with Syn and Tony Cobtree.

Brazlett, Hugh – Vol. 3. Smuggler/farmer who arranges to betray his colleagues to the Customs Officer, Fragg. Scarecrow makes a terrible example of him.

Briston – Vol. 4. Gambling friend of Sir Harry Sales. *Name taken from village in Norfolk, with family connection to Rosemary Thorndike (née Dowson).*

Bubukles – Vol. 4. Landlord of Mitre Inn, London, one of Scarecrow's major receivers. Name would appear to be taken from the description of Bardolph's face in Shakespeare's *Henry V*.

Buckshaft, Colonel (and Mrs) – Vol. 4. Invited to meet Prince of Wales at Lympne Castle.

Buckshaft, Fan – Vol. 4. Daughter of above. Unkindly referred to as a 'Dragoon in skirts' by Pembury.

Chesham, Admiral – (alluded to) Vol. 4. Successor to Troubridge.

Clinton, Colonel – Vol. 1. Commander of military in Albany (cousin of Governor of South Carolina).

Clouder, Abel – Vol. 2. Owner of Sea Wall Tavern. Killed in unsuccessful attempt to save crew and passengers of *City of London*.

Clouder, Meg – Vols 2, 5 and 6. Wife/widow of Abel. Coveted by Merry. Becomes owner of Sea Wall Tavern after death of husband. Subsequently married (for very short time) to Captain Vicosa (McCallum).

Cobtree, Antony (Tony) – Vols 1, 2, 3, 4, 5, 6 and 7. Boyhood friend of Christopher Syn. Born 1728 (and two years the senior of Syn). Tutored at Oxford by Syn. Attorney at Law. In younger days a reckless adventurer, gambler, duellist. Pompous Squire of Dymchurch following death of father, additionally assuming role of Chief Magistrate. Married to Caroline. *Cobtree family name reflects Cobtree Manor Park, a place near Aylesford of which Thorndike was fond.*

Cobtree, Lady Caroline – various passing references. Wife of Squire; niece of Agatha Gordon.

Cobtree, Charles – (alluded to) Vols 1 and 2. Father of Tony; Lord of the Level and Squire of Dymchurch. Chief Magistrate on the Marsh, a position formerly known as Leveller of the Marsh Scotts. Apparently met his death after breaking his neck in hunting accident (from information provided this would have been between 1763 and 1765).

Cobtree, Charlotte – Vol. 2 (death also alluded to in Vol. 6). Born 1756. Daughter of Tony; godchild and later lover of Syn. Shot when, dressed in Scarecrow's rags, she fires the beacon at Aldington Knoll. Dies in Syn's arms.

Cobtree, Cicely – Vols 2 and 6. Youngest daughter of Tony. Born 1760, four years after Charlotte. Rescues other sister (Maria) from French Revolution with Scarecrow's help and becomes Syn's lover. Also (as Charlotte) shot dead whilst impersonating the Scarecrow.

Cobtree, Denis – Vol. 7. Only son of Tony. Aged 18 at start of *Doctor Syn*. Suitor of Imogene (Tappitt) – whom he later marries. Held prisoner by Collyer as surety with threat of the press gang against Squire.

Cobtree, Maria – Vols 2 and 6. Selfish middle daughter of Tony, two years younger than Charlotte. Married to French aristocrat (Comte de Longue).

Coffin – Vol. 1. Whaling family with which Syn conducts business.

Collyer, Capt. Howard – Vol. 7. Captain of HM Navy and Coast Agent & Commissioner. Sank the *Lion d'Or* at mouth of St Lawrence (fictional reference). Comes to Dymchurch as Head of the King's Men and suspects that Clegg was not really hanged at Rye. Known as 'Collywobbles' to Mipps and some of his own men. Subsequently referred to in *The Slype*, where we learn that he was killed in the first few weeks of war with France. *Highly likely that the name owes something to John Collier, eighteenth-century Surveyor General of Riding Officers for Kent. Collier features heavily in the smuggling history* The Smugglers: Lord Teignmouth and C G Harper *(1923) – which was a source for a number of Thorndike's episodes. Collyer is also a Marsh name.*

Comte de Longue (Jean) – Vol. 6. Husband of Maria Cobtree. Victim of the guillotine.

Corday, Charlotte – (alluded to) Vol. 6. *In reality, French revolutionary figure, guillotined for assassination of Jacobin leader Marat.*

Cragg – Vol. 1. Gate-keeper for Bully Tappitt, engaged to spy on Syn.

Craigen – Vol. 3. Independent smuggler. Part-owner of boat with Evenden brothers, whom he murders in bid to secure sole ownership.

Creach, Gabriel – Vol. 6. Smuggler summarily hanged by Scarecrow and left on the Dymchurch gallows.

Culland, Major – Vol. 4. Gambling associate of Sir Harry Sales, to whom the latter is indebted to tune of 1000 guineas, which results in plan to catch the Scarecrow.

Cullingford, Viscount Clarence – Vol. 6. Gambler who attaches himself to Foulkes.

Dale, Betty – (alluded to) Vol. 1. Girl deflowered (in the language of the day) by Bully Tappitt.

Danton (Georges) – (alluded to) Vol. 6. *One of leaders of French Revolution.*

Decoutier – Vol. 6. Aide of *Robespierre*; one of three men deputed to ride with the Scarecrow to meet with Duloge.

Delacourt, Colonel – Vol. 2. Pseudonym of Nicholas Tappitt, when staying at the Mermaid with McCullum (alias Captain Vicosa).

Delacroix, Captain – Vol. 3. French privateer, responsible for numerous attacks on British shipping, who seizes cargoes of two of Scarecrow's luggers.

Desmoulins (Camille) – (alluded to) Vol. 6. *French journalist and politician who played key role in French Revolution.*

Dickenson, Joe – Vol. 7. Seaman serving under Collyer.

Dolgenny, Tarroc – Vol. 5. Handsome and arrogant north Wales smuggler. Murderer. On travelling to Dymchurch immediately identifies Syn as a likely candidate for the Scarecrow.

Duloge[19] – Vols 4 and 6. Organiser of Scarecrow's smuggling ring on the French side.

Dymchurch Preventative Officer[20] **(unnamed)** – Vol. 2. One of the first to try and effect the rescue of the *City of London*. Killed in bar of the Mermaid Inn by Tappitt as he tries to arrest him on suspicion of being the Scarecrow.

England – (alluded to) Vols 1 and 7. Notorious pirate, under whom Mipps allegedly once served. *Would appear to be real-life English pirate Edward England, although historical dates do not coincide.*

Esnada, Capt. – Vols 1 and (alluded to) 5. Spanish prisoner on parole in Sandgate who teaches Syn Spanish and assists greatly in his odyssey. Has ransom cleared by Syn.

Esnada, Senorita – Vol. 1. (Unnamed) daughter of Captain, at whose house in San Sebastian Syn lodges.

Evenden, Edmond – Vol. 3. Brother of John, murdered by brother-in-law Craigen for boat. *Name possibly based on informer Edward Edenden, a north Kent smuggler operating at time that novels are set.*

Evenden, John – Vol. 3. Brother of Edmond, also murdered by Craigen.

Evenden, Mrs – Vol. 3. Sister of Craigen, married to John.

Faunce, Capt. of Dragoons – Vols 2, 3 and 4. Involved in search for Grinsley (Vol. 2). Captured by Scarecrow (with two other Dragoons) so that he may witnesses the former's robbery

---

19. *Dulonge* in Vol. 6 (this most likely a perpetuated misprint).
20. Preventative Officers were also variously known as Customs Officers, Preventers or King's Preventive men.

of Bone. Promoted to Major by Vol. 3, when his coach (shared with the Archbishop and Troubridge) is held up by Bone. *Name presumably taken from the first wife of Thorndike's maternal grandfather, although may be partially based upon officer of the same name who led the Fourth (Essex) Regiment in the 1812 war with the United States.*

Faunce, Major – Vol. 6. Younger brother of above, who leads his own troop of Dragoons to Dymchurch.

Fielding, Sir John – (alluded to) Vol. 3. Boss of Jerry Hunt. *Real-life Head of the Bow Street Runners.*

Finn – Vol. 4. Farmer and landowner (owns Aldington Knoll).

Fitzherbert, Mrs – (alluded to) Vol. 6. Alleged acquaintance of Foulkes. *Historical society figure with link to royalty (see Chapter 2).*

Fletcher – Vol. 4. Elderly parishioner providing an excuse for Syn and Mipps to be on the Marsh after dark.

Foulkes, 'Bully' – Vol. 6. Successful gambler and soldier of fortune. Duellist with 19 victims (*see also* Barsard).

Fowey, Mrs – Vols 2, 3, 4 and 5. Housekeeper to Syn, 'found' by Charlotte Cobtree. As befits her name, hails from Cornwall (it is unclear why Thorndike decides that Syn should have a change of housekeeper: despite no reference to ill health or dispute, she is replaced by Mrs Honeyballs in *Shadow*; in the final novel there is no mention of a housekeeper although Mrs Fowey does appear in the London Films version of *Doctor Syn* – where she acquires the forename Prudence).

Fragg – Vol. 3. Undercover customs officer ('sea lawyer') who journeys to Dymchurch to buy information from Brazlett. Takes possession of list of smugglers but is lured to sluice gates, where he is murdered.

Gordon, Agatha – Vol. 6. Aunt of Lady Caroline Cobtree.

Granger – Vol. 2. One of two Dragoons (along with Metcalf) left on beach by Captain Faunce to guard smugglers whilst he pursues Scarecrow.

Grinsley – Vol. 2. Mean-spirited smuggler who murders Sandgate Riding Officer. Perceived at one time to be the Scarecrow. Hunted by both Dragoons and locals, who feel that he will squeal if caught. Escapes in rags taken from a scarecrow, which leads to Syn being drawn into the smuggling enterprise. Killed by Metcalf in incident that sows the seed for the belief that the Scarecrow has supernatural powers.

Hadley – Vol. 3. Dymchurch family (father and three sons) who become unfortunate victims of the press gang. One of the sons (whose wife is pregnant) is given the forename William by Buchanan.

Handaway, 'Mother' – Vols 2, 3, 4, 5 and 6. Old, sick Marsh woman. Archetypal witch (one-tooth; pointed chin and owner of both cauldron and cat!). Syn persuades her that he is Satan, and that she must stable his horse. Crucial to protection of Scarecrow's identity. Name is changed to Hathaway in the Disney film.

Handgrove – Vol. 4. Farmer and former smuggler who betrays two fellow Night-riders after extorting money under threat of exposure. Transported to Scarecrow's French dungeon, where he languishes for 11 years. When mutiny breaks out, makes break for England to try and claim a pardon for his colleagues and a share of the reward for breaking up the Scarecrow's operation.

Hargreaves, Mrs – Vol. 6. Villager greeted by Mrs Honeyballs.

Harker, Trooper – Vol. 2. Dragoon forced to give ride to Merry following Syn's fight with Bone. *Named after Thorndike family friend (Joseph Harker was a theatrical scene painter close to the Thorndikes whose son joined the Westminster Dragoons along with Russell at the outbreak of WWI).*

Hart, Fred – Vol. 4. Fisherman and smuggler interrogated and tortured by Blain; betrays Scarecrow and is shipped off to his hideaway in France.

Hart, Mrs – Vol. 4. Wife of Fred.

Hemminge, Sir Peter – Vol. 4. Gambling friend of Sir Harry Sales. *Name probably reflects English actor John Hemminge (1556–1630), who edited the first folio of Shakepeare's plays.*

Henley, Polly – Vol. 4. Girlfriend of cooper George Lee. Part of Dymchurch fishing family which owns the herring hang. *Name taken from real-life Dymchurch fishing family of Thorndike's acquaintance.*

Herman, Charles – Vol. 1. Brother-in-law to Sommers and cabinet maker involved in plot to rescue Imogene. Has grievance with Bully Tappitt.

Honeyballs, Mrs – Vol. 6. Syn's housekeeper. Appears to have succeeded Mrs Fowey.

Hunt, Jerry – Vol. 3. Bow Street Runner who travels to the Marsh to arrest Jimmie Bone but also sees opportunity to claim reward for capture of the Scarecrow.

Hyde, Nicholas – Vol. 6. Revenue Officer from Sandgate. Slow witted, but poses a potent threat to Syn, whose affair with Cicely Cobtree leads him to lower his defences.

Jackson, Sam – Vols 3 and 6. Outlaw living on stage route (at Stone Street) who is in league with both smugglers and highwayman Jimmie Bone. *Referred to only as 'Slippery Sam' within the novels, the character is clearly based upon the real-life smuggler, who did live on Stone Street.*

Jerk, Jerry – Vols 5 and 7. 12-year old schoolboy (at time *Doctor Syn* is set) and potboy at The Ship Inn. Sworn enemy of his tormentor, Rash the schoolmaster. Given the name Jack Ketch by Mipps on initiation to Night-riders. Lives with grandparents. Catch phrase: 'now, by all the barrels of rum', taken from a sailor. Grows up to become Maidstone hangman.

Jones, David Davis Llewellyn – Vol. 5. Lawyer who journeys from North Wales to Dymchurch to advise Syn of tontine. Guardian to Ann Sudden. Murdered by Dolgenny.

Jones, Hugh – Vol. 5. Brother of Welsh lawyer, also murdered by Dolgenny.

Joyce – (briefly mentioned) Vol. 6. Hythe saddler.

Kemble, Philip – Vol. 6. Takes part in conversation in Crockfords with Syn and Sheridan. *In real life, popular actor and manager of Covent Garden and Drury Lane Theatres, where his reforms improved the status of the theatrical profession. Played many Shakespearian roles (including that of Hamlet), as did Thorndike. Also trained for the priesthood.*

Knarler – Vol. 4. Slaughterman from Cranbrook engaged by Farmer Finn to level Aldington Knoll.

Lambton, Sir Harry – Vol. 6. Gambling companion of Cullingford and Foulkes.

Lee, George – Vol. 4. Dymchurch lad who becomes cooper at Brewery Cooperage in Hythe. Betrothed to Polly Henley. Used by Blain to try and obtain information to break up the Scarecrow's gang.

Lovell, Mrs – Vols 2 and 6. Housekeeper at Court House.

McCallum – Vols 1 and 2. Planter and ship owner entertained with Nicholas Tappitt and Imogene by Governor of Santiago at the time Syn commandeers Tappitt's ship. Owner of treasure ships to be escorted by the *St Nicholas*. Subsequently accompanies Tappitt to Romney Marsh using the name of Captain Vicosa ('Captain Vic') as part of Tappitt's plan to unmask Syn.

Maid of Kent, Holy – (alluded to) Vol. 4. Rumoured within novel to have placed curse on anyone trying to level Aldington Knoll. *In real life, a sixteenth-century servant girl (Elizabeth Barton), who lived at Aldington and had 'visions'.*

Mallett, Job – Vol. 7. Bosun serving under Collyer.

Marat, (Jean) – (alluded to) Vol. 6. *French revolutionary leader and journalist, heavily involved in Reign of Terror.*

Merry – Vol. 2. Dymchurch ne'erdowell who exploits the tragedy of the *City of London*, looting the dead bodies and murdering the captain (who stood to gain all valuables recovered from the ship). Later sees Jimmie Bone unmasked and contrives to obtain the reward on his head. Subsequently employed at the Mermaid Inn in Rye, where he becomes servant to Colonel Delacourt and Captain Vicosa (Tappitt and McCallum). Involved in the shooting of Charlotte Cobtree and is himself killed in bizarre fashion after being caught by Syn and Mipps trying to rob Charlotte's grave (in which the *City of London* pearls are buried). *Name possibly reflects the Barham character Mr Merryman in* The Leech of Folkestone.

Metcalf – Vol. 2. Dragoon left on beach (with Granger) by Captain Faunce to guard smugglers. Subsequently kills Grinsley.

Mipps, Septimus – Vols 1, 2, 3, 4, 5, 6 and 7. Septimus Mipps is a man of many parts, but an incredibly loyal, one-man servant. We know little of his formative years (although subsequently – in *The Shype* – his diary confides that he was raised in an unconventional family where his mother frequently attacked his father). He is introduced very early on in the saga as a smuggler and fugitive from justice, journeying to seek his fortune in piracy when he first meets Syn. Mipps is rarely addressed by his Christian name, which has changed to Didimus in *Shadow*. A carpenter by trade, is working at Wraight's Boatbuilding Yard at Dymchurch when he first encounters Syn. His partnership with Syn/Clegg on the high seas sees him employed as carpenter. When Syn and Mipps go their own ways, Mipps 'shanghais' a ship's carpenter in the Royal Navy, successfully applying for his post for the journey home to England. On return, he hears rumours of a new vicar at Dymchurch and travels down. Is re-engaged by Syn, initially as undertaker with the job of digging graves and making coffins (a duty that Wraight never liked). The duties of sexton, verger, bell-pull and clerk soon follow. Mipps takes up residence in Old Tree Cottage and further opens a small general store, but the quiet and respectable life soon palls. Through his general store he has become fully acquainted with the business of the village and becomes involved in the smuggling trade once more. His capture is the prelude to Syn's involvement and establishment of the Scarecrow empire. Within this, Mipps remains as Syn's right-hand man, in the guise of Night-rider Hellspite. Mipps's unusual appearance is frequently mentioned throughout the books: his face is described as 'ferret-like', with a long thin nose, and with scanty hair dragged back and twisted into a tarred queue (this is also described as 'looking for all the world like a jigger-gaffe').[21] Unkindly, is also described as 'rat-like and grotesque'. His distinctive looks and diminutive stature lead some to link him to Hellspite and thus his involvement with smuggling. Despite his appearance, Mipps appears to be popular with the ladies (particularly the widow Mrs Waggetts at The Ship Inn) although this is not reciprocated: 'I always did seem to attract the admiration of the females, probably because they never attracted me'. Mipps clearly has no eye for the ladies, and is seen to be distressed when Syn is in love. Mipps's fate is ultimately kinder than Syn's; he survives the bloodshed on the lugger by playing dead and swimming to safety. Reappears on the island of Penang, off the Malay Peninsula. The best epitaph for Mipps is provided by his master, who describes him as being: 'as faithful as a dog; as useful as a horse; as brave as a mongoose; as sly as a monkey; as fierce as a rat; as gentle as a lamb; and as wise and foolish, according to requirement, as an owl'.[22]

'Mountain Cat' – Vol. 1. Indian Guide to Syn and Mipps. Scalped and burned by rival Red Indian tribe.

Mulatto[23] **(unnamed)** – Vols 1 and 7. Alleged Cuban priest and dangerous practitioner of black magic. Sole survivor from the *Pit of Sulphur,* allegedly being struck dumb with the shock of the explosion. Subsequently turns up on the *Imogene,* causing unrest amongst crew by turning them against Clegg. Marooned by Clegg on coral island, is tied to a tree after having his ears cut off and his tongue cut out (by Shuhshuhgah). Somehow survives and, with the ability to sniff out trap doors and hiding-places during smuggling investigations, is employed by the Navy for investigation work under Collyer. Arrives at Dymchurch to haunt Syn. Despite his disabilities, manages to communicate to the bosun and Collyer a description of Clegg that does not tally with that of the man hanged at Rye. Various incidents bear testimony to his supernatural powers, although he is innocent of the murder of Rash – for which he is widely suspected. Achieves quest by burying Clegg's own harpoon into his adversary's neck before seemingly vanishing into thin air.

Murrain – Vol. 5. Farmer, instructed by Mipps in The Ship Inn. *Name is humorous reference to an infectious disease of cattle.*

---

21. Jigger-gaffe is a term for the after mast of a four-masted vessel.
22. *Courageous Exploits.*
23. A mulatto is the first-generation offspring of a white and black couple. We learn subsequently that this mulatto is a Cuban priest.

Noel, Lord, of Aldington – (fleeting reference) Vol. 5. Attends hearing into death of Hythe Revenue Officer. *Name rseflects Thorndike's friend Noel Coward (a one-time resident of Aldington).*

Osmund – Vol. 4. Officer of watch aboard Guard Ship on which smuggler Hart is held.

Pembury, Sir Henry ('Harry') – Vols 1, 3, 4, 5 and 6. Lord/Squire of Lympne. Justice of the Peace. Suffers from gout and regularly locks horns with Tony Cobtree.

Pembury, Lady – Vols 1 and 3. Wife of Sir Henry.

Pembury, Kate – Vol. 3. Beautiful daughter of Sir Henry. Marries (Philip) Brackenbury.

Pembury (other daughters) – Vols 4 and 5. In addition to Kate, there are at least two other daughters. Single, and described collectively and ungraciously as 'leaving much to be desired'. Used as bait to lure Dolgenny away from Dymchurch. Fan Pembury has designs on Blain, one of the Upton brothers and Bone (in the guise of the Scarecrow).

Pepper, Dr Sennacherib – Vols 1, 2, 3, 4, 5, 6 and 7. Dymchurch physician who makes frequent claims of seeing phantom horsemen on the Marsh whilst visiting sick patients at night. His fondness for drink allows smugglers to pour scorn on the notion. Murdered by Rash because he knows too much. *It is much quoted that Thorndike took name from a grave in Dymchurch churchyard.*

Peters – Vol. 6. Cullingford family groom.

Pettigrand, Silas – Vols 2 and 3. Leader of Romany gipsies, camped near Mother Handaway's. Man of honour who keeps the secret of Syn's dual identity (and also ensures the safety of Highwayman Jimmie Bone). *Forename probably affectionately reflects a favourite Churchwarden at Aylesford ('Silas Wagon – such a lovely name').*[24]

Phipps, Mrs – Vol. 6. Dymchurch bonnet-shop assistant.

Pitt, William – (alluded to) Vol. 6. *Minister of War at time the novel is set.*

Plattman, George – Vol. 5. Excise Officer who infiltrates Scarecrow's gang (in guise of Vulture) but is killed by Night-riders.

Prince of Wales – Vol. 4 (and other fleeting references). *Eldest son of King George III; 'First Gentleman of Europe'.* Visits Lympne Castle and rides with Romney Marsh pack (and at the kill, with the Scarecrow). Personally knows Syn and makes various undertakings to him. Quoted as saying that Syn is the only clergyman who can make him laugh.

Quested, Jonathan – Vol. 6. Fisherman and smuggler, part of Scarecrow's gang. *Surname is that of infamous leader of the Aldington Blues.*

Raikes, Captain – Vol. 3. Officer of Regiment of Foot; bully who provokes arguments and engineers duel with the younger Brackenbury.

Ransleys – Vol. 3. Grandmother is wife of smuggler transported to Tasmania; son **Shem** and two grandsons are also smugglers. Shem Ransley tries to deceive Scarecrow by diverting tubs. *Characters based on family of George Ransley, real-life eighteenth-century smuggler.*

---

24. A quotation from Russell's biography of his sister.

Ransom, Mervin – Vols 1 and 2. Master and owner of the brig *City of London* trading between New England and the Port of London, which brings Syn back in eventful fashion to Dymchurch. Murdered by Merry in the aftermath of the tragedy that befalls his vessel off Dymchurch Wall. Nicknamed 'Mayor' by Syn.

Rash – Vols 4 (fleeting), 5 and 7. Schoolmaster, fiddle player and leader of the church choir as well as Night-rider (Lucifer). Threatens to turn King's Evidence and betray the community if Imogene fails to marry him; is accordingly 'removed' by Marsh witches after having been attacked by Syn and is left hanging on Jerk's gallows near Littlestone Point. Buchanan bestows on him the forename Timothy. *It has been suggested that the character was based upon a mean-spirited master at Dymchurch school. If this is the case, it was probably a Mr Tanner, who taught there for a short period at the start of the twentieth century. His methods and predilection for the cane made him deeply unpopular and were the reasons for his subsequent dismissal. The name Rash could be associated with use of the cane, as indeed can Tanner; this arguably supports such a link as the naming would reflect Thorndike's sense of humour.*

River, Lady – (alluded to) Vol. 7. Host of party at which Tuffton snubs Mrs Whyllie.

Robespierre, Maximilien Marie Isidore – Vols 6 and (alluded to) 7. *Infamous leader of French Revolution.* Tricked by Scarecrow, who manages to disrupt his spying network.

Rowton – Vol. 4. Officer in charge of Guard Ship; drunkard.

Rudrum, Will – Vol. 7. Seaman shot by Night-riders whilst attempting to free the captured Collyer.

Sales, Sir Harry – Vol. 4. Young bachelor fond of gambling. Miscalculates his assets and incurs a debt he cannot pay, so determines to capture Scarecrow for the reward on offer.

Searly (poss. Searle) – (alluded to) Vol. 6. Dymchurch butcher.

Sheridan, Richard Brinsley – Vol. 6. Part of group in Crockford's, with Syn and Kemble. *Real-life playwrite who became manager of Drury Lane Theatre in 1778 (and Whig MP 1780–1812).*

Shuhshuhgah ('Blue Heron') – Vols 1 and 2. Red Indian (son of Chief) rescued by Mipps and Syn, who have mistaken him for Mountain Cat. Takes to seas with Clegg and Mipps and removes the mulatto's tongue and ears prior to his marooning on coral reef. After Syn and Mipps become blood brothers of his tribe, ventures to Romney Marsh to warn Syn that Tappitt and McCallum have returned to England to track him down.

Sommers, Esther – Vol. 1. One of a number of girls raped by Bully Tappitt.

Sommers – Vol. 1. Farmer and father of Esther. Holds grudge against Bully Tappitt and shows Syn means of unobserved access to Tappitt's Iffley estate via river.

Spiker, Bill – Vol. 7. Sailor (gunner) murdered by mulatto.

Strathway, Lord – Vol. 4. Gambling friend of Sir Harry Sales.

Stubbard – Vol. 3. Head of press gang that visits Dymchurch.

Sudden, Ann – Vol. 5. Niece of David Jones.

Swinnnerton – Vol. 4. Officer of watch on lugger from which Fred Hart has been removed to the Guard Ship. *Name probably derives from Arthur Swinnerton, an English novelist and critic, whom Thorndikek knew through his connection with H. G. Wells.*

Syn Christopher, Doctor of Divinity – Vols 1, 2, 3, 4, 5, 6 and 7. 1729/30–1793 (probably). Scholar and writer of ancient Greek; vicar of Dymchurch and Dean of the Peculiars; duellist; horseman/sportsman; pirate; smuggler; friend of the Prince of Wales; and great romantic. From a family of legal prolocutors and attorneys-at-law, based at Lydd and educated at Canterbury School. When he is just 15, his father Septimus is killed – heroically fighting for the Young Pretender (Bonnie Prince Charlie) at Culloden – and his mother dies of a broken heart the same year. The orphaned Syn is looked after by his uncle Solomon and Sir Charles Cobtree, Squire of Dymchurch. Accordingly, he forms a close bond with Cobtree's son Antony, which lasts until his death. At 24 becomes the youngest Don at Queens College Oxford and is youngest Doctor of Divinity in either of the Great Universities. At the start of Vol. 1, is resident classical tutor at Queens College, Oxford. Teased for his shyness with the opposite sex in his youth, this changes when he woos and weds Imogene Almago. She, however, cannot bear the thought of living at Dymchurch and elopes with Syn's friend, Nicholas Tappitt. This is the incident that sparks Syn's odyssey and, in pursuit of Tappitt and vengeance, he embarks on a bloody and highly successful piratical career, which lasts some 12 years. During this period, assumes the mantle of Captain Clegg. Returns to Dymchurch in dramatic fashion at the age of 45, his ship breaking up in Dymchurch Bay and Syn being the only survivor. The same storm also results in death of the local vicar (in an attempted rescue), which allows Syn to resume his former role. In addition, the Squire (his old friend Tony, who has succeeded his father) bestows the title of Dean of the Peculiars upon him, which gives increased status as a dignitary as well as more money and a legitimate reason to spend time away from Dymchurch. Within two years, the Scarecrow is born, as Syn is forced to bail out his faithful lieutenant Mipps, who has reverted to his former ways. Syn resolves to lead and organise the local smugglers for the benefit of the wider community. His increasingly daring exploits ensure that the notoriety of the Scarecrow assumes prominence way beyond Romney Marsh; the loss of income to the revenue authorities means that a large reward is offered for his capture. Although at various times there are those who suspect a connection between the Scarecrow and Clegg, Syn ensures that very few are aware that he is linked to the other two; not even his closest friend Tony Cobtree suspects until shortly before Syn's demise. This incident sees him witnessing Syn trying to remove his tattoo with a hot poker: one of the few errors of judgement that Syn made was – when drunk – to have his arm crudely tattooed with the scene of a man walking the plank and a shark swimming beneath – a mark that can immediately identify him as Clegg. His smuggling enterprise appears unstoppable until a figure from his past – the mulatto – returns to haunt him. The net closing in, Syn plans to flee and uncharacteristically issues veiled threats of turning King's Evidence in the event of villagers failing to support his last desperate flight. There is, however, to be no escape and the mulatto gains his revenge from beyond the grave. Syn is at least allowed to be buried at sea and by this act there is a poetic ending as, in the words of Clegg's own shanty, a pound of gunshot *is* tied to his feet and a ragged bit of sail *does* become his winding-sheet.

Syn, Christopher jnr – (alluded to) Vols 1 and 2. The birth of Syn's only child in 1755 is dealt with only very briefly by Thorndike. The inference is that he was murdered by Tappitt, although he (Tappitt) claims that the boy ran away with Red Indians. In Chris George's account,[25] Christopher Almago Syn dies in 1812.

Syn, Septimus – Vols 1 (Prologue) and 5 (mentioned by Jones). 1700–1745. Father of Christopher and younger brother of Solomon. Clerk to the Lords of the Level. Along with three other brothers, killed at Culloden fighting for the Young Pretender.

Syn, Solomon – Vol. 1 (Prologue). Uncle of Christopher.

Tandyshall, Capt. – Vol. 4. Gambling friend of Sir Harry Sales.

Tankerton brothers – Vol. 3. Half-breed gipsies and horse stealers. Sentenced to death after stealing horses used by the Scarecrow; 'reprieved' by Scarecrow and exiled to France. *Tankerton is a suburb of Whitstable and was commercially developed by the Tankerton Estate Company. Thorndike was not at all impressed by the development and his casting of the Tankertons as horse thieves is not concidental.*

Tappitt, 'Bully' – Vols 1 and (mentioned) 2. Squire of Iffley. Killed by Farmer Sommers following duel with Syn.

(Tappitt, Elinor) – Vol. 1. Fictitious wife of Squire of Iffley (invented to avert suspicion).

Tappitt, Imogene – Vols 2 and 7. Daughter of Nicholas Tappitt and Imogene Almago, born in Raratonga (Cook Islands). After death of father, is sheltered by Syn. Later becomes barmaid at The Ship Inn. Wooed by and eventually marries Denis Cobtree, after being adopted by the Whyllies. Sole beneficiary of Christopher Syn's will.

Tappitt, Nicholas – Vols 1 and 2. Squire of Iffley's nephew, dismissed from Syn's own college following an incident with a serving wench. Holds job in British consulate in Madrid but, when this post is lost, Imogene Almago's father provides a ship which allows him to remain in Spain (trading in fruit). Returns to Iffley at point where Esther Sommers's father kills his uncle. Initially becomes firm friend of Syn but the friendship turns sour as Tappitt elopes with Imogene. On turning to piracy adopts the name Black Nick and, as a pirate, earns a reputation for harsh treatment of his crew. Having been chased around the globe by Syn, subsequently tries to turn the tables by travelling (in the guise of Colonel Delacourt) to Kent to unmask him as Clegg. Is arrested, however, for the murders of Merry and a Preventive Officer; Syn undertakes to look after his daughter in return for Tappitt's 'confession' to being Clegg. Accordingly, Tappitt dies on the scaffold – as Clegg – in 1776. His body is hung in chains and buried in unconsecrated land at cross-roads by the Kent ditch.

Tapsole, Mrs – Vol. 7. Patient of Dr Pepper; works in bakehouse. Rash uses her alleged illness as cover when murdering Pepper.

---

25. See Chapter 3.

Tarragona, Juan – Vol. 1. Commissioned by Tappitt in Santiago, and briefs Syn as to the former's movements.

Thane, Henry ('Harry') – Vol. 5. Suitor of Ann Sudden, to whom Syn arranges marriage.

Tolling – Vol. 3. Smuggler sent by Mipps to spy on Fragg.

Tonti, Nicholas Lorenzo – (referenced) Vol. 5. *Neapolitan Banker who founded the Tontine process in 1684.*

Transome – Vol. 7. Valet to Capt. Tuffton.

Troubridge, Colonel/General – Vols 2, 3, 4 and 5. Leader of full squadron of Dragoons sent from Dover Castle to augment local force. Promoted to General (Vol. 3), and is traveller in stagecoach held up by Bone.

Troubridge, Admiral – Vols 3, 4 and 5. Twin brother of Colonel/General. *The Troubridge brothers are based upon the family of the same name, which included Thomas (Lord Commissioner of the Admiralty), who distinguished himself in both the revolutionary and Napoleonic Wars with France, and his grandson Sir Thomas, who served with distinction in the Crimean War.*

Tuffton, Capt. – Vol. 7. Head of the press gang, tricked into releasing Denis Cobtree.

Upton Brothers (Monty, Henry and Tom) – Vol. 2 (and other fleeting references). Leaders of Marsh smugglers prior to Syn's involvement; subsequently becoming the Scarecrow's lieutenants. Eldest (Monty) plays the part of Scarecrow in Doctor Syn's Christmas Mummers. *This is a Marsh name, and there remain a number of Uptons in the area today. Thorndike was friendly with the family, which was involved with fishing and a furniture business and which included a Henry.*

Vicosa, Capt. ('Captain Vic') – Vol. 2. See McCallum.

Waggetts – Vols 2 and (alluded to) 3. Proprietor of The Ship Inn, who suffers from poor health – dies in *Returns*.

Waggetts, Mrs – Vols 2, 3, 4, 5, 6 and 7. Landlady of The Ship Inn. Following the death of her husband, pursues Mipps. Unflatteringly described as 'large, ugly, vain but capable'. For a time becomes paid guardian to Imogene Tappitt. Meets a gruesome end, hanged from her own inn sign.[26]

Walters, Morgan – Vol. 7. Sailor on watch duty when Bill Spiker is murdered. Meets his death whilst impersonating Syn (on the instruction of Collyer).

Whyllie, Antony – Vol. 7. Attorney-at-law from Rye engaged by Collyer to prepare accommodation for a large number of prisoners. Waylaid and warned off by Scarecrow's men.

Whyllie, Mrs – Vol. 7. Battleaxe wife of attorney, who arranges to adopt Imogene.

Wooley, Mrs – Vol. 6. Another ageing parishioner of Syn's who provides him with an excuse to be out on the Marsh at night.

Wraight, Josia – Vols 1 and 2. Builder/boatbuilder engaged by Syn to make alterations to vicarage. Owner of boatyard that at one time employs Mipps. Initially also coffin maker (a job

---

26. In some subsequent editions of *Dr Syn* (re-publications) this ending has been changed.

he dislikes, allowing an opening for Mipps on his return to the Marsh). *Name taken from that of local boat builder in Thorndike's time, who also did act as the local undertaker (and from a family that had been involved in smuggling in the past).*

Young – Vol. 5. Owner of lugger used by Syn to cross Channel.

Characters referred to only by Christian name

Dolly – Vol. 6. Serving wench attending Bone at the Mitre Inn.

Edward – Vol. 5. Guard on mail coach.

Garcia – Vol. 5. Gaoler employed by Dolgenny.

'Old George' – Vol. 3. Coachman on stagecoach held up by Bone.

Harriet ('La Belle Harriet') – Vol. 6. Beau of Foulkes.

Jacques – Vol. 6. French go-between.

Jim ('Young Jim') – Vol. 4. Grandson of Fletcher.

Joe – Vol. 3. Acquaintance of Slippery Sam.

Joe – Vol. 4. Sailor whose clothes are taken to disguise Fred Hart on his journey to Guard Ship.

Old Katie – Vol. 4. 70-year old retail smuggler – the last left on the Marsh – from St Mary-in-the-Marsh. Tolerated and even protected by the Scarecrow. When arrested by an increasingly desperate Captain Blain, confesses to being the Scarecrow. Pleading guilty to the charges, sentenced to hang but reprieved by the Prince of Wales when Syn calls in a promise.

Lisette – Vol. 6. Frenchwoman who is maid to Agatha Gordon.

Pedro – Vol. 1. Landlord of the Staunch Brotherhood Inn, Santiago.

Pedro – Vols 5 and 6. Spanish valet of Tarroc Dolgenny (subsequently elevated to Captain).

Percy – Vol. 4. Village simpleton who fetches water for the villagers. Unwittingly becomes the carrier of messages for the Scarecrow, via the floats in his buckets crafted by Mipps. *Dymchurch was relatively late to enjoy the benefits of mains water and residents had to queue at standpipes. Between the wars, a local man set up a crude water delivery service. He did not use a yoke like Percy, but he did use floats in his bucket to limit spillage, although it is reported that the buckets leaked copiously! Whilst locals referred to him with affection, he was generally viewed – like Percy – as being of low intelligence.*

Pete ('Yellow Pete') – Vol. 1 and (alluded to) 7. Chinese crew member (cook) of Clegg. Assists Mipps in applying Syn's distinctive tattoo. Tries to stop Clegg from marooning the mulatto; in response has his back broken with a marline spike and his body is thrown to the sharks. Subsequently features in dream of Capt. Collyer.

Robert – Vol. 2. Footman at Court House.

Sam – Vol. 3. Another acquaintance of Slippery Sam.

Thomas – Vol. 6. Manservant of Squire.

Tiddy – (alluded to) Vol. 6. Squire's great aunt.

Tom – (alluded to) Vol. 3. Oboe player in church choir.

Other names (including nicknames)

'Boots' – Vol. 6. Junior servant at Court House.

Buttercups – various references. Syn's pony (although name is only revealed in *Shadow*).

Colindale – Vol. 4. One of Pembury's horses, used by Prince of Wales.

'Dandy Sleuths' – Vol. 4. Name given to Sir Harry Sales' party (comprising Sales, Briston, Tandyshall, Strathaway and Hemminge) by Capt. Blain.

Gehenna – Vols 2, 3, 4, 5 and 6. Scarecrow's jet-black horse (Charlotte Cobtree also subsequently adopts the name for one of her own horses). Name derives from biblical reference to Hell/place of torment – in Jewish beliefs a place where children were sacrificed (by fire) to the gods. Note that, in *Doctor Syn*, the Scarecrow's steed is described as 'a spectral grey'.

Horace – Vols 2, 5 and 6. Affectionate name used by Mipps for spiders and cockroach.

Judy – Vol. 4. Wooden idol acquired by Mipps in West Indies. Used to 'select' floats for Percy's buckets (to carry the Scarecrow's messages).

Lightning – Vols 4 and 6 (and other passing references). Mipps's donkey.

Mister Pitt – Vol. 6. Agatha Gordon's white poodle (named after the Minister of War).

Night-riders – Vols 2, 3, 4, 5, 6 and 7. Scarecrow's phantom horsemen who circle and give protection to the pack ponies on a 'run'. Names include Hellspite (Mipps), Beelzebub (Bone), Belch the Demon, Catseyes, Cormorant, Satan, Lucifer, Pontius Pilate, Curlew, Falcon, Owl, Raven, Eagle, Vulture and Seagull.

Red Pepper – Vol. 6. Cobtree horse on which Cicely 'teaches' Syn to ride.

Sirius – Vol. 2. Charlotte Cobtree's horse.

Stardust – Vol. 6. Cicely Cobtree's horse

Ships and boats

City of London – Vols 1 and 2. Brig on which Syn returns to Dymchurch. Formerly *The Gog*. Figurehead ends up in Wraight's Dymchurch boatyard.

HMS Crocodile – (mentioned) Vol. 4. Guard Ship of Tower of London, on which Blain was born and to whose command he later returns.

Ezekiel – Vol. 1. North American whaling ship into which Syn buys when pursuing Tappitt.

Ferret – Vol. 4. British Revenue cutter engaged by Scarecrow when commanding *Four Sisters*.

Flower – (alluded to) Vol. 4. Rye boat with false bow used by smugglers.

Four Sisters – Vol. 4. Littlestone vessel used by Scarecrow for transporting Handgrove back across Channel.

Gog – former name of *City of London*. *Although also a biblical name, taken from giant in Dickens's* Master Humphrey's Clock.

Greyhound – Vols 3, 5 and 6. Clipper used by Syn to take on Delacroix. Also sent to Wales to seize Dolgenny's ill-gotten gains.

Imogene – Vol. 1 and (mentioned in retrospective) 6. Clegg's ship. Formerly the *St Nicholas*, but name changed when commandeered by Clegg. Eventually blown up by Mipps to cover their tracks (the same fate as befalls the *Pit of Sulphur*), with loss of all lives.

Intention – Vol. 1. Ship on which Syn sails to Boston to first pursue Nicholas Tappitt.

Isiah (sic) – Vol. 1. Tappitt's whaling ship.

Louise – Vol. 5. French lugger used in smuggling operation in Wales (and on which Bone takes refuge).

Magog – Vol. 1. Former sister ship of *The Gog*, trading between Boston and London. Apparently sunk by Clegg. *Name again taken from giant in Dickens's* Master Humphrey's Clock.

Pit of Sulphur – Vol. 1. Pirate ship that intercepts the *Intention*. Syn kills captain in duel and assumes his role. Ship subsequently blown up by Mipps, seemingly with loss of all but one life (that of the mulatto).

Plough – Vol. 4. Hythe boat used to smuggle tobacco from France.

Providence – (alluded to) Vol. 4. Folkestone vessel. One of Scarecrow's fleet, fitted with false bow; broken up by Customs Officers (on finding no contraband, the Customs are forced to pay damages).

Resistance – (passing reference) Vol. 7. Collyer's ship.

St Nicholas – Vol. 1. *See Imogene.*

Sandgate Revenue Cutter – Vol. 3 (and other passing references).

Santa Celesta – Vol. 1. One of the two treasure ships to be escorted from Santiago to Spain by Tappitt. Subsequently looted by Syn.

Santa Mariana – Vols 1 and (alluded to) 2. As *Santa Celesta*. Also looted by Syn.

Strawberry – Vol. 4. Deal boat used to smuggle tobacco from France.

(Twin Sisters) – Vol. 6. Name of vessel falsely given by Syn when challenged by Sandgate Revenue cutter (when sailing the *Two Brothers*).

Two Brothers – Vol. 6. One of Scarecrow's fleet, seemingly moored in Rye Harbour.

HMS Vengeance – Vol. 3. Warship (man o' war) commanded by Admiral Troubridge.

Public houses/inns

Romney Marsh

Botolph's Bridge Inn, Botolphs Bridge – Vols 3 and 5. *Large inn within small hamlet in north east corner of Romney Marsh.*

City of London, Dymchurch – Vols 2, 3, 4, 5 and 6. Formerly Sea Wall Tavern within saga (name changed after storm of 1775).

Mermaid Inn, Rye – Vols 2 and 3. Occasional retreat of Syn's, when staying in Rye. *In reality, haunt of Hawkhurst Gang and boasts other smuggling links.*

Ocean Inn, Dymchurch – Vols 2, 3, 4 and 5. Another of the Dymchurch pubs frequented by Mipps.

Red Lion, Hythe – Vols 2,3,4, 5 and 6. Coaching inn favoured by Mipps and stagecoach drivers.

Royal Oak, Brookland – Vols 3 and 5. Used by Syn to hide contraband. *In real life, for a short time (in the early twentyfirst century) became the Yew and Ewe but has since reverted to its original name.*

Shepherd & Crook, Burmarsh – Vols 2 and 5. *Classic Marsh pub in village setting.*

Ship Inn, Dymchurch – Vols 2, 3, 4, 5, 6 and 7. Centre of village activity and Dymchurch pub of choice for Mipps and a great number of his smuggling colleagues; occasionally used by Syn. *Remains popular today and is something of a shrine to the Syn legend.*

Ship Inn, New Romney – Vol. 2. Yet another of the pubs used by Mipps.

Walnut Tree, Aldington – Vols 2, 3, 4 and 6. Popular with smugglers and visited regularly by Shem Ransley. *In real life, has played host to a number of smuggling gangs. A lamp was hung in the window on the night of a run to indicate that the coast was clear. A favourite haunt of the Ransleys.* The Walnut Tree also features in John Douch's smuggling novel *Moonlight Man.*

Kent (elsewhere)

Chequers, Aylesford – (alluded to) Vol. 2. Within the saga, the landlord was at one time Mipps's uncle.

George & Dragon, Fordwich (nr Canterbury) – Vol. 6. Coaching Inn on the London – Dover stage route.

Rising Sun, Stourmouth (nr Canterbury) – Vol. 3. Within novels, used to pass smugglers messages via the stagecoach.

Other

Golden Keys, Charing Cross – Vols 4, 5 and 6. *London Coaching House.*

Mitre Inn, Ely Place ('Ye Olde Mitre'), London – Vols 4 and 6. Landlord – Bubukles – is part of Scarecrow's smuggling network. *Pub with genuine links to the smuggling trade.*

Mitre Inn, Oxford – Vol. 2. *Coaching inn dating from 1630 (and a previous inn was on the same site from 1300). In the eighteenth century (i.e. within Syn's 'lifetime') it was possible to catch a coach from here to Holborn.*

Ship Tavern, Whitehall – Vol. 4. *Pub frequented by many actors (including Thorndike).*

Staunch Brotherhood, Santiago – Vol. 1. Tavern used by pirates and cut-throats.

All of above pubs (with the exception of the Staunch Brotherhood) are genuine establishments that are still trading at time of writing.

Appendix 13

Clegg's Shanty

Here's to the feet wot have walked the plank —[27]
Yo-ho! For the dead man's throttle;
And here's to the corpses afloat in the tank,[28]
And the dead man's teeth in the bottle![29]

For a pound of gunshot tied to his feet,
And a ragged bit of sail for a winding-sheet —[30]
Then the signal goes with a bang and a flash,
And overboard you go with a horrible splash.

And all that isn't swallowed by the sharks outside,
Stands up again upon its feet upon the running tide;
And it keeps a-blowin' gently, and a looking with surprise
At each little crab a-scramblin' from the sockets of its eyes.

Originally from *Doctor Syn* by Russell Thorndike, published by Arrow Books. (© Random House, Arrow Books. Reprinted by permission of The Random House Group Limited)

---

27. A double reference. Clearly an allusion to the piratical practice of forcing victims into the sea at swordpoint; but originating from Syn watching Mipps using a long plank to negotiate a Marsh ditch in *High Seas*.
28. Denotes sea.
29. A reference to the pirate Edward England allegedly cutting off a man's head with a cutlass; the unfortunate victim apparently bit through the glass of a bottle from which he was drinking, in shock. In *Doctor Syn*, Syn does the very same thing when he spies the mulatto.
30. This form of burial at sea is ultimately Syn's own fate.

Appendix 14

Doctor Syn (1937) – London Films:
Cast and Production Details

Production

Screenplay:	Russell Thorndike
Screen adaptation:	Michael Hogan; Roger Burford; Russell Thorndike
Director:	Roy William Neill

Cast

Doctor Syn:	George Arliss
Captain Collyer:	Roy Emerton
Denis Cobtree:	John Loder
Rash:	Frederick Burtwell
Mipps:	George Merritt
Squire Cobtree:	Athole Stewart
Jerry Jerk:	Graham Moffatt
Dr Pepper:	Wilson Coleman
Bosun:	Wally Patch
Mulatto:	Meinhart Maur
Mrs Waggetts:	Muriel George
Imogene:	Margaret Lockwood

Appendix 15

Captain Clegg (1962) – Universal/Hammer Major: Cast and Production Details

Released as *Night Creatures* in the UK.

Production

Producer:	John Temple-Smith
Director:	Peter Graham Scott
Screenplay:	John Elder (and Barbara S Harper 'based on Russell Thorndike')
Music:	Don Banks
Special effects:	Les Bowie

Cast

Rev Dr Blyss (Clegg):	Peter Cushing
Capt. Collyer:	Patrick Allen
Jeremiah Mipps (coffin maker):	Michael Ripper
Mr Rash (innkeeper):	Martin Benson
Mrs Rash:	Daphne Anderson
Harry Cobtree:	Oliver Reed
Imogene Clegg (serving wench):	Yvonne Romain
Navy Bosun:	David Lodge
Squire Antony Cobtree:	Derek Francis
Mulatto:	Milton Reid
Man claiming to have seen Phantoms:	Jack MacGowran
Pirate Bosun:	Colin Douglas
Old Tom Ketch:	Sydney Bromley
Sailor:	Jack Pott

Additional cast members:

> Peter Halliday
> Bob Head
> Rupert Osborne
> Gordon Rollings
> Terry Scully

Technical details:

Released by Universal Pictures
RCA Sound Recording
Made at Bray Studios England

Appendix 16

Doctor Syn Alias The Scarecrow (1964) – Walt Disney: Cast and Production Details

Production

Director:	James Nielson
Producers:	Bill Anderson: Walt Disney
Writers:	Russell Thorndike, Robert Westerby
Studio:	Walt Disney Pictures
Screenplay:	Robert Westerby
Song:	Terry Gilkyson

(Music composed and conducted by Gerard Schurmann)

Based on *Christopher Syn*, by Russell Thorndike and William Buchanan

Cast

Dr Syn:	Patrick McGoohan
Mipps:	George Cole
Simon Bates:	Tony Britton
Squire Banks:	Michael Hordern
General Pugh:	Geoffrey Keen
Mrs Waggett (sic):	Kay Walsh
King George III:	Eric Pohlmann
Joseph Ransley	Patrick Wymark
Frank Fragg (prosecutor):	Alan Dobie
John Banks (Curlew):	Sean Scully
Philip Brackenbury:	Eric Flynn
Harry Banks:	David Buck

Gaoler (Dover Castle):   Percy Herbert

Katherine Banks: Jill Curzon

Additional cast members:

    Mark Dignam

    Allan McClelland

    Bruce Seton

    Gordon Gostelow

    Richard O'Sullivan

    Simon Lack

    Elsie Wagstaff

Filmed at Pinewood Studios, Teddington (and on location)